The Tragic Thread in Science Fiction

BOOKS BY ROBERT H. WAUGH FROM HIPPOCAMPUS PRESS

The Monster in the Mirror: Looking for H. P. Lovecraft (2006)
A Monster of Voices: Speaking for H. P. Lovecraft (2011)
The Bloody Tugboat and Other Witcheries (2015)
The Tragic Thread in Science Fiction (2019)
A Monster for Many: Talking with H. P. Lovecraft (forthcoming)

THE TRAGIC THREAD IN SCIENCE FICTION

Essays on David Lindsay · Olaf Stapledon · Arthur C. Clarke
Mervyn Peake · William Gibson · Fritz Leiber
James Tiptree, Jr. · H. P. Lovecraft

Robert H. Waugh

Hippocampus Press
New York

Acknowledgments

"The Drum of Arcturus," first published (as "The Drum of *A Voyage to Arcturus*") in *Extrapolation* 26, No. 2 (Summer 1985).

"The Lament of the Midwives," first published (as "The Lament of the Midwives: Arthur C. Clarke and the Tradition") in *Extrapolation* 31, No. 1 (Spring 1990).

"Stapledon's Music of God: Spirals and Syntheses," first published (as "Spirals and Metaphors: The Shape of Divinity in Olaf Stapledon's Myth") in *Extrapolation* 38, No. 3 (Fall 1997).

"The Word in the Wilderness: Nehwon, Nowhere, and California" first appeared (as "The Word and the Wild: The Problem of Civilization in the Works of Fritz Leiber) in *Fritz Leiber: Critical Essays*, edited by Benjamin Szumskyj (McFarland, 2008).

Copyright © 2019 Hippocampus Press
Works by Robert H. Waugh copyright © 2019 by Robert H. Waugh.

Published by Hippocampus Press
P.O. Box 641, New York, NY 10156.
http://www.hippocampuspress.com

All rights reserved.
No part of this work may be reproduced in any form or by any means without the written permission of the publisher.

Cover art "Alienation" © by Robert H. Knox, used by gracious permission of the artist.
Cover design by Daniel V. Sauer, dansauerdesign.com
Hippocampus Press logo designed by Anastasia Damianakos.

First Edition
1 3 5 7 9 8 6 4 2

ISBN 978-1-61498-246-3 (paperback)
ISBN 978-1-61498-262-3 (e-book)

Contents

Introduction 7
The Drum of Arcturus in Lindsay's Strange Music 15
Lindsay's and Goethe's Celebration of the Pagan World 26
A Speculative Dictionary of *A Voyage to Arcturus* 38
Stapledon's Music of God: Spirals and Syntheses 53
Go, Tell It on the Mountain 70
The Lament of the Midwives in *Childhood's End* 89
The Lily and the Rose: Polarities in *The City and the Stars* 107
Titus Alone in the Waste Land 119
Neuromancer: The Fall Is the Case 133
The Word in the Wilderness: Nehwon, Nowhere, and California 144
Leiber Covers the Big Gambler Death 184
Stage Violence, Stage Resurrection in Tiptree and Leiber 192
The Deeps of Eryx 208
Works Cited 225

Introduction

In a prickly fashion this book is about heroism, grandeur, and tragedy among a number of science fiction writers in the middle of the twentieth century, a tradition that we can see rippling in a disconnected fashion from David Lindsay through Olaf Stapledon, Arthur C. Clarke, Mervyn Peake, William Gibson, Fritz Leiber, James Tiptree, Jr., and H. P. Lovecraft. It has a special flavor that cannot be mistaken.

Many people, however, would balk at the notion that Lindsay or Peake, to say nothing of Leiber in certain moods, wrote science fiction. No, they would say that these writers were writing at the least fantasy; but I would argue instead that they were writing modes of the Gothic, returning to the roots of fantasy and science fiction and greeting Edgar Allan Poe along the way. If they are not writing science fiction they are writing something that is a close cousin.

In addition, this collection is not simply a question of tragedy, however we shall define it. The collection is personal because it marks a moment for me, and I daresay for many readers of science fiction through the years, of religious conversion; suddenly science fiction became an article of faith for me, a genre to which I became devoted. For different readers I'm sure it was an encounter with different authors. For me it was an encounter with Olaf Stapledon, for after reading him I had to read every science fiction work I could acquire, whether good, brilliant, or truly awful; every book revealed something about the genre. I had received the Epistle to the World, an epitomy of faith, and thereafter I received every gospel of science fiction, of which there were many; every one of them meant something immediate and serious to me, something for which I would have sold my soul. In that sense it was and continues to be a Faustean moment.

It was not that I had not read science fiction before. I had read a good deal of Verne in the bad translations of my childhood, but children though moved may not understand the true purport of what they read and they pass swiftly on to other matters; and Verne himself, though he had written novels about a trip around the moon and a trip to the edge of the solar system, had not truly encountered the immensity of the universe and our finitude; perhaps only in *Vingts mille lieues sur les mers* did he show a true hint of that immensity. And such other science fiction that I read at the time, mainly space opera, had no understanding of our tragic place in the universe. Space opera has almost always been written in a triumphalistic tone, with no sense of the minuscule role humanity plays in the universe. Moreover, science fiction as it was written by Americans in those years between the First and the Second World Wars was essentially a utopian story in which a puzzle was given and solved. Stapledon, needless to say, brought that immensity and tragedy fully home to me. And this realization radiated out from him to such authors as Clarke, Leiber, and Tiptree. As for Lindsay, like Stapledon he had inhaled a tragic sense from Nietzsche and Schopenhauer, but it is not necessary to read the Germans when Macbeth, Hamlet, and Lear are treading the boards at home to an unsoluble melody; as for Lovecraft, he was reading as a child every astronomical text that was available.

These are the themes that excited me, and it is evident that Stapledon's two epics spoke to them all: what are we to make of the tragic destiny that is the subtext of our lives, whether human or alien; what is the meaning of our life for which we wrestle God, the paradoxes of good and evil; and what actually constitutes our life as we know it or as we guess it might be? No matter how specialized or peculiar some of these chapters may be, one or more of these questions will be at play in them, just as they were when I first read these authors years ago.

These chapters, then, are records of my encounter with the tragic and heroic in science fiction, that which converted me many years ago and that which I still read as holy texts. But when I ask what sort of tragic hero I have in mind, whether it is Achilles or Odysseus or Theseus, I would answer that it is Oedipus or Orestes, the man who searches for his origins and for truth no matter what befalls him. And he obeys the god Apollo no matter what befalls him. The theophany is a matter of faith.

In this question I have often found useful the Excursus that Gilbert Murray wrote in Jane Harrison's book *Themis*. He outlines there the order of parts that occur in Greek tragedies: 1. The *agon* or contest that we find so pervasive in Greek culture. 2. The *pathos*, a suffering that befalls the protagonist, at its extreme manifestation a *sparagmos* in which the protagonist is torn apart. 3. The messenger who relates the suffering of the protagonist, a long narration in which suffering becomes literature. 4. The *threnos* or lamentation. 5 and 6. The *anagnorisis* in which the protagonist discovers something vital about himself, so that a *peripeteia* occurs, a sudden shift in the plot. In this discovery and shift of the plot something numinous often appears, which we call the *theophany* (Harrison 343-44). I will not press this nomenclature in my analyses of these books, but on occasion they are doubtless helpful. I add to these moments the Night Sea Journey and the sense of the immensity and order of the universe, the sort of sense that we find in the words of the watchman at the beginning of the *Oresteia* (4-6).

The arrangement of the chapters in this book is broadly chronological, beginning first with David Lindsay, whose career began at a low point and became worse and worse through the years; the cordial support of C. S. Lewis could not save him. He could not stop, however, working with the themes that would not leave him because they seemed to point at everything in his body. The great triumph of his first novel is its concern with the body—what other protagonist of that time, other than Tarzan, is naked for most of the action? But the body in Lindsay is always changing. This may have been one of the lessons he taught Stapledon, who considered Lindsay one of his favorite science fiction writers (Crossley 351). Stapledon, however, extends this concern for the body to races and aliens.

The first two chapters of the collection are concerned with the structure of *A Voyage to Arcturus*, and they may not seem to speak to the heroic and tragic; they do, however, reveal the degree to which Lindsay responded to the tragic in Schopenhauer and Nietzsche. The second chapter plays with the extent to which the pagan in Lindsey responded to the pagan in Goethe, specifically material in the second part of *Faust*. The third chapter is concerned with Lindsay's style, more specifically with his invention of words. But the kinds of words he invents truly paint Arcturus as an image of the inescapable human universe.

The career of Olaf Stapledon was rather different; for though one could argue that his later works never matched the grandeur of *Last and First Men* and *Star Maker*, he remained a respected figure in British literature and a significant figure in American science fiction. The first chapter devoted to him is concerned once more with structure, in detail looking at the structures of those two books. The next chapter is interested in the place of mountains in these two books and to a lesser extent in his other books; this chapter leads directly to the experience of Dante when he meets Beatrice at the top of Mount Purgatory and at the top of the Paradiso. Tragedy in those first two works by Stapledon is racial; race after race attempts to reach its peak and fails—not always, but it is the failures to which Stapledon gives his greatest attention, and this tragic mode is even clearer in the later novels devoted to individuals, the mutant Odd John and the dog Sirius. There is a subtext in these first chapters that I should admit to. Both Lindsay and Stapledon had read George Mallory, the last great hope of England in the attainment of Everest and the great failure. His heroism, I believe, was a frequent presence in their writings.

Arthur C. Clarke testified often to the importance of Stapledon in his early work, especially in the way the older man introduced Clarke to the immensity of the universe and the possible varieties of alien life; Clarke's career, however, became increasingly significant in the public eye through his contribution to the movie *2001: A Space Odyssey* and to his presence as a commentator on the moon ventures throughout the 1970s. I will be looking at the complexities of his novel *Childhood's End*, a novel as sad as its title, and its companion piece *The City and the Stars*; in both novels we will be concerned with the theme of the second-rater and with the structures of the two books.

We will then turn to the last novel that Mervyn Peake wrote, *Titus Alone*, and investigate the ways in which certain themes and images in that book may be read in the context of T. S. Eliot's early poems through *The Waste Land*. We shall also give a nod to Peake's novella *Boy in Darkness*. Peake is one of those figures who straddle genres and arts; very respected as an eccentric illustrator, he became well known as a writer of fantasy in his novels of the castle of Gormenghast. This third novel of the Gormenghast series, however, clearly employs various science fiction tropes that had not been present in the first two; Titus leaves Gormenghast to face the world as it is, leaving behind family and ritual.

In the next chapter we investigate the novel that brought science fiction into the postmodern world, William Gibson's *Neuromancer*. Though much in the book is dystopian and parodic, suffering from a secret wound that parody cannot heal, the inner world and the outer world slowly, painfully open into the infinity with which we have been concerned. As AI speaks with AI and enters back into conversation with the new style of humanity, the mind of the new humanity suffers an expansion that is opening up the old boundaries of itself. It is difficult, however, to navigate this new infinity. Let us confess that *Titus Alone* and *Neuromancer* have protagonists who may very well seem strikingly modern in this collection. Are they tragic at all, and do they raise such questions as we faced in such plays as *The Iceman Cometh*, *A Streetcar Named Desire*, or *Death of a Salesman*? Is the modern world antiseptic to tragedy?

Fritz Leiber, much older than Gibson, was aware of Stapledon and of course aware of Clarke, but his career was darker than either Stapledon's or Clarke's because of his lifelong alcoholic addiction, which shines darkly through his story "Gonna Roll the Bones"; though his work is often playful, it is also a testimony to the power of Thanatos. James Tiptree, Jr., had also a dark career, since through most of it he was hiding his life as Alice Sheldon. The work is often ferocious; like Leiber she is very aware of the presence of Thanatos in our lives, deforming our bodies, and that will be the moment that we shall study in each of them, her late novel *Brightness Falls from the Air* and his autobiographical horror novel *Our Lady of Darkness*.

We will conclude with Lovecraft, the writer whom I last came to know. It took me some time to learn how immense the universe truly is in his late works, and it took me even longer to appreciate the extent to which his protagonists were tragic. I owe a good deal of guidance to the early Lovecraftians, especially Peter Cannon, Steven J. Mariconda, and S. T. Joshi; and it took me some time to carve out my own vision of Lovecraft's experience. Here then is the tragic Lovecraft in all his grandeur.

I should make one further observation about the authors these chapters treat. Several of them to a greater or lesser degree create a style through which the protagonist is forced to plow; the style presents a difficult thing, opposing a reader's response. It is as though the reader were like Mallory, plowing through the snow fields that surround the peak of Everest, or like Dante, bearing and sharing the horrible purgations that lead to the lintel of heaven, or like Lovecraft, wrestling with a variety of alien histories. It is a palpable, bodily medium that insists upon being understood, despite its difficulties. We do not experience style as a theme in Stapledon or in Clarke, but certainly it is present in the others; such a thick, dense style is not always the signature of the tragic—but often it is.

All the translations in this collection are my own. I have striven to make them as accurate as possible, though I have also tried to render something of their emotional force. Caveat emptor! I thank Pepper and Steven of the Research Department at the library of New Paltz for helping me through the digital intricacies of the modern media. My wife, Kappa, is a master proofreader, and I thank her more than I can say for saving me from the persistent and secret typos to which my computer is liable.

Wherefore let it hardly by any being thinking be said either or thought that the prisoner of that sacred edifice, were he an Ivor the Boneless or an Olaf the Hide, was at his best a onestone parable, a rude breathing on the void of to be [. . .], the canonicity of his existence as a tesseract.
—James Joyce, *Finnegans Wake* 100.24-35

Sometimes a thousand twangling instruments
Will hum about mine ears, and sometimes voices
That if I then had waked after long sleep
Will make me sleep again; and then in dreaming
The clouds methought would open and show riches
      Ready to drop upon me, that when I waked
I cried to dream again.
—Shakespeare, *The Tempest* 3.2.132-38

—Monsieur [. . .], j'ai divers chronomètres réglés sur les méridiens de Paris, de Greenwich et de Washington. Mais, en votre honneur, je me servirais de celui de Paris. [Monsieur (. . .), I have various chronometers regulated to the meridians of Paris, of Greenwich, and of Washington. But in your honor I will make use of that in Paris.]
—Jules Verne, *Vingt mille lieues sous les mers* 141

Damit scheinen alle Überlegungen, welche wir bisher über allgemeine Relativität angestellt haben, in Frage gestellt zu sein. In der Tat bedarf es eines subtilen Umweges, um das Postulat der allgemeinen Relativität exakt anzuwenden. [So, all the considerations that we have up to this point employed seemed set into question. Indeed, we need a subtle detour in order to make use of the premise of general relativity with any precision.]
—Albert Einstein 56

There is a Moment in each Day that Satan cannot find.
—William Blake, *Milton* 2.35.42

The Drum of Arcturus in Lindsay's Strange Music

> Das Auge hat sein Dasein dem Licht zu danken. Aus gleichgültigen tierischen Hülfsorganen ruft sich das Licht ein Organ hervor, das seinesgleichen werde, und so bildet sich das Auge am Licht furs Licht, damit das innere Licht dem äußeren entgegentrete. [The eye gives thanks to light for its existence. Out of indifferent, animal, auxiliary organs the light calls forth an organ that will become like it, and thus upon light for the sake of light the eye builds itself for itself so that the inner light will meet the outer.] (Goethe, *Zur Farbenlehre* 323)

I

Our first reading of *A Voyage to Arcturus* can be disconcerting. We are overwhelmed by two contrary impressions: that the book sports too much color and too much freedom and invention; but also that it obeys too strictly an abstruse form, an artificially imposed pattern or system that has led some readers to call the work allegorical. It is probably a sense of occult recurrences that led Colin Wilson to compare its construction to a set of Chinese boxes ("Introduction" 11). The suspicion of a hidden import remains, but the reader is wonder-struck by the book's riches and might miss its significance without a detailed account of its structure.

Nevertheless, a drum beat underlies the novel, sometimes clearly heard by the protagonist Maskull, sometimes only caught at the edge of awareness, as he hears it at the Gap of Sorgie: "It was very faint, but quite distinct. The beats were in four-four time, with the third beat slightly accentuated" (25). At the end of the novel that pattern is identified as Maskull's heart-beat, or rather as the beating of Krag on his heart and as the rhythm created in the titanic struggle between the gods Crystalman and Muspel (257-59). I intend to show how that beat affects not only the episodes of the novel and the characters but also the mythologies, the geography, and the suns themselves as well as the spectra that radiate from them. For the novel is heavily structured indeed, as we had suspected, and much of its significance lies in that pattern—that "dull, deadly repetition," as Krag describes it (259). He is, of course, skeptical of much, Nietzschean in his attack upon a good deal of music.

Before approaching the analysis directly, however, we should ask what kind of music this beat represents. It is certainly related to the many allusions to music pervading the text, often simply as bits of imagery, and sometimes in connection with the drum-beat: "It seemed to issue from an unearthly orchestra, and was strongly troubled, pathetic, and tragic. [. . .] The awful harmonies of the music followed hard one upon another, like the waves of a wild, magic ocean. . . ." (140). Near the conclusion of the novel at the rising of the sun Alppain Maskull responds to it, "agitated and tormented," as though to "the opening bars of a supernatural symphony" (255). Though Lindsay never becomes explicit about the structure of this music, I do not think we would be wrong in comparing it to the symphonies of Beethoven, in which so often the third movement is a scherzo, bearing an accent very different from the other three; and there is some support to this supposition. According to Murray Ewing the Wombflash Forest was influenced by Beethoven's Fifth Symphony, and Lindsay did believe that the third, fifth, seventh, and ninth symphonies "illustrate his passage from without to within," in four stages of the historical, the autobiographical, the sensational, and the psychical (Ewing). Beethoven did provide a model for the four-part movements.

The philosophic significance of this music also lies ready to hand, for Lindsay was an avid reader of the German philosophers, as the biographical essay in the Wilson-Visiak-Pick volume makes clear; it is Schopenhauer's understanding of music, as Nietzsche developed it in *Die Geburt der Tragödie aus dem Geist der Musik*, in which he cites the earlier philosopher, who wrote in *Die Welt als Wille und Vorstellung*:

> Die Musik ist [. . .] darin von allen anderen Künsten verschied, daß sie nicht Abbild der Erscheinung, oder richtiger, der adäquaten Objektität des Willens, sondern unmittelbar Abbild des Willens selbst ist und also zu allem Physischen der Welt das Metaphysische, zu aller Erscheinung das Ding an sich darstellt. Man könnte demnach die Welt ebensowohl verkörperten Musik als verkörperten Wille nennen" (1.346; sec. 52) [Music is (. . .) distinguished from all the other arts by the fact that it is not a copy of the appearances, or more correctly, the adequate objectification of the will, but an immediate copy of the will itself and therefore complements everything physical in the world and every phenomenon by representing what is metaphysical, the thing in itself. We might, therefore, just as well call the world embodied music as embodied will].

This music of the drum and of the symphony, an image of the will, conveys the primary apprehension that the world of Tormance, the very landscape through which Maskull moves, loves, kills, and struggles stubbornly to be pure, is itself embodied will and, more importantly for our immediate purpose, embodied music. It incorporates a relationship that is mathematical and emotional, analyzable and unanalyzable. In this understanding of its twofold nature, Nietzsche's characterization of music makes a further distinction:

> Wenn die Musik scheinbar als seine apollinische Kunst bekannt war, so war sie dies doch nur, genaugenommen, als Wellenschlag des Rhythmus. [. . .] Das Element [. . .] das den character der dionysischen Musik and damit der Musik überhaupt ausmacht, [ist] die erschütternde Gewalt des Tones, die einheitliche Strom des Melos and die durchaus unvergleichliche Welt der Harmonie" (1.28; sec. 2). [If music, apparently, had been known previously as an Apollonian art, it was so, strictly speaking, only as the wave-beat of rhythm. (. . .) The element (. . .) which forms the essence of Dionysian music and thus of music in general (. . .) is the emotional power of the tone, the uniform flow of the melody, and the utterly incomparable world of harmony].

Insofar as Crystalman is responsible for the rhythm of this music of Arcturus, that music is Apollonian and rational; but as incarnate will, as melody and depth, it is created through the violence of Krag, who scorns it, hammering it out upon Maskull's heart. Toward the music by which the novel is structured, therefore, Lindsay adopts a complex view that seems dual in this regard; as an Apollonian rhythm, the landscape of Tormance favors individualization and a state of appearances, as a condition that simply is (1.21–24; sec. 1); but as a Dionysian harmony, the counterpointed episodes of the four movements of the novel direct the reader's attention beyond themselves toward a state in which individualization does not exist, transformed beneath "den Meisselschlagen des dionysischen Weltkünstlers," for "der Mensche is nicht mehr Künstler, er ist Kunstwerk geworden" [the chisel-blows of the Dionysian world-artist], for [the man is no longer an artist, he has become a work of art] (Nietzsche 1.25; sec. 1). Confused and murderous as he often is, this is the light under which Lindsay would have us judge Maskull and his other actors.

    I am not sure where this imagery of the fourfold music originates, but I would like to suggest a possibility, given the frequent geography of the mountains in the book. In 1914 George Mallory wrote an influential essay that wrestled with the reasons for his high esteem of mountain-climbing, and his answer is a bit more subtle than the simple reason later attributed to him—because the mountain is there; and his answer is also more precise than the Romantic enthusiasm for the sublimity of the mountain, though it attempts to account for that sublime. He appeals to the aesthetic element in mountain-climbing, which he compares to a symphony in four parts:

> Andante, andantissimo sometimes, is the first movement—the grim, sickening plod up the moraine. But how forgotten when the blue light of dawn flickers over the hard, clean snow! The new *motif* is ushered in, as it were, very gently

on the lesser wind instruments. [. . .] And so throughout the day successive moods induce the symphonic whole—allegro while you break the back of an expedition and the issue is still in doubt [. . .]; and then, for the descent, sometimes again andante, because, while the summit was still to win, you forgot that the business of descending may be serious and long; but in the end scherzo once more—with the brakes on for sunset. (21)

The crucial phrase here is "the symphonic whole," for after this paragraph he examines in greater detail the way in which the various moments of the climb in their psychological richness are related the one to the other; and this sort of analysis is to be found in his other writings on his climbs. "The spirit goes on a journey just as does the body, and this journey has a beginning and an end, and is concerned with all that happens between these extremities" (21). And so it is for Maskull as he struggles through the various moments of his quest.

II

The simplest way to open this study of the music's simultaneous three- and four-part structure (noting the ambiguous placement of the accent upon the third beat) is to examine the three main characters. Maskull is "a kind of giant, but of broader and more robust physique than most giants. He wore a full beard. His features were thick and heavy, coarsely modeled" (7), and at first glance he seems to lead a merely physical existence. Nightspore seems utterly his opposite, "of middle height, but so tough-looking that he appeared to be trained out of all human frailties and susceptibilities. His hairless face seemed consumed by an intense spiritual hunger, and his eyes were wild" (7). Spirituality is the key to this man. Krag, set apart from Maskull and Nightspore when he enters the novel, seems a combination of them both, yet different; like Maskull he has "a surprising muscular development," though his head is too large; and like Nightspore he is beardless, his yellow face indicating "a mixture of sagacity, brutality, and humor" (10). Most arresting, as the only character who really acts in the study of Prolands, he waits upon no ceremony but kills the apparition and invites Maskull and Nightspore to the voyage.

We see the same pattern of the three men in the characters of Polecrab's children:

> The eldest was tall, slim, but strongly built. He, like his brothers, was naked, and his skin from top to toe was ulfire-colored. [. . .] The second showed promise of being a broad, powerful man. His head was large and heavy, and drooped. His face and skin were reddish. [. . .] The youngest child was paler and slighter than his brothers. His face was mostly tranquil and expressionless. (156-57)

When the eldest points at Maskull and asserts brashly, "I would like to be like that big fellow" (157), his correspondence to the protagonist is established. The rest of the relationship unfolds when we read that "the oldest boy was carrying the youngest on his back, while the third trotted some distance behind" (156). Thus Maskull, when climbing Starkness Tower, seemed to be carrying upstairs not one Maskull but three" (26); and Nightspore in Muspel Tower "felt as though he was carrying a heavy man on his shoulders" (262). Three characters are presented here, two of whom are polar and cannot exist upon Tormance without the invisible other. The third mediates between them: Krag relates, as does Amfuse in Corpang's mythology, though Krag would seem to be interested only in tough love (197). Following the order of the children's ages, as Polecrab relates them, we see this trinity of characters in the order of Maskull, Krag, and Nightspore; and in this order they are the first three beats of the drum.

With this order in mind, let us turn to the novel's events and the order of its episodes. We should follow Krag's advice, that there is no necessity to "stop and gape at illusions" (32), and ignore the pre-Arcturan scenes, which function as a rudimentary thematic prologue and illustrate incidentally the variety of isolated human self-interest. We will investigate the prologue in much greater detail in the next chapter. In the first movement, then, after he has been ferried to Tormance in that remarkable torpedo, Maskull encounters the innocent Joiwind, who with her artistic husband instills in him a desire for purity and a sexless existence (44-45). Next he meets the seducers, Oceaxe and Tydomin, the murderous goddesses of will, whose very different taunting challenges contrast with the empathic relations of Joiwind and her husband (Pohl 168). Last Maskull meets the ascetics, Spadevil and Catice, with their calls to duty or mutilation (125-33). From the height of these episodes the direction falls, for a short intermission, to the Wombflash Forest—the region of an auroral darkness, true dream, reality, and a sucking at the breast (139-40, 148). The action's pattern, a trinity of episodes concluded by a fourth, corresponds to the full rhythm of the drum and, in the first three elements, to the three main characters. In these events the reader is directed from Maskull's eager ignorance, through Krag's mockery and growth, to Nightspore's tense, cold, spiritual withdrawal. From these three well-defined confrontations the action moves to a collapse, a death, and a rebirth, presented not in terms of action, as in the first three episodes, but in terms of landscape and tone.

I would not insist upon the presence of this pattern in the book if it were not repeated, in precisely the same order, in the second presentation of the episodes. First, Maskull must take a ferry again, and as the peculiar Back-Rays of Arcturus drove the spaceship (21-22), so the Sinking Sea's to-and-fro currents carry Polecrab's raft to Swaylone's Island. Morever, this island, a retreat of beauty for the sake of art that recalls the region of Panawe, who had also been an artist (52-53), displays an art that has been touched by Krag and now produces, cracked and discordant, "beauty in its terrible purity" (162). The effect on Maskull is violent: "A hideous pain hammered away inside his brain [. . .]. In his agony he stumbled and fell again; this time on the arm which Krag had wounded" (167). Terror—to tremble or to shake, perhaps to shake apart—has a particular significance here, for Krag, the violent beater on hearts, does indeed shake things apart, and the art under his aegis is that of "exposure to the tensions and problems of a false world" (Peckham 314). Just as, in retrospect, we can see that the first movement of this symphony had been played under the look of Maskull in his first, innocent apprehension of this new world and its opportunities, so this second movement is played by Krag, transposed into his own key. From Swaylone's Island Maskull goes to Matterplay, the land of generation and change, analogous to the land of the Ifdawn Marest of Oceaxe where change had been rampant there in the brutal, mountainous landscape; but in Matterplay it resides in the organic forms themselves. The sudden generation and mutability of inorganic rock has shifted to that of organic rock, from the torsal physicality of Maskull to the beardless, vital head of Krag. The ambiguous otherness of Leehallfae's sexuality also suggests Krag's presence: in Starkness, after the three men had stripped for the voyage, Krag had dropped to the floor, "kicking his legs in the air. He tried to drag Maskull down on top of him, and a little horseplay went on between the two" (32). Leehallfae's death upon confronting the demands of spirituality echoes the death of Tydomin and anticipates that of Sullenbode.

Threal, the third part of the second movement in this scheme, is outlined in black and white, the habiliments of morality (192). Corpang, the aching heart, is the representative figure of this region; his name is based upon his comment on the third person of his trinity—"Feeling is Thire's world"—and he has no organ that physically determines his moral life, precisely as in Sant Maskull had been driven to castrate his own organ, the sorb (131). In Threal too, moralities and idealities, the concerns of the distracted and distant Nightspore, are given bodies, but now also the passion for service is embodied, insofar as a primary function of Krag is mediation (197). An intermission follows, in which Maskull dreams and is born again: "The angle became one of forty-five degrees, and they had to climb. The tunnel grew so confined that Maskull was reminded of the evil dreams of his childhood" (207). He has passed through the Wombflash Forest again, on another level, from a second perspective.

The Drum of Arcturus in Lindsay's Strange Music 21

Now, as we ought to expect, the pattern begins anew. Haunte's boat, flying through the air by its male stones' repulsion, resembles the torpedo and Polecrab's raft; and Haunte's separatist sexual philosophy suggests Joiwind's purity and Swaylone Island. His hunting, boat-building, and science represent arts that are directed toward knowledge (211-14). The difference lies in the control of this third movement by the asceticism of Nightspore, and Haunte's purity is signaled by the mutilation that has characterized the third parts of the first and second movements (210); beyond any question, "in Lichstorm the sexes are pure" (211). Facing this storm of light and knowledge, that darkly suggests a tumult of corpses—that distance from Nightspore's typical distance from physicality—Maskull denies Haunte's sexual rift by casting forth the male stones and being "oppressed by a black, shapeless, supernatural being," going "through torture to love" (223) in the same way he had loved Oceaxe and beheld Leehallfae's long yearning. Again with Sullenbode he experiences will and change: "Her lips seemed like a splash of vivid will on a background of slumbering protoplasm" (224). In Maskull's moral being in the Ifdawn Marest, the rocks seemed to grind against one another (226), confronting as it were in Sullenbode the naked abstraction of sex proper to Nightspore's movement. After this confrontation she climbs toward Muspel-light, as had Tydomin and Leehallfae, and dies. Maskull turns away, for "he cared no more for Muspel" (242). He turns to the land of Barey and Gangnet's allure, the allure of acquiescence and the womb, and the allure of death.

Yet also in Barey and beyond it, the final beat of the four-beat rhythm accomplishes itself. Now Maskull dies, as Leehallfae had prophesied, and his corpse vanishes, since, as Krag remarks to him when the stout man reappears for the first time since their departure from earth, Maskull "has run the gamut" (244). Gangnet, in battle with Krag, is revealed as Crystalman and flees; and through Krag's mediation, Nightspore arises above Maskull's corpse. A reference here to Gangnet as a common thief deflates not only his Promethean aspiration (254) but also the aspiration of Crystalman's alter ego, Maskull himself, with whom the Promethean myth had been associated early in the Panawe section and in Dreamsinter's words (51, 139). But Maskull's death does not affect the essence of the structure: "Der Held, die Höchste Willenserscheinung, wird zu unserer Lust verneint, weil er doch nur Erscheinung ist, und das ewige Leben des Willens durch seine Vernichtung nicht berührt wird" [The hero, the highest appearance of the will, for the sake of our pleasure is negated, because he is only an appearance and the eternal life of the will is not disturbed through his destruction] (Nietzsche 1.92; sec. 16). The third movement has ended; but in a ferry across the ocean Maskull, Krag, and Nightspore are entering the fourth—the transcendental light of Alppain and

Muspel—until Nightspore, incorporating Maskull, proceeds into the tower while Krag remains on the raft at the gateway.

This fourth movement, heralded by the dawn of Alppain, presents itself "like the opening bars of a supernatural symphony" (255): rhythm gives way to totality, the Apollonian measured beat to the Dionysian wraparound lightshow. In a large part this last episode, which is the final beat of the drum, has given way to the night and germination of a real dream, a true birth, of the actual experience of the work. Through the decision of Nightspore, who must now choose this return for the sake of battle, Maskull will obviously be reborn. This state of rebirth for which Lindsay reaches in the last pages—a state of re-engagement and change when the pattern of life has been seen whole—is the same process that he attempts to describe in the last pages he wrote: "It was as if he had completed the revolution of a spiral, to come again to Urda's changed beginning. And now his perpetual approach to her also was recommenced; yet nothing could be repeated" (*The Witch* 391). Nightspore is spirit (Pohl 164), within that relationship suggested by *The Witch* of personality, soul, and spirit (354, 368), but an operative, active spirit. In this rebirth Nightspore requires Krag, the figure of sexuality, as the true demiurge and mediator of the way to read the book and its episodes, because the work is first an experience. Though it overwhelms us, we can now see how necessary the rich invention of the novel actually is: we are given what appears too much so that we must struggle through the experience and discover for ourselves what lies on the other side of this experience.

III

So before we read the world of the tower, we must cast ourselves back into the book again. We have seen that it is composed of four movements, the first three corresponding respectively to the three main characters and each movement recapitulating the threefold pattern—innocence, sexuality, and spirituality—and the fourth transcendent vision. The Trifork of Hator is another version of this triad, seen from the point of view of an aggressively ascetic Nightspore: "The first fork is disentanglement from the sweetness of the world. The second fork is power over those who still writhe in the nets of illusion. The third fork is the healthy glow of one who steps into ice-cold water" (122). We may regard these moments from another perspective, mindful of Nietzsche's short account of tragedy: "sie horcht einem fernen schwermütigen Gesänge—er erzählt von den Müttern des Seins, deren Namen lauten: Wahn, Wille, Wehe" (1.113; sec. 20) [it listens to a distant melancholy song—it tells a story of the mothers of being, whose names are illusion, will, woe]. Art as illusion and purity; will as individuation and opposition; and anxiety as distance and separation. We find a similar pattern in Lindsay's last novel, in which the three musics of Urda "will be the history of our soul after death" and move from liberating passion, through the oneness of the soul, into the loneliness of spirit (*The Witch* 353–54). Little wonder that Krag comments, "Deadly repetition" (236)! But we realize, from these and several other parallels in the book, that this pattern is not an allegory in which one character stands for one quality, as such terms as innocence, will, and spirit seem to imply, but a generator of symbols, a music in which each figure ambivalently reverberates because of the pattern's multi-layered syncopation; or we might say that this is a psychomachia, in which the warriors die and live again, the one contained within the other. The book refuses to bear one clear, decisive reading because of the very process by which each movement encapsulates the total structure, and by which the structure affects the relativization of moods, characters, landscapes, and themes.

This complex intent becomes especially pressing if we consider the color symbolism, which Corpang describes in detail:

> There are two sets of three primary colors [...], but as one of the colours—blue—is identical in both sets, altogether there are five primary colours, [the two sets] produced by the two suns. Branchspell produces blue, yellow, and red; Alppain, ulfire, blue, and jale. [...] Blue is existence. It is darkness seen through light; a contrasting of existence and nothingness. Yellow is relation. In yellow light we see the relation of objects in the clearest way. Red is feeling. When we see red, we are thrown back on our personal feelings. . . . As regards the Alppain colors, blue stands in the middle and is therefore not existence, but relation. Ulfire is existence; so it must be a different kind of existence. (220–21)

Two points are of interest initially in this account. Tormance is lit by two different color wheels, two cycles of threes; and yet the wheels are connected by this blue in motion, this peripatetic Maskull. His impression of the two new primary colors is at first vague; ulfire seems "wild and painful, and jale dreamlike, feverish, and voluptuous" (43). More remarkable is the information that dolm, a color composed "of ulfire and blue" (220), stands "in the same relation to jale as green to red" (210); that is, green is complementary to red, and dolm is complementary to green. Green is the color either seen before Muspel-fire (264) or associated with it; in fact, it represents the back-rays of Muspel (265). Green and dolm, therefore, as complementaries to red and jale, represent the fourth beat of the dream. Red and jale stand in the third place and point beyond themselves, northward on the map of Tormance.

This direction may seem odd, but it follows from the reversals that inhere in Lindsay's scheme; green, lying between blue and yellow on the color wheel, lies in addition beyond red, the third beat, although resulting from the mix of blue and yellow, insofar as they are the two colors of relation. Thus green, in its conventional significations of growth and hope, is a potentiation of Krag in the form of Surtur, guarding and struggling for the fire that lies to the north and beyond the north; for as we are told in the Eddic account of Ragnarok, Muspel lies to the south, and it is from the south that the destroying monster Surt comes (*Edda* 10, st. 51 and n. 73). The green that approaches Muspel points a way toward the actual flux of complementaries and symmetries in the book. Despite Crystalman's grin, Maskull seems to be going from life to death and as Nightspore into the unendurable light of Alppain—into the Alps indeed, for he has chosen always to go north (207). That is the reason the voyage is to a star that circles the North Pole. And Lindsay is probably quite aware that "Alp" in German means "nightmare," besides of course referring to a range of mountains.

There is a difficulty with all these colors and suns in the pattern I have been describing, and we should now try to face it. The beat of the drum is fourfold, but there are only three main characters, whom I have identified with only the first three beats. The contrast of the two accents is emphasized when Nightspore hears the two musics in the tower; one is a march in four-four time, "bitter and petrifying," and the other is a waltz, "gay, enervating, and horrible" (262). How does the polarity of the two suns arise, and how are we to explain its significance? The last pages of the book, in fact, turn often to a polar structure in the vision of the eternal war between Muspel and Crystalman. What are we being taught in the tower that Nightspore, the inner core of Maskull, ascends?

The answer to these questions must lie in a further consideration of the mythologies of Shaping and Crystalman, Surtur and Krag, and Muspel. From the beginning Shaping and Crystalman are associated with matter and physical life, and in this aspect, especially in the long first movement, they are regarded positively (40). But also, from the beginning, Crystalman has a sinister side, represented by the grin of a corpse. He is death-in-life, Shaping merely his more innocuous, superficial aspect; and he with the sun Branchspell, which apparently refers to the magic of organic life, as a symbol of these disparate, meaningless growths and decays, stands for the general state of the first three beats of the drum. Thus it is possible for Shaping and Surtur to be confused—green on green (67)—because even Krag, whether as sexuality, soul, or will, is insufficient as a category to the reality represented by Muspel-light. Nightspore too is insufficient insofar as he is associated only with the third beat, whether it be religion, spirit, or anxiety. From the viewpoint of Muspel, which is to say from their viewpoints (to the extent that on the last pages of the book Krag and Nightspore are identified with Surtur and Muspel [266-68]), Krag and Nightspore are also judged and found wanting with Maskull, the incorporation of Crystalman, in whom they are rooted (257-58). One of the consequences of this realignment of the three-four pattern is that all the arts presented—those of Panawe, of Swaylone, and of Haunte—stand indicted in the judgment of Nightspore's vision: "The sweet smell emanating from it was strong, loathsome, and terrible . . . it seemed to spring from a sort of loose, mocking slime, inexpressibly vulgar and ignorant" (266). The characters, therefore, do not signify simply a series of parallel meanings in one pattern, as we believed in our explication of the order of the episodes. The three-four pattern must be re-evaluated from the aspect of Muspel into a polarity in which the same characters are assigned new values that qualify the initial pattern. The same resolution is adumbrated in the polarity of the triune spectra, which are opposed yet are linked by that blue which is both existence and relation. And so Muspel, although a part of the entire symphony and forming its last movement, is really and rightly "the opening bars" (255).

Lindsay intended that his readers should see Maskull as a hero. As he leaves Joiwind and Panawe he already feels that he was a man of destiny, on Tormance not for his own purposes (68). He later insists to Tydomen that the blue glare of Alppain "is exactly like the eye of fate. It accuses us, and demands what we have made of our life. [. . .] The joy consists in this—that it is in our power to give freely what will later on be taken from us by force" (102). The person who lives in such a way will force fate to be "astonished at us" (102), and this he claims in faltering words is heroism (102). This is the way that Maskull plays the irontick, as though he were Beethoven, "heroically" (170), giving shape to his musical ideas. Shortly before his death he realizes what he has done, setting himself "against the Infinite." When the accusing Alppain "like an awful eye . . . watching him" (256), rises above the horizon, he cannot escape his death, but his joy lets him give his death up freely. He is like Odin, giving his eye for wisdom. The eye of fate misses nothing, but the hero endures its accusation.

In the last formulation of the pattern he was able to write, in the unfinished pages of *The Witch*, Lindsay insisted that though this pattern seemed static it did represent a process: "These three, life and ancientness and deathly being, together, shall become living meaning in translation" (395). This counterpointing, fugal rhythm is the actual difficulty of the symphony in four movements that composes the structure of *A Voyage to Arcturus*, and until we have begun to grapple with the counterpoint the book will continue to seem baffling. Many years after the book's unsuccessful publication, this chapter remains an early view from the tower.

Lindsay's and Goethe's Celebration of the Pagan World

> Blicke ruhig von dem Bogen
> Deiner Nacht auf Zitterwogen
> Mildeblitzend Glanzgewimmel
> Und erleuchte das Getümmel,
> Das sich aus den Wogen hebt!
> Dir zu jedem Dienst erbötig,
> Schöne Luna, sei uns gnädig!
>
> [Look in peace from the arch
> Of your night on the trembling waves
> Tenderly pouring your teeming
> Light and illumine the crowd
> That lifts itself out of the waves!
> Ready to serve you in every way,
> Beautiful Luna, be full of grace!] (Goethe, *Faust* 8037-43)

Without denying the structure of *A Voyage to Arcturus* that I have outlined, there is another way to regard its characters and themes. This perception arises from asking what Mr. Faull, his estate and his friends, all that busyness of the first chapter, means for our reading of the book. To make sense of this problem we will turn to the remarkable events of Goethe's *Faust II* that lead into his *Klassisches Walpurgisnacht* with all the historical, scientific, and elemental material that that work is composed of. Patricia Marivale attempted a plan of this sort, comparing Mozart, Goethe, Flaubert, Cabell, Ibsen, Lindsay, Hesse, and Fowles in terms of the genre of the Gothic pedagogy; but in the event she spends little time on Lindsay, except to assert that Mephistopheles is the stage-manager of the work, as doubtless he is at certain points in *Faust I* and *II* (150-51). I mean to show that the comparison between the two parts of *Faust* and the comparison between *Faust* and *The Voyage to Arcturus* is much sharper than we have previously imagined.

I

We are led to this comparison through the similarity of the two works as they begin the direction of their main narrative. After the analysis of court life that we find in the first act, its finances and its foibles, the action in *Faust II* truly begins when the emperor off stage asks Faust the magician to bring to life for entertainment of the court the spirits of Paris and Helen. This narrative was long a part of the Faust tradition. At great risk he performs the request, apparently unaware what this might mean for him, descending into a strange underworld where the Mothers rule, while the court reveals its silliness in matters of sexuality and taste; some of this section of the play within a play may have had some debt to Friedrich Schlegel's ironic *Der gestiefelte Kater*, in which the action is more about the audience than about the play. In *Faust II* the hall in which the spirits shall appear is arranged as a temple and music begins; Faust is a willing impresario. When the performance does begin he violently falls in love with Helen, attempts to break into the action as Paris begins her theft, and falls unconscious as the stage dissolves in an explosion and smoke.

The action in the beginning of Lindsay's novel is not dissimilar. The medium Backhouse has been hired by the gentleman Montague Faull of "Prolands" to perform the appearance or materialization of a spirit (though Backhouse seems an invented name, the first of the many invented words of the novel, it may be based upon the name of Lodolf Bakhuysen, a Dutch painter; his name probably meant the bake house). Their names indicate that in some fashion they are opposites; the consciousness of Backhouse is in the back of the house, with a good deal of him not visible; Kathryn Hume believes the name is "an openly sardonic comment on spiritualism" (81), but I am not so sure. Backhouse seems quite forthright in admitting that "I dream with open eyes, [...] and others see my dreams" (2); he denies that he is in any way in control of the drama. In the upshot it is as though he dreamt a small part of the main action of the book. He is certainly not aware of the significance of what he has brought about. As "a fast rising star in the psychic world" (1) he does command a certain price, which to some extent taints the evening, though there is little doubt that no hoax is involved. His opposite is Montague Faull, who is foul, lazy, or rotten (cf. *faul* in Cassell 150)—he often sprawls, a man clearly unworthy of his illustrious baptismal name—and he is in front of the house; what we see of him is all there is to see, and there is no indication that he dreams. Music is performed and a theatrical scene arranged, much to Backhouse's distress, and the guests arrive, described with the same satirical hand that Goethe had employed in their various problems of sexuality, taste, class, and financial obsession. The performance leads to an apparent murder—only in the main action of the novel do we discover that it is a murder indeed, more than a dream—and thereby to a breakup of the performance, though Faull pays the Medium who has done more than anyone had expected of him. He leaves, not to appear again. However, since he has no proper name, none that the narrative mentions, his name Backhouse is very much in the style of the characters that live on Arcturus and very much in the style of Maskull, Nightspore, and Krag. Arcturus, then, already extends into Faull's mansion of "Prolands" before the nameless apparition forms.

These preliminary comments suggest there may be a series of valid comparisons between the characters in Goethe's work and those in Lindsay's; but though I do mean to investigate such comparisons I want to warn us against any simple comparison. Only in a few cases do these relations seem clear, as between Krag and Mephistopheles. If from Faust's perspective Mephistopheles comes from the fires of hell, Krag as Surtur comes from the fires of Muspel. It is Krag and Mephistopheles who mock and draw out the protagonist; they laugh at anything that the other characters think holy, but they spur the other characters into action; they are the comic, critical voices. In the first scene Mephistopheles mocks and draws out the Lord God. It is, of course, Maskull whom Krag especially mocks and draws out, so we are led at first to think of Maskull as the Faust of Lindsay's work; in Goethe's work it is Faust who disrupts the performance of Paris and Helen, whereas in Lindsay's work it is Krag. Maskull, however, at the beginning of the work is suffering from a severe case of ennui, just as Faust suffers at the beginning of *Faust I*; and Maskull is the character who is often led by Eros, several times over. But at the end of the two works it is Faust who dies, caught by his death in the middle of his work beside the ocean, and who is lifted up; Maskull also dies beside the ocean and suffers a transformation. The nature of these deaths and transformations, however, remains in both cases ambiguous.

I do not claim to identify Nightspore in this comparison. He stands much too aside to bear comparison. But that reticence may be the key to our understanding of him if we consider the stance Faust assumes in *Faust I* when the confident Mephistopheles takes the elderly professor, having hardly doffed the cap yet, to Auerbach's Keller, where the devil believes Faust will easily fall to the temptations of "Ergo Bibamus." He does not, of course, fall to such temptations; and even in the passion of love he still stands back. Nightspore, then, is that part of Maskull which stands back, that in the darkness of the earth waits for his rebirth into the pain of life and finds nothing else of any worth. It is Maskull who could often say, echoing Faust, "Zwei Seelen wohnen, ach! in meiner Brust" (1112), but he never realizes that his second soul is standing next to his elbow, despite certain hints such as Krag's response to Maskull's question where Nightspore is: "Not far away" (244). Whether he learns anything from his reticence and proximity is a moot point.

An action that leads directly to the performance in *Faust II*, an action without which the performance cannot take place, is Mephistopheles' mention of the Mothers, archetypal figures who enable formation and transformation in the world. Something of the same moment occurs in *Faust I* when Mephistopheles mentions Mother Night, though we need not believe that she is truly the patron of the destruction for which Mephistopheles fervently hopes (1349-58); and also in *Faust I* Mephistopheles brings Faust to the Witch who transforms the elderly scholar into a young man; and though Faust finds her disgusting, standing as much aside here as in Auerbach's Keller, she does have a mirror in which Faust sees the reflection of Helen, or of Gretchen *qua* Helen, each of them becoming for a moment for Faust the "Inbegriff" (2439), the internal meaning and epitome of the Ewig-Weibliche. The *Klassiche Walpurgisnacht* proper is introduced by the witch Erichtho as she walks beside the night fires of Caesar and Pompey; and the final scene of the *Walpurgisnacht* is introduced by the Sirens in their invocation of the moon. The Ewig-Weibliche is to be seen wherever we turn in this section of Goethe's work. Mephistopheles is not impressed by the power of the Witch's mirror, claiming that after Faust has drunk her concoction he will see Helen in any woman that he encounters; and in truth that is how Faust encounters Gretchen.

In both parts, then, Mephistopheles, without quite knowing what he is about, brings Faust to ambiguous, underworld mother figures who preside over the transformation that gives Faust what he wants and needs, though the relationships in which he then engages himself with Gretchen and Helen take him much further in his life's work than he had expected. These two patterns conclude in the same way: in the first part Gretchen's child and Gretchen die; and in the second part Helen's child dies, though Euphorion is no longer a child, and Helen dies also, once more, just as the mystery of beauty dies in our world of contingency many times.

Another ambiguous story concerns these children, one that takes place on stage. When Faust prepares himself for his first night with Gretchen, Mephistopheles says, "Hab ich doch meine Freude dran" [I have my pleasure in it too] (3543). We cannot say what he means by that, whether it is his pleasure looking ahead to the disaster that shall result from this night, or whether he means that in some way he will be present at the lovemaking. But in Part Two he is present and perhaps necessary for the conception of Homunculus, whose gratitude to Mephistopheles is almost overwhelming: "Du aber Schalk, du Vetter, bist du hier? / Im rechten Augenblick, ich danke dir.

/ Ein gut Geschick führt dich zu uns herein'" [But you rascal, you kinsman are you here? / In the true moment I thank you. / A good fate brings you to us] (6885-87). No doubt every wise child knows its father; but the significance of the passage would seem to lie in the idea that in every conception there is something magical and aggressive involved. Goethe never surrendered the idea of the daemonic power, outside human consciousness, in human affairs.

Does any of this make sense in *A Voyage to Arcturus?* Two women, hardly mother figures of course, are present for the séance; one is Faull's very aesthetic sister Mrs. Jameson, who first appears swooning over a piano work of Scriabin, and the other, Mrs. Trent, who is apparently Faull's mistress, given the peculiar "half-glance" (4) she casts at Faull, which reveals to Backhouse "the concealed barbarian" (4) in him. The two women are so different from each other that we must consider them contraries, and this difference will play out frequently in the novel proper. Mrs. Trent resembles works of art herself, a decadent version of the pale women with red lips whom we find in such paintings as Dante Gabriel Rossetti's *Body's Beauty* (1864-73). The husband of neither attends the séance. Mrs. Jameson the aesthete has arranged the room for the séance according to her own aesthetic values, making the scene an imitation of an Egyptian temple such as might appear in a production of *Die Zauberflöte.* To Backhouse's distress, since he does not believe that art has anything to do with his actions and may deter him from them, a small orchestra plays "the beautiful and solemn strains of Mozart's 'Temple' music" (6), presumptively Sarastro's invocation, "O Isis und Osiris," in the second act of *Die Zauberflöte.* It is a prayer asking the gods to protect Tamino in his quest and to take him to them if he dies; it is a song that might well be applied to Maskull's situation as well as to Faust's. We are often distressed by the misogynist vein in Mozart's opera, but surely the invocation that foregrounds Isis balances the murderous Queen of the Night.

The names of the two women are interesting. The husband of Mrs. Jameson, whom we never see, is the son of James, most famous during the Middle Ages for the pilgrimage to St. James in Campostella at the far peninsula of Spain; and the neurasthenic Joiwind supports Maskull in the pilgrimage that he undertakes in three days so disastrously. Mrs. Trent, whose name recalls the Trent River, possesses a sexuality that throughout his pilgrimage attracts Maskull in the figures of Oceaxe, Tydomin, whose appearance is maternal, and Sullenbode. Mrs. Trent we should note is the person who has invited Maskull, Krag, and Nightspore; without her mediating powers the voyage to Arcturus would not have taken place. Both women in "Prolands" cast their shadows upon the rest of the world.

Though these two women are present at this séance, they are hardly in balance with the six men, not counting Maskull, Nightspore, and Krag, who are clearly outside the balance in arriving late. However we count the sexes, there is no doubt that the women are outnumbered; they have an effect upon the proceedings, but it is a private effect, and one of them, Mrs. Jameson, almost faints twice, as does the pure Joiwind on Tormance. At one point in the action they both leave the room, not to return. The men belong to the public world and no doubt exercise their weight in such a manner.

The proportion of women to men is very different in the séance that the court of the Emperor attends. The first extended commentaries to the scene belong to the Herald, the Astrologer, Mephistopheles, the Architect, and Faust; but then a much curter dramatic episode follows as six ladies comment upon the features of Paris, a commentary that swiftly becomes erotic. Two knights and a chamber man interrupt these remarks, but the commentary is taken up again by three ladies, young, older, and oldest. When Helen enters, Mephistopheles, the Astrologer, and Faust take up their commentary once more, again to be interrupted by a variety of people, of whom we should take especial note of the older and younger woman, the first lady, and the duenna. Unlike Lindsay, Goethe has taken great care to maintain a balance of the sexes as they comment upon the phantasmagoria that Faust produces.

The Herald behaves as he ought with careful, benign neutrality, observing the audience and the emperor as much as the stage. Especially he takes note of the erotic tension in the audience: "Auch Liebchen hat, in düstern Geisterstunden, / Zur Seite Liebchens lieblich Raum gefunden" [Also the lover has in the dark hour of the spirits / Found a charming space next to his lover's side] (6387-88). The astrologer mounts the proscenium, agreeing with the Herald superfluously that magic is here at hand (6393) as the room begins to transform itself into a theater. From the cue box Mephistopheles speaks to him confidentially, ready to speak through him and mocks his magic of the stars, since his own magic is so much more powerful; and the astrologer seems to agree, describing the temple that now appears through this magic "Wunderkraft" [miraculous power] (6403). The architect now speaks because this classic architecture is not to his taste at all; his Romantic world, which Goethe no longer cared for, prefers thin pillars, "strebend, grenzenlos" [striving, limitless] (6412). The astrologer, however, defends the temple, though his defense is not very well thought through, and he concludes with a touch of Tertullian's obscurantism, "Unmöglich ist's, drum eben glaubenswert" [It's impossible, so it must be worth belief] (6420). Goethe finds many opportunities for satire in this Gothic audience that misunderstands so much about this classical world. Lindsay's satire, for which Goethe's made the occasion, is of course aimed at different targets; we need to look closely, however, since in our first reading we do not know the world, the Arcturan world and the world of Muspel that lies beyond it, against which his satire arises. Broadly speaking, his satire belongs within these categories: an aimless mysticism and an aimless purity; a will that expends itself to destroy others; a religiosity that exists to destroy others; a will to life and shaping that conceals a will to death; the opposite of music.

As Faust enters from the other side the astrologer continues his commentary, but now he is more engaged. He describes the magician, robed like a priest and with him a tripod that reminds us of the Delphic oracle. Faust invokes the mothers, using a language that is new to him, religious, aesthetic and musical:

> Euer Haupt umschweben
> Des Lebens Bilder, regsam, ohne Leben.
> Was einmal war, in allem Glanz und Schein,
> Es regt sich dort; denn es will ewig sein.
> [The pictures of life, moving, without life, circle your head.
> What once was, in all glitter and brilliance,
> Moves there; because it wants to be eternal.] (6429-32)

At the conclusion of this prayer the astrologer steps in again, describing how a mist arises and divides into spirits that make music as they move and how at last, out of this mist, unmistakably steps Paris.

Upon his appearance one theme is carried from the first comments of the six ladies and Lindsay's ladies, the theme of full lips. Consider the dialogue of these four Ladies as they comment on the appearance of Paris:

> O! welch ein Glanz aufblühender Jugendkraft!
> Wie eine Pfirsche frisch und voller Saft!
> Die fein gezognen, süß geschwollnen Lippen!
> Du möchtest wohl an solchem Becher nippen?
> [O what a shimmer of blossoming young strength!
> Fresh like a pear and full of juice!
> The finely drawn, sweetly swollen lips!
> You would perhaps like a sip from such a goblet?] (6453-56)

Yes, though the four women react with very different languages, sublimated, healthy, sensual, and aggressive, each of them would like a bite of those full lips. The men have a different reaction to Paris, finding in him as a shepherd *Flegelei*, uncouthness (Cassell 158), not at all fit for the armor that they would wear in any war of the late Gothic period. They see Paris in the light of their professional life, with no sense that art or culture shall change as the ages pass. In a gender reversal one of Lindsay's characters, Mrs. Trent, the mistress of Faull, has very full lips; and several of the women on Arcturus, as we shall see, have very full lips also, especially Sullenbode, eating a piece of fruit, whose lips "in their richness [. . .] seemed like a splash of vivid will" (224). All these descriptions are aggressive in their natures. Unlike the healthy sexuality of Paris that rests upon its own strength, Mrs. Trent and the other women represent a sexuality that is aggressive and diseased. But something more may be at work here in Lindsay's work, expressing a distrust and disgust of the world of nature.

The room in which Faust's summons of Paris and Helen resembles "Ein tief Theater" [a deep theater] (6396), in which the pillars of the temple resemble a series of Atlases that bear up heaven. Faust needs no orchestra, for as the figures in a mist move they seem to make music and melody so that "der ganze Tempel singt" [the entire temple sings] (6448). Is this sublimated music in any way like the music in Mozart's opera? Goethe was never bothered by a touch of anachronism, letting a classical music resound in a Gothic surrounding. We cannot therefor answer our question with any certainty, but it is suggestive to remember that Goethe was so moved by Mozart's opera that he devoted some time attempting to write a sequel to it. This moment in *Faust II* and in Lindsay's work, the creation of a theatrical background, is more resonant than we would at first think despite Backhouse's resentment.

In this setting the first reactions to Helen's appearance are the curt, dismissive words of Mephistopheles, the measured, just words of the astrologer, and Faust's confession that he feels immediately this passion for beauty. Mephistopheles the wise stage-manager warns him not to fall out of his role, but he is already not in a role but in an intimate experience. To one of the ladies Helen's head is too small; once more the audience cannot experience the classical world. She is nothing but a "Buhlerin" [a whore] (6525) who has already gone through the hands of many men. The best the audience can do is to compare the tableau of her and Paris to the story of Endymion and Diana. Faust leaps onto the stage, grabs her, and touches Paris with the key that had led him into the world of the Mothers. The moral would seem to be that we must not confuse art and reality; perhaps Backhouse was right to sense that there was something dangerous in the stagecraft of Mrs. Jameson.

This danger certainly lies in Goethe's poem at first in the witch in the first part who rejuvenates Faust and who more particularly introduces him to the mirror in which he sees the image of Helen or of Gretchen. In the second part Goethe frames the *Klassische Walpurgisnacht* by the presence of significant witches. Walking the plain of Pharsalia, the witch Erichtho meditates upon the cyclic nature of human aggression that cannot seem to escape from civil war. Opening the finale of the poem, the sirens recall the Thessalian witches who could summon the moon, and these sirens invoke the moon to bless them as it lingers for a moment in the zenith. These daemonic women—whom humanity, not knowing better, call witches—are necessary for this grand work of Galatea. They sing the line that introduces the celebration of the elements: "So herrsche denn Eros, der alles begonnen!" [So let Eros rule, who began it all!] (8379). Though Mrs. Jameson and Mrs. Kent are pale versions of these witches, servants of the moon, they do remain potent versions.

The male guests at Montague Faull's entertainment are so typical of their class and their professions that it is difficult to read them as individuals. The first to arrive is Mr. Kent-Smith, who bears a very nondescript name, a retired magistrate working on his autobiography; on the one hand he is ready, nay eager, to observe any "deception" that might occur on the part of Mr. Backhouse, but on the other hand he expresses a certain "cunning" as far as his own writing is concerned—rightly so, since we doubt that it will be very interesting (3). Is this hypocrisy, or simply an expression of the rigorous thought that has atrophied in his retirement? Or is this the doubt we should cast, in Lindsay's eyes, upon the *Dichtung und Wahrheit* that Goethe wrote as an aged bureaucrat?

The next people to enter, probably business acquaintances of Mr. Faull, are Mr. Prior (he who came first?) and Mr. Lang (the German word for "long"). These two men are quite the opposites of each other. The first man, a coffee-importer who exudes the smell of wine and tobacco, attempts to bring a certain atmosphere of joviality into the evening, but soon sobers up (4). He would not find a place in a priory; he is not made for the events of the evening. The second man, tall and thin and beginning to grow bald, is a professional stock-jobber; but the real reason for his presence is as an amateur prestidigitator (4), taking it upon himself that no deception on the part of Mr. Backhouse should take place. He shall not be taken in by any supernatural fakery; yet "to his own disgust" (6) he confesses that he cannot see anything underhanded in the medium's work. Though invited to touch the apparition, he holds back, and at the end of the evening he follows Backhouse to find a drink, as though he and Backhouse were comrades. In addition, as we see in retrospect, before Maskull and Nightspore have entered the novel, these two men, Prior and Lang, unconsciously take upon themselves the personalities and the bodies of those two main characters. Maskull like Mr. Prior is definitely an extrovert; Lang is like Nightspore insofar as he "said little, but stared a good deal at Backhouse" (4).

The last person to enter is Professor Halbart, the eminent psychologist. Small, meager-looking, and mild, he is nevertheless "the most stubborn brained" (4) of anyone there. Though he does not have a beard, his name means "healthy beard." It is probably no surprise that he knows Kent-Smith, the two professionals calling out to each other, soul to soul; the two of them represent a professional competency that is very careful not to recognize a world outside of their competence. The other two men who belong to the world of business, Mr. Faull's world, are neither of them people who respond to the seriousness of the evening's work; the two women are much more liable than these men to accept the evening as it appears to be, even to the point of fainting.

Maskull and his two companions leave earth in a torpedo powered by Solar Back-Rays and Arcturan Back-Rays, all the accoutrements of science fiction that we find in the 1920s, and all the more obviously fake, since we find the theme of back-and-forth repeated at crucial moments later in the work. How does Goethe manage such moments of escape and return in *Faust*? In the escape from Auerbach's Cellar, Mephistopheles and Faust simply vanish, but Goethe is referring to an actual wine cellar in Leipzig that sported two murals of the doctor, in one drinking with the students, in the other riding a flying wine barrel. To arrive at the Classical Walpurgis Night, Homunculus has Mephistopheles wrap himself and Faust in his mantle, while the little man, the product of Wagner's science and Mephistopheles' magic, flies ahead of them. In his return to Germany and Gothic times Faust rides a cloud. In all these cases the two characters, doctor and devil, ride something dubious in order to fly; but in none does the ironic writer, neither Goethe nor Lindsay, take the method seriously. The truth is that Tormance and earth are radically discontinuous the one from the other; they do not exist on the same level of reality.

II

It takes a greater stretch of the imagination to ask whether anything happens thereafter in the two works that I believe parallel each other. Mephistopheles is shocked by the nakedness of the classical world, but Faust accepts it immediately, asking as soon as he touches the ground and wakes, "Wo ist sie?" [Where is she?] (7057). Goethe is always fascinated by Eros, but in this *Walpurgisnacht,* unlike the obscenity of the witches in the first part of *Faust*, Eros is sublimated into the praise of Galatea, a *theophany* of the four elements of fire, water, air, and earth (8474-87); and in a further *theophany*, a subtler praise of the ambiguous eidolon of Helen, who belongs partially to life and partially to death, the four elements are once more praised, now in their relationship to human activity (9985-10038). This is the way Eros plays in the world of art. In Lindsay's work Eros is either radically purified, as in Mrs. Jameson, Joiwind, or Panawe, who feels the sublimity of awe in all things. Or more often it lives a rampant existence in the lips of Mrs. Trent, which are "so crimson and full that they seemed as if bursting with blood" (4), or in the mouth of Sullenbode, which crossed the lower half of her face "like a gash of fire" (227). Perhaps in these two women we can see what is hinted about the necessity of Mephistopheles' presence in Faust's love-making and in Wagner's fumbling attempt to create the Homonculus.

In Goethe's work the *Klassische Walpurgisnacht* proper opens upon the battlefield of Pharsalia, and several other moments in the work are reminiscent of human warfare, especially the emotional and intellectual ambivalence of civil war. When Faust and Mephistopheles return to the Gothic time of the Emperor, returning from the parenthetical time of the *Klassische Walpurgisnacht* and the Helen tragedy, they find the Emperor involved in a civil war also. Next to that violence there is the violence of geological change as mountains erupt from the earth and the ants, dactyls, and pygmies, reacting to that violence in which gold is discovered, initiate a war in which Goethe would like us to see the European wars initiated by the French Revolution; we see nothing of this sort of thing in Lindsay, where the deaths are quite personal. Nevertheless, we are always reading him against the background of the Great War, which several people at first regarded as a civil war. John Clute has pointed out the inescapable significance of that war to Lindsay's generation (viii).

In counterpoint to this martial violence, in Goethe two Pre-Socratic philosophers argue the question of origins, whether the world began in volcanic or oceanic phenomena; in Lindsay we have philosophers argue the moral world in the silent context of Schopenhauer's *Wille und Vorstellung*. The phantasmagoria of Goethe's work concludes in the transfiguration of Homunculus as he is shattered in the ocean at the feet of Galatea, just as Maskull in self-abnegation dies at the end of the novel in order to give birth to or make way for the elusive Nightspore, his true self. The drama of the *Klassische Walpurgisnacht* concludes in a paean of praise to the four elements and to the wonderful dynamic evolution of the physical world: "Heil dem seltnen Abenteuer!" [Hail the rare adventure!] (8483), a moment that is repeated when Helen's entourage, transformed to dryads, oreads, naiads, and maenads, vanishes in the mysteries of Dionysus (9992–10038). For "Wer keinen Namen sich erwarb noch Edles will / Gehört den Elementen an" [Whoever achieves no name yet desires something noble / belongs to the elements] (9981–82). Lindsay's novel does not end in a paean of praise, not at all, but it certainly constitutes a "seltnen Abenteur" as Maskull dies into the life of Nightspore.

What, then, are we to say of A *Voyage to Arcturus* in regard to the battlefield? We have no echoes of a distant war, though as some commentators argue this is a work that is reacting strongly to the mass deaths of the First World War (Clute viii–ix). Beyond that violence, the geological change that the novel records, as mountains erupt and collapse under the feet of the characters, is one of the single horrors of the novel. Also, the novel does seem to have the transformation of its characters very much to heart; Lindsay is not writing far from the Victorian concerns, still reeling from the world of Darwin and trying to find some comfort in the *élan vital* of Bergson, as Loren Eiseley believed (271). Goethe had ideas in this matter of evolution, but he had not yet received the gospel in these matters from the man who took ship in the *The Beagle* a year before the German author's death.

A more concrete example of an action shared by the two works at this point concerns the remarkable mountains that erupt across the landscape. In Goethe's *Walpurgisnacht* they are examples of Plutonian science, the theory that the earth has originated in orogenesis rather than in a slow action of water. Goethe is thus playing with an important component of evolution as his age was arguing these theories, a scientific battle ground in which he himself took part. We might argue that the mountains in Lindsay's work probably have little to do with the arguments of evolution but instead seem projections of the passions of the characters. In addition we should note that though everything in Goethe's work comes down to the ocean and the celebration of life and change with which his *Klassische Walpurgisnacht* concludes, there is no ocean in Lindsay's rocky work until Maskull comes to an immense expanse of water in the last pages of the novel, in the country of Barey, a word unlike so many of Lindsay's inventions because it is not difficult to read at all, for there Maskull dies. Unlike Goethe's ocean, which is a symbol of life, Lindsay's ocean is a symbol of death. If a rebirth lies beyond the pages of the novel we cannot be assured of it; but within the pages of the novel a rebirth has taken place, for at the moment of Maskull's death Nightspore stands beside him. No narration shows how this is possible or how it occurred. Quite simply, as Nietzsche citing Pindar several times insisted (Oehler 370), Maskull has become what he is. We have often admitted the density of Lindsay's narrative, a density that lies at the basis of his structure. The rocky, challenging, allusive structure of his words is basic to our vision of the world through which Maskull so chaotically, heroically, finds his way to the meaning of his death.

A Speculative Dictionary of *A Voyage to Arcturus*

Those that dally nicely with words may quickly make them wanton. (Shakespeare, *Twelfth Night* 3.1.14-15)

En ekki er að gleyma eð ósanna svo Þessar frásagnir að taka úr skáldskapnum fornar kenningar, Þær er höfuðskáldid hafa sér lika látið. [Though we do not heed or believe these stories, we should not remove from poetry ancient kennings which the great skalds of old allowed themselves to enjoy.] (Sturluson 108)

Having come so far in examining *A Voyage to Arcturus* in its own light and in the light of Goethe's *Faust*, I want to return to the body of the novel and its peculiar nouns, asking what they mean in themselves and what they mean for the novel. It is a violent, exciting book—in the minds of some readers a violent, unintelligible book. We have come closer to its nature, but there is no doubt that problems still exist. One of the problems is our understanding of the nouns and personal pronouns, which in a radical fashion present the problem we face in so many science fiction and fantasy books. What sort of names shall the author invent? Shall they be alien, utterly alien, and thereby unpronounceable as in Lovecraft, or shall they be only too pronounceable and familiar, hardly alien at all? J. D. MacClure believes that some names are apt and some names partially apt; some names, though not literally apt, do have "some degree of metaphysical or associative appropriateness"; some are composed from real words that, however, have no connection to the things they name; and some are "utterly meaningless" (30). Kathryn Hume admits that some of the words "elude me entirely" (81). The words are invented according to no overarching principle. MacClure would not think that my program announced in this chapter of a speculative dictionary can be achieved, and Hume would be dubious. In its rich inventions *A Voyage to Arcturus* is often challenging, nearly overwhelming; but several of its alien words are only challenging, and not so challenging, insofar as he draws them from Norse mythology, which is where we should begin in the hope that they will offer some guide to our understanding of his vocabulary.

I

We do understand a few words that appear in the Eddas. Muspel and Surtur are associated with the fiery apocalypse that concludes the *Völuspá*. Muspel is the region of fire in the south, and from Muspel the monster Surtur comes to set the Norse universe on fire. The peculiar aspect to Lindsay's use of this material is that his Muspel and Surtur are associated with the north, where Maskull is always proceeding, and they are challenging states toward which a person must proceed. In any case, we readers are always going north linguistically. But as far as Krag is concerned, something else is happening. Muspel and Surtur are the creatures of Norse mythology, but Krag, beating with a hammer, belongs to Lindsay. He beats with a hammer when Maskull sees him on Swayone's island (167), and Maskull sees that hammer again, climactically, shortly before his death when he sees Krag hammering on his heart, halfway up a perpendicular cliff (257), surely a reference to Nietzsche's announcement on the first page of *Götzen-Dämmerung*; it is all a matter of "Wie man mit dem Hammer philosophiert" [how a person philosophizes with the hammer] (2.939). And on Tormance an individual is forced to philosophize in that manner, for as Oceaxe comments, "Nature is all hammer-blows with us" (78). Krag is that moment when on a crag life judges itself at every heart-beat; and as Surtur he would be only too happy to set the world on fire.

Many of Lindsay's inventions are kennings. A kenning, whether in the Anglo-Saxon or Scandinavian tradition, is a combination of two nouns, sometimes very bold, like swan's way for ocean as we find in *Beowulf*. One of the first kennings of Lindsay's book is Nightspore, though we feel none of the true sense of invention or of wit that we usually find in a Germanic kenning; on the other hand, it is not until later in the book that we begin to understand why Nightspore should be named so. There is a radical difference, however, between the kennings of the Germanic and Scandinavian traditions and of Lindsay's book, for within these traditions the kenning is immediately understandable, since it is a communal experience; but there is no communal tradition that clarifies Lindsay's kenning. Readers are left to their own devices. I hope to help us in this problem, but I offer no assurances. There is a tension in the word that attempts to reveal its meaning at the same time that it attempts to conceal it; in this way *A Voyage to Arcturus* approaches the problems of meaning that we find in *Finnegans Wake*. From this point of view Krag is a simple pun, combining a crag and a collar (Cassell *Kragen*). That is rather disconcerting, but there is no doubt that Krag often collars Maskull; several slang expressions in German employing *Kragen* are desperate in meaning, such as: "It will call him to account," or "It will cost him his life" (Cassell

276). In one of his first acts the playful Krag kills the phantom from Arcturus "with a double-turn" (11), twisting its neck completely around. We should also mention that the Icelandic *kraga* means "Flare" (Sigurðsson 437), significant given his connection with the fires of Muspel; but he does not play with any other Icelandic word. This is a very concrete language, incapable of disclosing itself.

Other inventions in the book with similar problems are kennings that work as portmanteau words, in which two or more nouns are treated more violently, layered upon one another. Sometimes it is relatively easy to identify the words, sometimes less easy. The name of the central protagonist, Maskull, is such a word, combining "mask" and "skull," but also suggesting "my skull" or "my skill" and "Mu+spel" and perhaps suggesting "mascul[ine]," for this protagonist, though not as purely male as are the males of Lichstorm, is passionately drawn to a number of women as the novel proceeds. The word masculine indicates the gender concerns of the novel. We understand these possibilities in an easy fashion, but we do not understand why he should be named so until the final pages when Nightspore realizes that Muspel is fighting for its life against everything that is a emphatically a masquerade (265; cf. Hume 82). But what are we to make of such names as Tydomin? A tide that is an omen? Or is this rather a portmanteau contraction of the proverb, "Time and tide wait on no man"? Or is this a contraction of "a tide of men"? Or should we see in the word the infinitive "to dominate"? As far as this ambiguous character is concerned, I do not think we can have a definitive answer; and I do not think that Lindsay meant that we should.

Several of these words apparently suffer mutilation; they are kennings, no doubt working as portmanteau words, but letters are left out for no other reason than to challenge the reader to insert the simple letter that has been cut from the text. It is actually no challenge; it is simply a trace of the mutilation. Slofork and Lusion are examples of such words. I suggest they are mutilated because of so many moments in the action when a character is in fact mutilated. It is as though the violence of the narrative had entered into the syllabic details of the text. This phenomenon is obviously more than a mere contraction of a word.

II

To trace these problems in detail and to offer possible solutions to some of these problems, as we keep in mind the characters in the first chapter and the shadows they cast over the characters of the novel proper, I now want to examine these characters' names, stage by stage of the action. Thus I will ignore certain words describing areas of the landscape until Maskull has arrived to grapple with them.

We have already dealt with the names of Maskull, Krag, and Nightspore, so let us examine the beginning of the action in Scotland. These words purport to be Scotch, but they are something other. "Starkness" (like goodness and horridness) accentuates the word "stark," which in the Anglo-Saxon means strength, rigid as in death, absolute, unadorned, or strongly delineated. Much on Arcturus is stark in death, presenting in an instant the stiff guise of Crystalman; and much appears stark as black and white (Webster 1150). "Ness" means peninsula. Nightspore takes Maskull on a mysterious quest to the Gap of Sorgie, where Maskull first hears the drumbeat I have discussed earlier. Sorgie sounds Scotch, but I suspect it has more to do with the Anglo-Saxon *sorg* or the German *Sorge*, both of which are related to the English sorrow (Partridge 645). Certainly upon Arcturus there is no escape from sorrow, just as in the late pages of *Faust II* the elderly Faust on the verge of his death finds no escape from the spirit Sorge except by energetically engaging in action.

No such great problem occurs with the couple Maskull first meets on Tormance, Joiwind and Panawe, though her name has that slight twist to it in its French accent, *joi* rather than *joy*, that alienates us from her purity; we are reminded of Mrs. Jameson, pure and given to fainting. On the other hand, we should be moved by the joy she takes in each peculiar creature that flies past her and Maskull; one of these creatures, however, is a flying worm that lands upon the blossom of a crystal bush that like all the blossoms is crying, "To me! To me!" and begins to suck its nectar (54). This worm is very like the worm that "flies through the night" in William Blake's poem "The Sick Rose" (213); in the innocent world of Joiwind nothing seems to be wrong until we look more closely.

In his encounter with Joiwind, Maskull learns that he now has three new organs, the breve upon his forehead, the poigns under his ears, and the magn, a tentacle reaching from his heart. Like Joiwind and Panawe, these words are not far from Romance words we are familiar with, breve, poignant, and magnus. Breve is the most peculiar, for on the one hand it introduces the musical imagery of the book, but on the other hand it points out how seldom things in the world of Joiwind and Panawe are accented.

Joiwind explains a good deal of her world to Maskull. According to her the god Shaping is also known as Crystalman, but the two words suggest very different states of being, the vegetable and the crystal, that which grows and that which is static. In later pages the face of death is called Crystalman, whose face presents "a vulgar, sordid, bestial grin, which cast a cold shadow of moral nastiness into every heart, [...] a sickening stench of the graveyard"

(11). The discord between the name and the appearance is palpable. The two suns are Branchspell, again that which grows or permits growth through its enchantment, and Alppain, that which suffers. Alp may point to the several mountains that Maskull must climb, but in German *Alp* is a nightmare, cognate to *Alb*, an elf (Cassell 18) or a threatening, ghostly creature (Wasserzieher 112). It is useful to point out now that, since we learn on the last page that on earth Krag is known as Pain (268), the other name of this sun is Alppain, the overhanging crag in the nightmare Alps; he is a mountain that is very difficult to climb. When Joiwind explains the two suns Branchspell is in the ascendant, its light very painful to Joiwind at the time of Blodsombre, thickening the blood and causing her and Maskull to seek shade; the blood in this state is not only somber, it is *sub umbra*, beneath the shadow.

She also introduces Maskull to the two colors ulfire and jale, and later he learns there is also dolm, "a compound of ulfire and blue" (220). Ulfire may make use of the prefix "ultra," "situated beyond" or "the most distant" (Partridge 749); possibly we can feel here the force of "to turn" (Partridge 964-65), as in the imperative the color utters, "This is the fire at which you must turn." "Jale" may allude to "jade," whether the jewel or the flirtatious woman, or to "jewel," or of course to "jail," which in English proper would be spelled "gaol," so we should not perhaps make too much of this meaning. Jale may also be an allusion to Jael, the woman who nails the head of the defeated Sisera to the floor of her husband's tent (Judges 4:18-22); the description of jale may then be apt, "dreamlike, feverish, and voluptuous" (43), or we might understand that here Joiwind, who appears so passive, is the woman who nails her husband's brain to the floor. "Dolm" may be an allusion to the German *Dolmen*, a menhir or a cairn (Wasserzieher 159), a proper skin color for a character whose name is Haunte; the Gaelic word *cairngorm* means "azure of a cairn" (Partridge 70) and thus associates a color with the menhir.

Joiwind and Maskull arrive at her home on the Lusion Plain, a phrase that suggests a wealth of meanings: elusion, a state of clever escape; allusion, pointing toward another word or phrase playfully; or illusion, not real (Partridge 367-68). Maskull asks Panawe, "What work do you allude to?" and receives an elusive answer [65]); an illusion may be a mistake or a delusion, which is a profound mistake. All these words have their base in the Latin *ludere*, "to play." Allusion is a fairly neutral word, but elusion, illusion, and delusion have each of them something suspect. Lusion Plain may of course be an allusion to the Elysian Fields, where the heroes of the classical world enjoy their afterlife. Each of these words casts a shadow on the simple life that Joiwind and Panawe lead.

In what seems to be a digression, Panawe recounts how he came to the

Lusion Plain where he met Joiwind, a story that introduces Broodviol in the Wombflash Forest, Slofork on Shaping's Causeway, and Muremaker in the Marest. We will deal later with the geography to which Panawe's story refers. Broodviol is accounted "the wisest man in Tormance"; doubtless in his brooding he comes upon a thought that gives birth; "viol" carries on the musical imagery and may suggest that his thought is musical in nature, but "viol" may also pun on "vile" or introduce the word "violent." He is first discovered sitting in a pit of mire. Slofork may branch slowly as the astringent sloe berry, but this fork may also be an instrument with which one digs; the imagery of the fork is carried forward later by the sacred instrument Trifork. But Slofork may also contain slough, a mire if pronounced "slo" or the skin of a snake if pronounced "sluff"; certainly there is much in himself that Maskull must slough off as the novel proceeds. In the name of Muremaker mure suggests both "demure" and "demur," both of which apparently spring from the Latin *morari*, "to delay" (Partridge 146, 388). Broodviol, Slofork, and Muremaker each pause and consider; they offer Panawe a means of holding back and reconsidering his deep desire to simply worship the natural world, three alternatives to his innate mysticism. Without quite realizing what he does, Panawe offers these alternatives to Maskull, who refuses them.

Much more overtly challenging than the paradoxes Maskull met in Joiwind and Panawe is the portmanteau word of Oceaxe, the woman he stumbles upon when he leaves the two children of innocence. Not that we do not understand the two words, ocean and axe, but it is difficult to see how they join together in her name or in her being. She seems to be a violent contradiction of meanings, offering on the one hand an oceanic experience of sensuous love in a land where there is no water and on the other hand a violent blow of the axe; in the terms of the time when Lindsay wrote the novel, she is both feminine and masculine. We do not see a reconciliation in her name. Tormance is also problematic; on the one hand we see torment and romance, on the other hand a tor and a manse, the wild, steep hill upon a moor and the civilized, spiritual retreat. These are obvious problematic moments we meet in the narrative.

Oceaxe has new organs; in the place of the magn and of the breve she has an arm and a sorb, which may recall "sorbum," a red berry cognate to Surtur, both of them connected to burning (Tucker 226). The sorb is the important insight here, for through it the man or woman can absorb someone else; it is an instrument of the will, which becomes perhaps the most important action of the characters upon Tormance and which is central to Lindsay's analysis of human compulsions. But he retreats from Nietzsche's *Wille zur Macht* to Schopenhauer's *Wille und Vorstellung*. Maskull achieves his transformation through placing a radiant stone called a drude onto the former organs and cauterizes them through "healing pain" (71). The drude may recall the druids, the priests of the oak, or it may recall the Welsh word drud, "strong, violent, audacious" (Partridge 168).

Something of a "paradox" (76) to his mind as the sound of her name suggests, she guides him into the erupting mountains of the Ifdawn Marest. At this point we have a good example of Lindsay's rough humor in the description of the shrowk, a creature reminiscent of Geryon, the emblem of fraud that bore Dante and Virgil into the eighth circle of the *Inferno*. It is not a shrike, but it does shriek, perhaps for good reason, since its word contains the interjection "ow," the human interjection for pain. The dawn (derived from the Anglo-Saxon word *dagan*, "to begin the day") and the day would seem to be in some doubt in this landscape; and even more we might doubt that the countryside is devoted to the virgin Mary or to the ocean. Marest is perhaps suggestive of the demonic mare that rides through our nightmares, and that in a most intense fashion. The highest mountain in this country is Disscourn, "an enormous natural quadrilateral pyramid" (86). A reader probably hears this word as "discord" or "discourse," and rightly so. When we unpack it we see the word "Dis," one of the names for the god of the underworld or simply the underworld itself. Not for nothing is it a pyramid! "Scorn" is also here, reflecting the general temper of Oceaxe, and "scour," doubtless a distant word, yet it resides in Disscourn and might point at the scouring Maskull endures as he goes forward. At their destination she introduces him to the ghastly young boy Crimtyphon, the crimson or the criminal typhoon, who is training an older man, Sature, to become a tree, a living espalier. The Latin *satis* means enough: a nature that is compelled to be more than enough; but the word also recalls Saturn, who devoured his own children—Crimtyphon is simply getting ahead of the man. Though this leafy man might as well be the younger man's father, however, he has no voice but the younger man's. This episode seems to be a variation on the frequent theme in the novel that opposes nature and art; but more importantly it comments on the relation of the generations in the years after the Great War.

Tydomin now appears, whose name we discussed earlier, but we must reconsider her name just as we must reconsider Crimtyphon's. Both characters' have names of three syllables, unlike most of the other characters. Let us then understand his name as grim+tie+ phon, "Tied in grim bondage by a voice." Tydomin, then, who shares a significant syllable with him, "ties [people] in her dominion." Whereas the voice of Crimtyphon has no effect on Maskull, her voice does. At first he cannot distinguish her words. "The sounds, however, lingered in his ears, and curiously enough seemed to grow stronger, in-

A *Speculative Dictionary of* A Voyage to Arcturus

stead of fainter" (96). Both Crimtyphon and Tydomin represent an ominous bondage of the voice. In her case we have "tied by the dominion" [of a mother?]. The description of her exposed, "small, ivory-white breasts" (95), resembles the appearance of the Cretan mother-goddess; she has considerably more power than we ascribe to her quiet voice.

After Maskull kills Crimtyphon, in an act that seems a reprise of the moment when Krag kills the young phantom in "Prolands" and thereby adds to the musical structure of the work, he picks up the body at the order of Tydomin who wants to see the body cast into the fiery lake on the other side of Disscourn; but as they walk there they meet Digrung, the brother of Joiwind, and upon his clear intention to tell her the truth of Maskull's actions that man kills him. His name has the clear shape of a kenning, a verb and a noun. The man is a digger or fighter after truth; "rung" originally meant a staff or cudgel (Partridge 575). The man appears to be simply a lover of truth, but in fact he assumes an aggressive stance that in the hands of Maskull leads to his death.

Tydomin leads Maskull to Sant, a word not difficult to unpack, "holy," exhibiting once more the mutilation that so many of Lindsay's words exhibit; for Sant is neither a saint nor a santa nor a sanctum. The Latin *sacer* is an ambiguous word, for it means both sacred and accursed (Partridge 579), an ambiguity that is played out in Lindsay's narrative. The text also refers to the Levels of Sant, emphasizing the hierarchical structure that is an important component of the Sant experience. The central symbol of the cult is the Trifork that signifies an insistent, unrelenting version of Buddhism: "The stem [. . .] is hatred of pleasure. The first fork is disentanglement from the sweetness of the world. The second fork is power over those who still writhe in the nets of illusion. The third fork is is the healthy glow of of one who steps into ide-cold water" (122). The prominent characters in this section are Hator and Spadevil. Hator is the man who hates, as is required in the first stage of the Trifork, the protestant of this religious landscape; he is a very clear and distinct character; haste is often characterized as being "hostile towards" (Partidge 280). Cf. Hatz: hetzen is to hurry, like the man who is the Hetzer of the hounds, driving them to destroy the game (Wasserzieher 225). Hator is implacable.

Spadevil is more complex, formed from a portmanteau word in which two words claim a prominance, "spade" and "evil." In the reading of the cards the spades are the death cards: "La carte impitoyable / Répétera: la mort! / Encor! Toujour la mort!" [The merciless card / will repeat: death! Again! It is always death!] laments Carmen, turning the cards (18). But this figure of death is digging out evil as best he can, as far as he understands it. He insists that Maskull enter his new world, by transforming his sorb into a probe, through which his vision of the world is now dominated by duty, indifferent to pain or pleasure (120). Through this change Spadevil claims to be more than a man: "He that is not more than a man is nothing" (122), a statement that alludes perhaps too openly to Nietzsche's challenge early in *Also Sprach Zarathustra*, "Der Mensch ist etwas, das überwunden werden soll. Was habt ihr getan, ihn zu überwinden?" [Humanity is something that should be overcome. What have you done to overcome it?] (2.279). In the same manner Spadevil's goal of a "divine apathy of soul" alludes to the ataraxia of Stoicism.

Two more figures become important at this point, Maulger, who has died, and Catice. Maugré is an archaic form of malgré, "despite," and so much in this fiction is despite something else. "Maul," however, German for mouth or muzzle, puts a nasty complexion upon this name, suggesting a devouring mouth; despite his death Maulger is very present. Catice, according to the kenning, is a cat of ice, or perhaps it is an oxymoron, connecting the lively organic and the deadly crystal. But we are told that he is "destroying evil" (131): this is, then, no cat to which we pay kindly attention. So we should consider the possibility that "Catice" alludes to "cicatrice"; this word for a scar through a mutilation of the word produces "Catice." One reason for thinking this is his face, "disfigured by a number of longitudinal ruts, a quarter of an inch deep, the cavities of which seemed clogged with ancient dirt" (128).

Maskull leaves Catice to descend from Sant and encounters Dreamsinter, who lives in the Wombflash Forest, one of the wise men of that place. The narration has already told us of Broodviol in the Wombflash Forest, and these words take us further into this state. Dreamsinter, a man quite different in appearance from Broodviol and larger than Maskull by a head, introduces us to the center of dreams, that focus in which all individual psyches discover their coherence. It is also that place in which we are interred, and thus the word introduces us to the funereal imagery of the last section of the novel; it may also be that place in which we are reamed. At one point in the text the name occurs very close to the word "intends" (139). Dreamsinter tells Maskull, in words that are dark to him, that he shall act as Prometheus and steal the Muspel fire; and he is quite likely the medium through which Maskull sees the tableau of himself, Nightspore, and Krag marching to the drum-beat, a small version of the novel's action. All this being more than Maskull can bear as he witnesses his death at the hands of Krag, "he tumbled over in a swoon which resembled death" (140), rather like Dante falling "come corpo morto cada" in pity for Francesca (*Inf.* 5.142). Does Dreamsinter, then, play Virgil to Maskull? In a manner of speaking, for he is Maskull's internal voice that knows much more than Maskull.

After Dreamsinter vanishes for no clear reason unless it is simply the logic of dreams, Polecrab takes his place as a practical guide, leading Maskull down to the Sinking Sea. He is another instance of the kenning in Lindsay's work; the word "sinking" has a special meaning in the book, connected to the back and forth rays that bring Maskull to Arcturus. Polecrab, however, is nothing more than a crab who makes use of a pole and an arg, a creature that fishes for him, bringing up six fish in his six claws. Several words are suggested by "arg": argentum, "silver," which is a simile for argue; argon, derived from the a+ergon, absence of energy; and Argo, the ship that bore Jason to the golden fleece. Polecrab does not argue, but he does present an argument for the rest of Maskull's journey; as Hume puns nicely, he "keeps a low profile and leads a litoral existence" (84). He does not have the energy himself any longer, though in the past he has journeyed; and his raft may be no Argo, but it does sail the Sinking Sea.

Polecrab's wife has a more peculiar name, Gleameil. "Gleam" is the evident word here, with its cognate "glimmer," but "eil" alludes to the German root for "hurry," to hasten, to be in a hurry. After years as a wife and mother she is now determined to "Follow the Gleam" (Tennyson 550). We might also read her name as glee+meil. "Glee" is a cognate of "gleam" (Partridge 256); and according to the way we pronounce the word, "meil" is close to "meal" or to "mile," for she is determined to go many a mile.

Together Maskull and Gleameil are taken by the raft to Swaylone's island. To sway is to move back and forth gracefully; but to hold sway is to govern, sometimes with a tyrannical connotation (Webster's 1191). Insofar as we are speaking of art, Swaylone and anyone who desires to take his place holds sway alone under the moon, "loonely in me loneness" as Anna Livia Plurabelle laments (Joyce 627). Much of this section seems to agree with Theodor Adorno in his analysis of the tyrannical, exclusive nature of the work of art (75). A cognate of sway is swag, a treasure in a bag, or to swagger and boast (Partridge 684).

The quotation from *Finnegans Wake* reminds us that the moon is often treated in the Western World as a symbol of art, so it is not surprising that the moon of Tormance rises over this scene, rising now for the one moment in the book. This is Teargeld, and certainly much is torn apart in this episode, just as there is much to give tears for also; it all depends on how we shall pronounce "tear." Gleameil claims that "to see beauty in its terrible purity you must tear away the pleasure from it" (162). "Geld" is more difficult: the word means money in German; we cannot escape the role that money plays in the arts of our culture. More ominously the word also means to castrate, pointing us to the extreme mutilations in the words and in the narrative. Purity, one of the themes of the novel, may take a person this far as the poem of Catullus in which a character goes this far in the service of the Great Goddess. It is perhaps the violence of money in our art that this kenning expresses.

The art that Maskull experiences on Swaylone's Island is music, played by Earthrid on Irontick. Earthrid is a portmanteau word, expressing the art that allows us for a short time to be rid of earth, or it is an art that threads the ear and then heart. It may also be useful to remember that "thridda" is Anglo-Saxon for "third," a number that we have found important in the structure of the novel. Also Þriði, the third (*The Poetic Edda* 63), is one of the names that Odin is known by; there is something potentially divine in attempting to play this music. Both in English and in German iron derives from roots that more generally refer to almost any metal (Partridge 456-57). The description of the instrument irontick says, "it resembled a mirror of liquid metal" (164), suggestive of the metal mercury, which is used as the backing of mirrors, and the slippery, ironic god, a messenger of Zeus, who leads the souls of the dead into the underworld. Tick has a wealth of meanings. It is a bloodsucker, and so is art, sucking out the blood of its audience and of its creator; it is one of the components of a bed, putting its audience to sleep, though that is not what happens in this case, for this art kills; it is a rhythmic click or beat, a sign of primitive music (Webster's 1232-33); and it is the sound that a deathwatch beetle makes when a person is close to death (Webster's 328). The irontick, it would seem, is that primitive metal that takes us between heaven and earth, timed to the second of an individual's fatality. It destroys us, and time, and meaning, though it pretends that it destroys none of these.

Coming to Matterplay, the region where matter (probably derived from mater, mother), the apparently most palpable and basis of our makeup, is released from its inertia and changes, free to change, as though it played, did something striking with no evident purpose—coming to Matterplay, Maskull meets a series of people whose names are strikingly different from those we have met so far. Perhaps part of our confusion with Leehallfae comes from its trisyllabic nature, rather like the word Tydomin. "Fae" is Old French for fay or faery (*OED* "Fay"). A person who acts in a fay manner is probably due to die soon, as Leehallfae prophesies that both ae and Maskull will be dead on the morrow (192). Ae explains that "in olden times the / world was peopled by *phaens* [sic]" (182-83), but that ae is now the last of aer race; we may catch here an echo of the nostalgia expressed by the Wife of Bath: "But now can no man see none elves mo" (l. 864). The same nostalgia is expressed in the description of aer voice, "suggestive of a mystical forest-horn, heard from a great distance" (182). What, then, are we to make of the more personal name "Leehall"? Surely ae is now the dregs of aer race. Partridge points out that **kel-*

, to hide, is the root of several words; hall, a great house with a noble connotation; hell, where the dead are hidden away; and a hole or cavern (275-75). Leehallfae is shortly to lead Maskull into an intricate cavern. Leehallfae is the fae, the dregs of his race, who shall die soon and leave no notice of himself behind. Ae is the lealfae, the loyal fay of his race.

He has much to teach Maskull, however, before he dies. He explains that Shaping or Crystalman should actually be called Faceny, through whom they are to search for the region of Threal. Corpang, whom Maskull meets upon the death of Leehallfae, explains that Faceny, Threal or Thire, and Amfuse are not so much regions as a triune deity. Now let us put names to these entities. Faceny according to Leehallfae faces nothingness in all directions, being all face; "ny," however, is an odd suffix; perhaps it stands in the place of "nigh" or represents a primitive "ness." Threal should thrill us, but instead its reality dips into an underworld that is no more than black and white, compared to a lunar landscape; it is "*th* real," but its reality is expressed by the accustomed mutilation. Amfuse sounds like "infuse," "abuse," or "amuse." We might keep in mind the name of Ambrose, the archbishop of Milan, who was to be so important to St. Augustine and to his mother. Maskull complains—quite justly, some readers would think—that "this is mere nomenclature" (195). Its root, however, would seem to be the prefix "amphi-" on both sides or of both kinds. Amfuse is the second in the trinity and stands for relation (197), the power that mediates between Faceny and Thire, which is related to thorough and thrill (Partridge 714) and which Lindsay may have mistaken as a cognate for three.

Corpang, who is deeply in love with Threal, is the spasm of the heart, or perhaps it is the suffocating, tightening ache of the body, if we read the word as corp+ang. The pang in the heart is the result of Krag beating on Maskull's heart with a hammer, though that image has not yet been introduced. "Pang" looks as though it is of English origin, but in fact it confuses "pain" and "prange," which is a fork or a tine of a fork (Partridge 467). We do not escape the fork and its act of digging.

Maskull and Corpang leave the cavern and enter Lichstorm, where the lich-wind blows, exciting sexual passion. "Storm" is once more, immediate, good old Anglo-Saxon. "Licht" in German means light, and we may keep in mind lichen; but "lich," as in the lich-gate for the corpse to enter the church grounds, derives from Anglo-Saxon "lic," body (Partridge 358). Sexuality and death are closely bound together here. They meet Haunte, whose name recalls the modern word "haunt," either a noun for a place one often frequents or the verb "to haunt," that is most often associated with ghosts. When the men are flying to Sullenbode, Haunte feels that "the phantoms come trooping in on [him] already" (222). Maskull remarks that Haunte is a hunter, but the two words are not related; they work together in a lucky accident. He has speared a wold-horse, which is "about the size of a large sheep" (210). Wold, derived from the Old English and cognate with the German *Wald*, is still common in England, so in Haunte's mouth it simply indicates the place in Matterplay where he killed the animal (Partridge 788).

Haunte outlines for the visitors the geography of Lichstorm: Adage, the highest mountain, and Sarclash, the next highest mountain where Sullenbode lives, with between them a long ridge that at its lowest point has the Mornstab Pass, below which lies Barey, where Maskull shall be buried like a berry. An adage is a proverb, usually rather simple in nature. We need to pay attention to its Latin components, ad+ago, urged or compelled toward, to realize that the word is an admonition. It is said that a person can see Muspill from the top of Adage; and Haunte says that a man called Lodd once came from the east to climb the mountain. His name may allude to the loadstar that guides us on our way and is itself the way and the load (361); in any case, the man Lodd never returns.

Sarclash we need to take apart as sarc+lash: the Greek word sarx means flesh or meat, as in sarcophagus or sarcasm—"to eat a dead body or to tear a dead body" (Partridge 587). The lash is another aspect of the compulsive nature of Lichstorm. We might also understand the word as the French sarclage, which means weeding, though the "clash" within it emphasizes the violence. We might also read this as sore-clash. The Mornstab Pass merely indicates the horror and pain, the suffering passion, of waking up into reality; after Maskull has walked through the pass he meets Krag, who tells him he will die this morning (244).

Before he meets Krag, however, he meets Sullenbode, the last woman in the novel. According to a false derivation, the "bode" suggests an abode, a small, comfortable structure to live in; but since "bode" means to foretell or portend (Partridge 52), an event now seldom bodes anything good. Sullen is derived from "sole," alone, the state in which she alone abides; only Maskull is able to break through her solitude (Partridge 638).

Gangnet appears, an amiable young man to accompany Maskull onto the ocean where he dies; but in the final agony of that death, as a pang goes through his heart, he sees Krag fighting with Gangnet to reveal him as an aggressive gang with a net or a deformed indication of gangrene. *Gegangen* is the past participle of *gehen*, "to walk"; and net implies "nice, pleasant, kind," all of which Gangnet seems to assume to himself as he walks with Maskull and Krag (Cassell 181, 339). One of Odin's names in the Grímnismál is Gangleri, which is to say "The Way-Weary" (*The Poetic Edda* 63). Gang may also signify a gallows, one of the signs and kennings of Odin. This is the last appearance of Crystalman in the work and clearly identifies him with physical and spiritual death.

III

We can make several points on the basis of this survey. First, let us mention how often these words use the sound of the letter *k*, in which we would include such forms as *sc* and *x*. I will not give an exhaustive list of these words now, but any list would include Krag, Arcturus, Starkness, Slofork, Trifork, Catice, and shrowk. This is Lindsay's music, a significant component of his style, as rough and ready and rocky as the action through which Maskull storms.

More often than not, certainly more often than a casual reader would expect, there is a sentence or phrase in the passage in which one of these kennings alludes to the word and elucidates it; it can be taken as a guide to how we are to understand the kenning. I have made use of such phrases in my investigation of the words. As we slowly recognize such passages we realize that Lindsay is not so stubborn an author as we at first thought.

Let us consider what we are to make of jale, ulfire, and dolm, these colors that Lindsay has so carefully inserted into the color wheel as we know it. The effect of these new colors and of the suns under which they exist, words that are repeated often in the novel, is to sensitize the reader to the phenomenon of light to which we are so thoroughly accustomed. But this is not the light to which we are accustomed. In this novel an interior light is strikingly significant. In this matter I find Gaston Bachelard very enlightening in his disquisition upon the difference between esprit and âme, arguing that âme may be best understood through the work of Roualt, which possesses "une lumière interieur" (5), that which shines out of the poetic image, in contrast to the esprit, which is at work in the structure of a work. In Lindsay's novel esprit is very much at work, both in the work's structure of the drum-beat and in the structure of the colors. But the invention of the words, ulfire, jale, and dolm, Branchspell and Alppain, Lindsay touches upon resonating poetic images that vivify the work.

A further important point is the degree to which Lindsay partakes in the imagery of digging in such words as Slofork, Trifork, Spadevil, and Digrung; it is important in Panawe's explanation of the different forms Maskull meets on Tormance: "the will forks and sports incessantly, and thus no two creatures are alike. [. . .] Then sporting is the blind will to become like Shaping?" (54). Yes and no. Lindsay is attempting to discover what lies beneath the buried culture of the Celtic peoples in Wales, Ireland, and Scotland, though most of his kennings are Germanic in origin. This is an imagery that is shared in common by James Joyce, William Butler Yeats, Seamus Heaney, Hugh Macdiarmid, and David Jones. They are digging up words from the midden heap and cairn of history, the garbage and the grave, and it is difficult to discern the difference between death and fertility. Something has been buried and lost that the languages we play with now are traces of. As far as Lindsay in *The Voyage to Arcturus* is concerned, he is digging into the metaphysical substratum that lies beneath the polite "Prolands," the contemporary world of English society in which the urgent questions are never asked. In this world, however, though words often conceal, they can also with some effort reveal. With good luck. They rush by and drench us.

Language is a storm.

Stapledon's Music of God: Spirals and Syntheses

> Nascentes morimur, finisque ab origine pendet.
> [In the act of birth we die, and the end hangs from the beginning.]
> —Manilius 4.16

The reputation of Olaf Stapledon remains one of the most singular in science fiction. Detailed and expansive, with little sense of literary propriety, ecstatic, clinical, on occasion verbose, he is a phenomenon to which readers respond with very strong, often belligerent, reactions. When he is mentioned in histories of the genre, as he must be, it is either with a nod to the influence of his ideas, an influence that may be overrated, or with a gasp at what has been vaguely called his sense of wonder. In 1974 David Samuelson wrote that Stapledon made "no concessions to artistic form" (96). In 1981 John Huntington summarized several such reactions to *Last and First Men* ("Olaf Stapledon" 352) in an essay that insisted upon the aesthetic significance of that work; but Huntingdon is dubious about the success of *Star Maker* ("Remembrance of Things to Come" 264n9), which he characterizes as "a kind of unprogressive anthology of social ideas" ("Olaf Stapledon" 363). In any case, he does not perceive in the events of *Last and First Men* any "firm, consistent shape" ("Olaf Stapledon" 353); for him the "dialectical mode of thought" in *Last and First Men* operates only "at the level of the sentence and the paragraph" as a form of irony ("Olaf Stapledon" 355). More recently, Cheryl Herr has discussed the ideology of the two works; Eugene Goodheart has argued that in regard to *Last and First Men* Stapledon's "gift is for telling the story of an idea rather than analyzing it" (92); Robert Crossley has emphasized literary genealogies (189-91, 240-42); and Edward James has characterized the books as "oddities" (44). By 1993 Roland Fischer described the two books as "largely ignored and quickly forgotten" (15). Despite Huntingdon's insistence on the aesthetic value of *Last and First Men*, therefore, the question of aesthetic form still seems pressing in the case of Stapledon. And in none of his works is the question so pressing as in his most individual, *Last and First Men* and *Star Maker*.

I

It is natural to investigate the question of form in the case of *Last and First Men*, which seems a mere chronicle of humanity, ending two-billion years in the future when the eighteenth race is destroyed on Neptune by an astronomical accident. And an appreciation of *Star Maker* seems even more difficult, which recounts the eighty-billion-year annals of the universe and of an infinity of universes, in which two paragraphs summarily allude to the events of *Last and First Men* (379). These books do not work like novels, with characters whose psychology produces the intricacies of a coherent plot; nor, of course, does Stapledon claim that they are novels: his preferred term for them seems to be myth (9), although their historical aspects do concern him, a situation that should probably be seen in the light of their being written at a time when Toynbee's *Study of History* and Joyce's *Finnegans Wake* were still works in progress. But if a myth, as Stapledon seems to argue, is a history that has been submitted to various aesthetic demands for the sake of particular values, the question yet remains to be answered what shapes are made of the materials in the two books and, further, what relation these shapes bear to one another. This chapter attempts to demonstrate that the books are indeed tightly structured, but in very different ways: *Last and First Men* is organized by the image of the spiral; but *Star Maker* is more broadly conceived in a complex dialectical pattern. Yet each work employs within its smaller segments the main organizing principle of the other, so that their relation is polar rather than opposed. Like medieval altar-pieces, the two books present diptychs of possible myths.

An overview of the proportions into which *Last and First Men* is divided provides a useful point at which to begin. The work falls into five parts, after each of which a catastrophe overwhelms humanity, the final one totally. The first and second parts, and the third and fourth, are balanced internally and externally, whereas the fifth part recapitulates the first three on a higher level and by implication criticizes and corrects the fourth. The first part, approximately 100 pages, traces the five million years of the first race, marked by too great an advance of technology ahead of spirituality; civilization falls through its waste of energy resources and a nuclear accident in Patagonia. The second part, concerning the second race, involves fifteen million years and some 40 pages; here the spiritual predominates over the intellectual, though a fusion is imminent when the race meets the Martians and both peoples are ruined in the unhappy war that follows. The third part lasts over two hundred million years, composed of 50 pages, concerning the third, fourth, and fifth races and introducing genetic engineering and telepathy, basic topics of Stapledon's fiction; the utopian society that results in the fifth race is forced to migrate to Venus as the moon, spiraling closer because of the density of the spiritual superstructure that the race has created (183, 230), threatens to destroy Earth. The fourth part, a mere 10 pages long, chronicles again three races through six hundred million years; none rise as high as had the fifth race (though the race capable of flight is accorded a special place in the metaphoric structure of the novel, rather like the disastrous race of intelligent plants in *Star Maker*), so that the civilization is destroyed by an expansion of the sun, genetic constructs being transported to Neptune. The last part, 40 pages long, narrates the billion years of the next ten races until, in a utopia that as one telepathic mind searches the galaxy for other life, the eighteenth race is extinguished by a stellar infection, the lurid light of stars' going nova. To observe, as Patrick McCarthy does, that the book "describes the histories of five species of men on Earth, three on Venus, and ten on Neptune" (34), accurate as he is, obscures the thematic regularity of Stapledon's future, which falls into five parts marked by five cosmic accidents—the atomic explosion, the Martian attack, the lunar spiral, the solar expansion, and the stellar disease.

When we note the formal significance of the catastrophes, the expansion of objective historical time and the contraction of text devoted to it are clear. But before we investigate the meaning of the pattern, we should see how the pattern is generated; especially we should examine whether it is a mere repetition of the same dull round, as Krag in *A Voyage to Arcturus* believed, or whether the basic contention of the Neptunian narrator is true, that "though time is cyclic, it is not repetitive" (229).

The principles that generate the pattern are stated clearly in the terms of the first human race as the apparent opposition of Socrates and Jesus: "Socrates, delighting in the truth for its own sake and not merely for practical ends, glorified unbiased thinking, honesty of mind and speech. Jesus, delighting in the actual human persons around him, and in that flavour of divinity which, for him, pervaded the world, stood for unselfish love of neighbours and of God. Socrates woke to the ideal of dispassionate intelligence, Jesus to the ideal of passionate yet self-oblivious worship. Socrates urged intellectual integrity, Jesus integrity of will" (17). The looseness of terminology allows for a certain slippage; it is not, for instance, clear how Socrates' delight is to be distinguished from his dispassion or how his honesty of mind differs from Jesus' integrity of will. And Stapledon is quick to add that with different emphases each principle involves the other in a polar relation (17) and cannot in fact be achieved, as the myth will show, without both being expressed. In the case of the first humans, their imperfect neural system can seldom intuit the ideals with ease (17); thought doubts love, and love clouds thought. Through a resolution of the apparent dichotomies, however, the narrator steadily elides the difficulties which the fifth and the eighteenth races encounter.

A further dichotomy frames the chronicle, apparently parallel to the first, between the "vision of an alien and supernal beauty," akin to fate or divine law, perceptible when the intelligence of Socrates and worship of Jesus are fused, and the "intransigent loyalty to Life" that is proper to flesh itself (18). A proper attitude toward fate arises out of a synthesis of the Socratic and Christian principles. But Stapledon stubbornly opposes the tendency, which his own philosophic language cannot help but express, of abstracting the polarities and rendering them intelligible to the reader, who as a representative of the first race is postulated by the fiction as incapable of the ideals. The "intransigent loyalty" that flesh offers itself prevents a rationalization of the material and the triumph of the Socratic principle that such a rationalization would involve. This inertia of flesh may be the reason the resolutions of this dichotomy achieved by the fifth and eighteenth races—the only rest notes to the progress of our "fluid nature" (13)—are provisional and interrupted.

This relation, therefore, is not static, for each principle approaches synthesis with the other in an "admiration for Fate," expressed in Greek tragedy and in Israel's worship of divine law (18). This fusion has difficulties, however, because a conflict arises "between this worship and the intransigent loyalty to Life" (18). The intellectualist impulse achieving the synthesis transgresses it, so that the demands of the irrational organic body become pressing once more; the Apollonian settlement must answer to Dionysus and the cross. Another expression of this pattern arises in Stapledon's description of his own art in the "Preface." After he insists that history and art find their synthesis in a true myth, he admits that no myth can seem true unless it transgresses what our society believes are the facts of the world and unless the myth is in fact a particular kind of art, a tragic art that contemplates injury to human consciousness; both upon the side of history and of art the irrational powers protest in the name of experience. As Eugene Goodheart nicely says, Stapledon "is attracted to the adventure of remaking, but he craves at the same time the resistances which make the remaking difficult. He wants both the experience of radical transformation and that of resistance and limitation" (86). This is the equivalent of the stylistic resistance we have discussed in our introduction and we saw at work in our chapter on Lindsay's diction.

The imbalance of the first race reveals itself. In its technology it has run beyond the abilities of its spirit. "Animals that were fashioned for hunting and fighting in the wild were suddenly called upon to be citizens, and moreover citizens of a world-wide community" (18), and nuclear power leads twice to a catastrophe (35-41, 88-90). Related to this technological imbalance is a sexual repression that reacts upon the intellect, arousing tribal lusts (23) and, at a later date, an adoration of blind energy (54). The opposition of the skepticism of Europe and the "uncritical romance" (25) of the rest of the world occasions a clash in which all that remains is an Americanized World State, devoted to a heartless technology and a selfish sensuality; Socrates and Jesus are simplified and shorn (69-70), to decline, in the frenetic end of the World State and the exhausted Patagonians following it, into a childish senility, to which will be contrasted the youthfulness of the final, eighteenth race. Unable to respect either principle in its actuality and totally unable to fuse them, the first race falls from the tightrope that Nietzsche in *Also Sprach Zarathustra* had strung across meaninglessness to summon forth the Übermensch (2.285-90; "Zarathustras Vorrede" sec. 6-9).

Stapledon devotes so much space, however, to the first race, a section we are liable to misunderstand because it has been so thoroughly overtaken by the history of our contemporary, nonfictional world, that we need to examine more closely how the section is structured. It is composed of five conflicts: the Franco-Italian war, the Anglo-French war, the Russo-German war, the Euro-American war, and the Sino-American war. We clearly have here a chain of events, each taking up an element from its predecessor and each broader in its scope and impact. Each element, moreover, seems transformed in each conflict. France, which behaved as though it were a practical adult in its conflict with Italy, in its conflict with England finds its values of personality polarized as sensuality vis-à-vis its perception of the island's hypocritical judgment. Germany, the new representative of the European critical spirit, though itself romantic, becomes intellectual vis-à-vis the collective, mystic personalism of Russia; and Europe itself is critical in regard to a childish, romantic America. But America itself represents a critical spirit, albeit debased, in its encounter with China, as that nation represents a continuity and epitome of the principle encountered in Russia. The world conflicts exemplify a dialectical process that embodies a broadening explication of the principles of Jesus and Socrates.

In contrast to the hollow intellectualism and youthful exuberance of the first race, Stapledon inserts an interlude that describes its late heirs, the Patagonians, a people "more capable of dispassionate cognition" because "the sexual impulse was relatively weak" (78). In them and their prophet, the Patagonian Boy, Stapledon makes explicit the thematic contrast between the age of Socrates and the youth of Jesus. The image of the *puer senex*, to which John Kinnaird has called attention (50) and which I will examine further in the next chapter, is another way in which Stapledon is working out the consequences of his dialectic as youth and age find it impossible to reconcile their values and make a martyr of the Patagonian Boy.

The second race has "an innate interest in personality" (102) that shields it from the effects of a runaway technology. Yet it too has problems, the greatest being that its physiology, insufficient to its ideals, leads it once into a brilliant despair, unable to reconcile the worship of Fate within its flesh (109), and into a religious war (110). To overcome the difficulty it must undertake two projects: the genetic engineering of its own flesh, an objective sadism in the manner of Socrates; and an attempt to achieve telepathy, to make the ideal of Jesus wholly intuitive. But before these programs are accomplished the second race encounters the cloud-intelligences of the Martians, and, uncomprehending each other, the races are destroyed. Although it rises higher than the first race and is on the threshold of a resolution, the second race fails through not yet being sufficiently aggressive in its technology (113, 135). Delight in the variety of spirit, through which the race misunderstands the Martian lust for unity, is as careless as the first race's obsession with functionalism. The physique cannot rise to the opposite challenge.

The third and fourth parts of the book about the next six races are divided into contrary triads, schematized in this way. The first triad is comprised of spirit, intellection, spirit and fusion; the second triad of intelligence, ecstasy, and a technological imbalance that results in failure. The third race, tormented by its passion for genetic manipulation, torn "between the tender-hearted" and those who wish "to create at whatever cost," reveals "an almost mystical reverence for sensory experience" (145). It creates the fourth race, its opposite, the Great Brains who, divorced from the body, explore the data of the universe with intellect alone; they ignore the accidents for the substance, thereby missing what is clearly for Stapledon an important and actual component of the world's existence. Realizing their sterility, the Great Brains construct the fifth race, which with its potential for a group-mind begins to explore the past and confronts the despair of the lost generations behind it. Stapledon is here concerned over the same problem that Edward Schillebeeckx confronts at the conclusion of his two volumes on the meaning and import of Christ:

> For millions of men who in the past or the present have already been excluded because they have died or have been martyred, have been snatched away by illness and killed in road accidents or earthquakes, and so on, any form of liberation however successful, will come too late. And if salvation means *perfect* and *universal* wholeness, do we then no longer include those in our modern conception of salvation? Are they the chaff in our history that we throw away?

There is no liberation unless these forms of suffering which are not accessible to human liberation are also overcome. (764)

Stapledon had recognized the problem in a letter to his fiancée, Agnes Miller: "Think of all the pain and defeat and 'badness' that has been mounting up through the centuries. Not a speck can be destroyed" (*Talking Across the World* 35). Only a finesse of empathy and judgment saves the fifth race from the despair to which such irremediable and eternal sufferings could lead. Forced to migrate to Venus, the race slaughters its alien population and attempts to transcend its guilt, as the second race was unable to do with the Martians, but succumbs to the new environment.

In the second triad the sixth race, confined to a little land, admires flight, and after achieving the first race's technological level creates the winged seventh race (195), which loses itself in a dispassionate ecstasy of the air (198-200); devoted as much to mysticism as the fourth race of the Great Brains was to intellection, the seventh race ends as a mass suicide by flying into the crater of a volcano as had Empedocles. Its servant and successor, the crippled eighth race, struggles on with a technology that fails in the face of the expanding sun, as the fifth race had failed before the threat of the falling moon. The two triads of parts three and four barely rise to their challenges; moreover, Stapledon contrasts the fourth part to the third in the same way he contrasts the first to the second, from trough to wave to trough.

On Neptune the history is retraced, only to reach the first race's achievement with the fourteenth race and the second race's with the fifteenth, which assumes a responsibility for evolution until the eighteenth race is produced (210-14); the Neptunian history represents what should have been accomplished earlier, had not the second, fifth, and eighth races, to employ the theatrical metaphor of the Patagonian Boy (83), muffed their lines and been retired to the dressing room for another rehearsal. Having achieved a group-mind, the last human race senses the steeper burdens beyond the solar system, comprehends the agonies of the past with worship, and accepts its own destruction as a grace note within that "alien and supernal beauty" (18).

How are we to judge such a work? It is not a novel, for there is neither plot nor character nor landscape, and it is not a chronicle—though it poses as one in its early pages—for there are remarkably few of the frayed edges we discover in historical accounts. It operates, rather, as a prose poem, with the several internal echoes we have observed; but its structure seems mathematical rather than organic. And this spiral, like the "formulae expressive [. . .] of the innumerable rhythms of shells, fronds, leaflets, grass-nodes" collected by the children of the second race (102), suggests a mathematical divinity that approaches infinity.

A spiral is a circle that is not closed; because it is potentially infinite, it may be broken off at any point—hence the cosmic accident that concludes the book. A spiral may be read either outward or inward, as a shell or as a whirlpool; and Stapledon's book represents these opposing tendencies through the more and more spacious times and capabilities of his races and the less and less space devoted to them. Gaston Bachelard speaks of "les dialectiques du grand et du petit, du cache et du manifeste, du placide et de l'offensif, du mou et du vigoureux" [the dialectics of the large and small, the hidden and manifest, the placid and aggressive, the soft and energetic] (111) inherent to the nature of a spiral shell. It incorporates microcosm and macrocosm within one form and thus realizes Louis Tremaine's point that for Stapledon magnitude enables us to understand that relation (250). For Valéry, "Like a pure sound or a melodic system of pure sounds in the midst of noises, so a *crystal*, a *flower*, a *sea shell* stand out from the common disorder of perceptible things" (7); the spiral involves an observer in a "controlled vertigo" (9) in which every part accords with every other part (14). Like the skull that Hamlet throws away, it attracts thoughts that cannot be concluded (20-30). The spiral may be emblematic of resurrection. A logarithmic spiral is inscribed on the tomb of Jacques Bernoulli in Basel with the words, "Eadem mutata resurgo" [In the same way changed I rise again] ("Bernoulli" 804). The spiral is a symbol of continuity and change, of stasis and of transcendence, of "a variety of self-reproducing aspects of the natural and theological worlds" (Davis 19). Bachelard argues that we can recognize these possibilities even in the spiral of the humble snail (115). Though one aspect of the shell is that it represents the joy of living alone in a great solitude (120), it represents also "un grand rêve de cosmicité" [an immense dream of the cosmic] (119). And this is the dream that Stapledon offers, nothing less.

The spiral may also be regarded as an emblem of that conation, or effort, which Stapledon believed basic to the structure of the universe, so basic a principle that it is difficult to conceive without contradiction. Though he thought it is "prior to feeling" (A Modern Theory 49), it is also "conscious activity" (51). The discrimination between pleasure and unpleasure arises from conation (45), but "what we *mean* by 'good' is the fulfilment of teleological activity, whether or not consciousness plays a part in that activity, and whether or not there is awareness of its fulfilment" (81). Analogously in Spinoza, conation (his word is *conatus* [*Die Ethik* 3.6]), the attempt of a thing to persevere in its being (3.6), is the actual essence of a thing and its power (3.7). Moreover, without any final cause being implied (1.Appendix), when conation is manifest in the mind it appears as will and appetite.

> Deinde inter appetitum, & cupiditatem nulla est differentia, nisi quod cupiditas ad homines, plerumque referatur, quatenus sui appetitus sunt conscii. [...] Constat itaque ex his omnibus, nihil nos conari, velle, appetere, neque cupere, quia id bonum esse judicamus; sed contra nos propterea, aliquid bonum esse, judicare, quia id conamur, volumus, appetimus, atque cupimus. [And therefore there is no difference between appetite and desire, except that desire is usually related to men insofar as they are conscious of their appetites. [...] Given all this, we do not strive for, will, want, or desire anything because we judge it good; on the contrary, we judge something to be good because we strive for, will, want, and desire it.] (3.9 Scholium)

How neatly put in the Latin! Manifesting itself through the material and moral worlds, conation finds a fit emblem in the spiral, *more geometrico*.

But in Stapledon's thought Spinoza's worldview also carries overtones of the agonistic and aesthetic Übermensch. Twice in *Die Geburt der Tragödie* Nietzsche insists that "nur als *ästhetisches Phänomen* ist das Dasein und die Welt ewig *gerechtfertigt*" [only as *aesthetic phenomenon* is existence and the world eternally *justified*] (1.40; sec. 5; cf. 1.131; sec. 24). Mark Rose has pointed out the relevance of Nietzsche for Stapledon's conceptions (116), but more should be said. In *Die Geburt der Tragödie* the description of the relationship between artist, work, world, and divinity is remarkably like that of the Patagonian Boy:

> Nur soweit der Genius im Aktus der künstlerishen Zeugung mit jenem Urkünstler der Welt verschmilzt, weiss er etwas über das ewige Wesen der Kunst; denn in jenem Zustande ist er, wunderbarerweise, dem unheimlichen Bild des Märchens gleich, das die Augen drehn und sich selber anschaun kann; jetzt ist er zugleich Subjekt und Objekt, zugleich Dichter, Schauspieler, und Zuschauer. [Only insofar as the genius in the act of artistic creation melts into the form of this urgenius of the world (Dionysus), does he know something of the eternal essence of art, for in this state, miraculously, he is like the weird picture of the fairy-tale which can turn its eyes and behold itself; he is now at the same moment subject and object, at the same moment poet, actor, and spectator.] (1.40; sec. 5)

To this description we need only add the later characterization which includes in the matter of the world and the work all negative experiences: "Selbst das Häßliche und Disharmonische ein künstlerisches Spiel ist, welches der Wille, in der ewigen Fülle seiner Lust, mit sich selbst spielt" [Even the ugly and discordant is an artistic game which the will, in the eternal abundance of its joy, plays with itself" (1.131; sec. 24). For, as the later Nietzsche insists in *Zarathustra*, "Lust will sich selber, will Ewigkeit, will Wiederkunft, will Alles-sich-ewig-gleich" [Joy wants itself, it wants eternity, it wants return, it wants all things eternally like itself" (2.556; 4 "Das trunkene Lied 9); and anyone who affirms joy also affirms pain and grief, for it is "alles von neuem, alles ewig, alles verkettet, verfädelt, verliebt, oh, so *liebtet* ihr die Welt" (all new, all eternal, all linked, threaded, in love, oh, thus you love the world" (2.557; 4 "Das trunkene Lied" 10). In the closing pages of *A Modern Theory of Ethics* Stapledon seems to adumbrate this vision as he discusses ecstasy: "We seem to stand above the battle in which we ourselves are eager and hard-pressed figures, and to admire it as a work of divine art, in which tragic aesthetic excellence overwhelmingly vindicates all the defeat and pain even of those who may never have access to this vision" (249); thus, at least in this early book, he found a solution to the problem of unredeemed pain. The essential condition for this achievement is that for Stapledon the artist and historian, as for Yeats, the eternal return should assume the solidity of the gyre.

II

In *Star Maker*, even more than in *Last and First Men*, are we to be impressed by "the wastefulness and seeming aimlessness of the universe" (316) at the same time as by "the wild fountain of creations, and all the spray of worlds" (420). Because of this extreme tension between waste and fertility, the magnitude of ruins and growths to be intimated, the aesthetic risk is higher than in the earlier book and the demand upon a reader's cognition of pattern all the more arduous.

Star Maker also attempts the absolute, but its outlines are broader, employing the dialectic internal to the first book; Stapledon divides it into two parts, each of which he subdivides into two sections. The first section, half the book, of the first part is a catalogue of typical alien creatures of the galaxy; the second section traces their history to the establishment of a galactic utopia. In the second part this history is interrupted by the lives of larger creatures, the stars and the nebulae; and the last section, further divided into two subsections, describes how the symbiotic mind of planets and stars envisions the history of their creator and views its static nature. And like *Last and First Men*, as the breadth of the narrative grows the amount of space devoted to it shrinks; the problematic of infinitesimals approaching a limit—the debate of Leibniz and Newton—once more structures the work. A stasis of analysis gives rise to the dynamism of history, which interrupted by a broader stasis gives rise to a broader dynamism, in which the static and dynamic converge to indicate the duplicity of any vision of the Star Maker, hidden behind dualism.

A further detail about these sections needs to be pointed out. As the narrative proceeds we are at certain crucial points cast backward into greater depths of the past. The original catalogue is divided into two subsections, devoted first to the Other Earth, the Echinoderms, and the Nautiloids, those creatures that seem closest to the crisis in which Earth finds itself, and second to those creatures more distant from the human, the Ichthyoid and Arachnoid symbiotes, the composite creatures, and the intelligent plants. The history of Other Earth occurs some ten billion years before that of *Homo sapiens* (294), but the history of the symbiotes some five billion years even earlier, as Time Scale 1 indicates (436). The histories of the stars and of the nebulae, which the second part catalogues, occur necessarily even earlier and are introduced by the vision of the group mind of the narrator, "at an earlier stage of its existence, in fact at a time before it was really a galaxy at all" (376).

The vision of the Star Maker returns the narrative to a time before the creation of our cosmos (if we can call it a time), to the first cosmos of the Maker, and ahead to the last cosmos, which seems coincident with the first. This large-scale reversal and spatialization of time that structures the entire book is exemplified in the small details also, especially in the variations worked on the phrase, "has happened (or will happen)" (301, 311, 334, 360, 402). It is as though Stapledon employed as a large-scale structure of *Star Maker* those analeptic and proleptic gestures which Huntingdon perceives in the sentences of *Last and First Men* ("Remembrance of Things to Come" 257-59). It may be this experiment with time that moved Virginia Woolf to see in *Star Maker* effects and concerns preoccupying her (Crossly, "Olaf Stapledon" 29). We need to see *Star Maker* in the context of Modernism, the structural and verbal experiments of writers like Conrad, Ford, Joyce, and Woolf (McCarthy 49). It is not a structure that Stapleton achieved haphazardly; the publication of the early version, *Nebula Maker*, reveals a narrative that meant, as most traditional narratives do mean, to begin at the beginning with a good deal of circumstantial detail. That fragment does not resemble the complex and metaphoric work we now have before us, which challenges us to understand the purposes of the structure that Stapledon finally developed. Leslie Fiedler discusses problems intrinsic to *Nebula Maker*, its anticlimactic structure, the vagueness of its narrator, and its growing digressiveness (123-25); in *Star Maker* Stapledon placed the climactic vision at the end, created a functional narrator, and embedded potentially digressive histories within the structural flesh of the work.

But the catalogue and history of the universe and the Star Maker do not provide the only plot of the book. This aspect is counterpointed and framed by the folktale of the human who, falling asleep on a hill, wakes to a vision of faery outside time; several interludes describe how he and the alien minds with him react toward one another and the vision unfolding before them. Their experience specifies two themes: the necessity and difficulty of realizing community; and the difficulty and necessity of worshipping the Star Maker. Their experience is spiral, in the abstract sense that the more they can see the harder the vision is to contain morally and intellectually; when they are overtaken by mental fatigue, panic (295), and nostalgia (375), the vision falters. The book, therefore, is a fragment and falsification of the experience, its difficulty akin to that which like many mystics Dante faces in the last canto of the *Paradiso*. Thus the growing magnitudes of *Last and First Men* are mirrored in the moral triumphs and failures of *Star Maker*; but the possessed narrator of the first book, who has lost his voice to the confidence of the speaker from the last race, is replaced in the second book by a more humble, more groping, more disappointed narrator, so that the pathos of the second book is more palpable.

In *Star Maker* both plots, the histories of the galaxy and of the group mind of the observers, are generated by a polarity that may at first glance seem similar to that of Jesus and Socrates in the earlier book; this new frame, however, is subtler. It is most explicitly discussed in the Preface concerning the author, who in order to serve the pressing needs of his society, faced as he feared by another world conflict, must detach himself from that struggle to offer a broad view of the human condition; but detachment is necessary to service and may "also strengthen our charity towards each other" (250). If, however, such detachment "does not produce, along with a kind of piety towards fate, the resolute will to serve our waking humanity, it is a mere sham" (250). Service by itself is blind partisanship (250). When detachment and service are fused, at once a cool criticism and a loving contact, Stapledon is discussing community, of which the galactic metaphor is symbiosis and the local metaphor marriage; but marriage itself may be described as an "intricate symbiosis" (255). It is at that point that the book actually begins in the first sentence, when the narrator leaves his home because he has "tasted bitterness" (255), uncertain whether marriage is possible. *Star Maker* has a greater tension than *Last and First Men* because, though the scope in space and time is broader, the immediate issues of marriage and an imminent war are closer; the abstract and the concrete are radically juxtaposed in *Star Maker*.

Apparently opposed to community, symbiosis, and marriage is detachment, vision, and worship; the relationship is symbolized at the beginning and end of the work by the light of the home and the light of the star (255-56, 434). But the star is most problematic, at the beginning of the work an epiphany of "no Love, no Power even, but only Nothing" (256); the heart's praise, the very slight evidence that something may exist in that condition represented by the star, becomes a principle of negation that expresses itself as criticism. Its relationship with the home, however, is actually polar, since detachment is, as we have seen, a necessary component of true community, "coolly critical, shrewdly ridiculing" (256); when the narrator shakes off the problem of the Star Maker he nevertheless brings its temper into the marriage: "Thrusting aside worship, and fear also and bitterness, I determined to examine more coldly this remarkable 'us'" (256). The first polarity, of detachment and service, is resolved by the achieving of community; the second polarity, between community and divinity, resolves itself outside time and assures, by the drag of flesh in service, the impossibility of rationalizing any of these principles totally.

I will not detail the histories of the aliens as we did with the earlier book; they weave variations around the two polarities we have described. Closer to the purpose of *Star Maker* is the way in which aliens prepare a reader for the vision of divinity. They provide the narrator metaphors with which to handle a myth that in a single moment includes the atemporal and its infinite temporalities. It is as though Stapledon determined to work out concretely Aquinas's assertion that "cognoscimus [essentiam Dei] secundum quod repraesentatur in perfectionibus creaturarum" [We understand the essence of God to the degree that it is represented in the perfections of creatures] (1.13.2). And insofar as *Star Maker* depends upon its imagery for a part of its coherence, the more it behaves as poetry.

Other Earth, for instance, the first world encountered, exemplifies in a simple fashion the cyclic and spiral aspects of *Last and First Men* (286-88), but also emphasizes the aspect of the destroyer revealed by the Star Maker in this book's conclusion. The narrator's friend protests: "That all struggle should be finally, absolutely vain, that a whole world of sensitive spirits should fail and die, must be sheer evil" (291). What, then, would he say if he knew that the Star Maker destroys not only individuals and races but one cosmos after another?

Of the next two subsections in the catalogue, each concerns three types of creatures. Strange Mankinds wean the narrator away from his physiological bias to an appreciation of diversity; evolved from starfish, the echinoderm humanity with its "coronet of five eyes" (305) reinforces this point, broadening the sense of creatureliness from a dual to a radial symmetry. More importantly, echinoderm reproduction by budding depends on the complexity of the pollen cloud emitted by the whole tribe, a sexuality illustrating the need of the individual for a rich and various community, not a monolith that could "degenerate into an instinctive animal herd" (307). The last aliens described in this subsection are the Nautiloids, an intuitive, oceanic life, mediated by unfamiliar senses: "to taste the bitter or delicious currents streaming past one's flanks, to feel the pressure of air on the sails as one beat up against the breeze, to hear beneath the water-line the rush and murmur of distant shoals of fish, and indeed actually to *hear* the sea-bottom's configuration" (312). Such an emphasis in this subsection on smell, taste, and synaesthesia disorients and reorients meaning and prepares for the transvaluations within the Star Maker.

The next subsection deals with symbiotic and composite races and the plant beings. The ichthyoid and arachnoid symbiosis, improved by genetic artifice and telepathy, develops the basic theme of service and detachment, modulated to the Jungian modes of extrovert and introvert (322) and to the medieval topos of the active and contemplative lives (325–26); the symbiosis also suggests one aspect of reality in the symbiotic deity, "a symbol of the dual personality of the universe, a dualism, it was said, of creativity and wisdom, unified as the divine spirit of love" (326), an emblem that looks forward to the Maker's relationship to the cosmoses, but also in the Maker a duplicity.

The composite beings, avians and insectoids, extend the sensory reorientation: "to see with a million eyes at once, how to feel the texture of the atmosphere with a million wings" (330), or to labor "with innumerable manipulatory antennae"(332). Whereas in the echinoderms it was necessary for Stapledon's rhetoric to present a variety of the group, in these composite races it requires a multiplicity and specialization of the senses; and the senses are also temporalized, in that potentially *immortal* "the civilized swarms had vague and fragmentary memories of every historical period" (332). It has, of course, been common in science fiction since at least *Flatland* and *A Voyage to Arcturus* (with both of which Stapledon was familiar [Crossley, "Olaf Stapledon" 23, 26]) to insist on those larger aspects of the physical world that lie beyond the limits of the human senses; for Stapledon, such spatial and temporal extensions implies an approach to divine omnipresence. The direct comprehension of wider spaces and longer and smaller durations that these races exemplify begins to describe the perception *sub specie aeternitatis* of the Star Maker.

The last race dealt with in the second triad is that of the intelligent plants, whose planet having little gravity possesses no atmosphere, so that the sky in full sunlight is "black with the blackness of interstellar space" (336), in which the stars blaze down. With three eyes, arms, and legs (337), they like the echinoderms have transcended dualism; what dualism they experience is a reversal of ours, in that, being mobile and individual by night, by day they sleep and flooded by sunlight wake into an apparent "ecstasy in which subject and object seemed to become identical, an ecstasy of subjective union with the obscure source of all finite being" (339). Unfortunately, these natural mystics ignore the polarities of true community, in their losing a sense of mutual critique, and pass "from ecstasy to sickness, despondency, uncomprehending bewilderment, and on to death" (340–41). Their experience warns the future Galactic Utopia not to ignore the details of its physical, fleshly basis; when it embarks on its great project "to see as though through the eyes of a creator" (372), it realizes that the task can only be achieved through an internal and external diversity.

The third section elevates these themes to the stars and the nebulae. Stars wish "to execute perfectly their part in the communal dance, and [. . .] to press forward to the attainment of full insight into the nature of the cosmos" (389). The icy raptures of old stars prefigure the icy temper of the Star Maker (390, 429); and the union of stars and planets recapitulates themes of diversity and symbiosis (394). The description of the dance attempts to resolve the dichotomy of necessity and free will through a remarkable blend of Spinoza and General Relativity (387-88), for which Stapledon may have found useful Eddington's four treatments of general relativity, each true from its particular frame, in terms of the earth: it is trying to go in a straight line; it is taking the longest possible route; it is accommodating its track to the existence of the sun; it goes anyhow it likes (148). The aesthetic nature of the dance provides the basic metaphor of the Star Maker as an artist, which as we have seen in *Last and First Men* is a development of Nietzschean ideas. The plight of the nebulae, those "celestial megatheria" (402), desiring "union with one another and [. . .] to be gathered up into the source whence they had come" (400), but confined to their separations within an expanding universe, recalls the withering of the plants at the end of the first catalogue, "annihilated, giving place to stars" (402). Also, the fate of the nebulae repeats the theme of spatial and temporal expansion. Dying at the beginning of the universe, but only contacted near its entropic conclusion, they suggest the abrogation of time revealed in the Star Maker.

What, then, is the Star Maker? The narrator envisions the creator as "an echo, a symbol, a myth" (412) that must be regarded dually, outside and inside time: "In my dream, the Star Maker himself, as eternal and absolute spirit, timelessly contemplated all his works; but also as the finite and creative mode of the absolute spirit, he bodied forth his creations one after the other in a time sequence" (413). A paradoxical language becomes necessary in order to affirm a proposition containing both these aspects: "Thus it was that in the end he became what, in the eternal view, he already was in the beginning, the ground and crown of all finite existence" (414). The debt of this formulation to Hegel is evident, for Hegel does not contemplate a passionless, static conception. It is not simply that "das Wahre ist das Ganze" [the true is the whole] (22; "Vorrede" XXIII). Truth achieves substance only through becoming, and the Spirit "gewinnt seine Wahrheit nur, indem er in der der absoluten Zerrissenheit sich selbst findet" [wins its truth only insofar it finds itself in absolute dismemberment" (29; "Vorrede" XXXIII-IXL), that is to say, in death. Only through such negativity is found the "in sich zurückgehende Kreis, der seinen Anfang voraussetzt, und ihn nur im Ende erreicht" [the circle that is returning into itself, that presupposes its beginning and reaches it only in the end] (442; 757).

But Stapledon has made a myth, not a philosophy. Besides a metaphysician, the Star Maker is a passionate artist: "Though there was love, there was also hate comprised within the spirit's temper, for there was cruel delight in the contemplation of every horror, and glee at the downfall of the virtuous. All passions, it seemed, were comprised within the spirit's temper; but mastered, icily gripped within the cold, clear, crystal ecstasy of contemplation" (429). A part of the grandiosity of the language proceeds from the assimilation of the Star Maker to the author, for, as Dorothy L. Sayers intimated, the experience of an author as a maker both in theory and practice may influence the author's theology (141-65). The narrator, now a part of the Cosmic Mind that assumes the Star Maker will accept his worship, as though the divinity were a god of love, launches itself forth as the Church cosmical, the bride that, in the figural interpretation of the Song of Songs, is the church made for her savior; the biblical language is a sign of the myth. It ignores Spinoza's warning: "Qui Deum amat, conari non potest, ut Deus ipsum contra amet" [He who loves God cannot strive that God should love him in return" (5.19). So in this myth the bride is "blinded and seared and struck down," as Semele was by Zeus, by the "effulgent star" that the narrator has seen on the first pages of the work, but a star that is "the centre of a four-dimensional sphere" (409). Yet knowledge and adoration cannot be refused, for "as I slammed and bolted the door of the little dark cell of my separate self, my walls were all shattered and crushed inwards by the pressure of irresistible light, and my naked vision was once more seared by lucidity beyond its endurance" (429). This "once more" is, however, precisely the vision that has been; the vision bites its own tail in a fashion that recalls the formulation of *Last and First Men*, "cyclic, but not repetitive."

The symbiosis of the Star Maker and its universes is, like all true community, a close and critical, bitter, yet most valuable of experiences, like all myths "a dread mystery, compelling adoration" (430). We had to have expected this conclusion, for these catalogues and histories of alien races are listed only in order to point beyond themselves, duplicitous metaphors that are meant to be broken. And among other metaphors, the Star Maker is a spiral. The structure is represented by the last of the famous time scales (438), now going inward. It is not possible, however, to give a formula for this spiral; we cannot say whether it is Archimedean or logarithmic because the cosmoses that compose it, in which the Ultimate Cosmos and the First Cosmos coincide, are infinite (438). Possibly that places a torsion on the structure that makes it helical. But Euclidean space will not confine the Star Maker, for which even its representation as a curved tesseract is undoubtedly symbolic. In the end mathematics fails as well as language. In the light of this rhetoric, the book is very orderly indeed.

What kind of orders are these that structure the two works? They are not organic, unless it is the organicism by which pine cones are formed to the Fibonacci sequence; nor are the books baggy or mechanical. They partake of music, which with the concept of game is the main source of Stapledon's controlling metaphor, and thereby of mathematics. In reading him we should be ready to be fulfilled, in part, by the dance of number, pattern, and a strenuous order. And if we are in any way aesthetically convinced by these structures that creation, process, and destruction are one, eternal actuality, within which as Nietzsche argued humanity ought to be both "ein *Übergang* und ein *Untergang*" [a surpassing and a descent] (2.281; *Zarathustras Vorrede*, sec. 4), then we can be moved with the eighteenth race to think that "it is very good to have been man" (246) and with the lonely narrator on the hill, walking home to his wife and his community at the end of *Star Maker*, that we have had "some increase of lucidity before the ultimate darkness" (434).

Go, Tell It on the Mountain

> Col viso ritornai per tutte quante
> Le sette spere, e vidi questo globo
> Tal, ch'io sorrisi del suo vil sembiante.
>
> [With my face turned down through all
> The seven spheres, I saw this globe
> Such that I smiled at its vile appearance.] (Dante, *Par.* 22.133-35)

An illuminating detail in Robert Crossley's biography of Olaf Stapledon is the man's avid devotion to mountain-climbing, illuminating because the imagery of the mountain-climber appears so often in the fiction (6, 223). When in *Last and First Men* the Patagonian Boy is trapped by a blizzard in the Andes and has a vision, he is fulfilling an archetype of Western culture, both in terms of religious tradition, in terms of literature, and in terms of the historical meanings with which mountain-climbing became invested as it developed into a sport. In *Odd John* the young mutant becomes initiated into his calling through a stay in the Scotch Highlands. In this chapter I want to investigate both *Last and First Men* and *Odd John* as well as *Star Maker* in terms of this archetype of the mountain-climber; but in the midst of this investigation it will also be necessary to employ and extend John Kinnaird's insight that the Patagonian Boy and the Last Man fulfill the archetype of the *puer senex*. Stapledon's perennial protagonist is a visionary mountain-climber, whether individual or racial, who in various fashions fails in the implicit quest.

I

Mountain-climbing is a natural symbol. It implies a detachment from the level plain of the earth, a broader vision as the climber sees more of the earth than can a person on the plain and sees the earth as a person on the plain cannot; it implies an increase of light as the clouds are left behind—but again an increase of detachment, as from the viewpoint of people on the plain the climber disappears into the clouds, and too much light is liable to blind the climber; and mountain-climbing implies authentication, as the climber selects the self and, given all the danger, begins to feel as though the self were selected—and thereby once more a startling detachment. To none of these influences was Stapledon blind. As an avid climber he could not have escaped what mountain-climbing had become in England during the nineteenth century; and after 1924 the heroic example of Mallory on Everest was inescapable.

Let us survey, as from a mountain peak, the tradition of the mountain and its visionary experience. This tradition begins with the experience of Moses on Sinai as he receives a structure for life directly from God, so directly that his face shines; but something of a failure is implied in this story, since the people who have been left behind revolt for the sake of the golden calf, for the sake of mere flesh, and also implied in his anger when he breaks the tables of the law. At the end of his life he ascends Nebo, from which he sees the Promised Land, which he cannot enter. There he dies and his body is lost from the earth but secure in the eye of God; in his authentication he is removed from human sight. Figuratively speaking Jesus repeats these moments on a mountain where he walks transfigured with Moses and Elijah and on a mountain where he is taken from the midst of the apostles. As we shall later see, it is not insignificant that Moses is also a liberator, as is Jesus; liberation from the fleshpots is inextricably associated with these two mountain-climbers.

We should also take note of the place of mountains in the Greco-Roman mythologies. The gods take their homes at the peak of Mt. Olympus, emphasizing the superiority of Zeus as well as his near-omniscience. The summit of poetry is to be found at the top of Parnassus and Helicon, where Apollo and the Muses are often to be found. Humans are seldom to be found on these peaks, though Heracles is transformed into a god who has married Hebe; a very important god in Roman times, he has not climbed a mountain; he marries her on Olympus but has not climbed it. If there is any visionary experience involved here it is through the aesthetic experience by which the poet imagines these peaks. These mountains demonstrate the distance between the gods and humanity; so the closest the pagan world comes to the Hebrew world is in Hesiod's encounter with the Muses on Helicon. "Wretched shepherds," they say, "we know how to speak many false things, and, when we wish, we know how to chatter many true things too" (*Theogony* 26-28). They do not condescend to discriminate between truth and fiction, certainly not for the sake of humans; the visionary experience of the Hebrew world is not to be found on Olympus.

After Moses and Jesus we would be hard put to find a mountain experience in the European tradition. In 181 BCE Philip of Macedonia decided to climb the Haemus Mountains because of the rumor that from the peak he could see the Pontic and Adriatic seas, a panorama possibly useful for the plans of a future war. The climb proved so difficult, however, and the view so impossible because of the trees and fog, that he returned to the plain not wishing to say anything of the disappointment of the climb (cited by Petrarch 2). Climbing a mountain provides neither a strategic advantage nor a transcendent moment when played out in the classical world.

Though this story had no further effect for many years, Petrarch mentions it as a reading that incited him to climb Mont Ventoux, the Windy Mountain, a climb he had contemplated for years. His ascent of the mountain on April 26, 1336, proved quite different from King Phillip's, an adventure he swiftly moralized. He climbs because he grew up with the mountain; and so this climb is at first as naïve as the later climbs. It begins with the warning of an old man, which youth naturally regards as a challenge and ignores; in Wagner's opera, Siegfried reacts in the same way to Wotan at the base of the fiery mountain. As Petrarch attacks the mountain he wanders, and his brother mocks him (the adventure has comic touches). We might guess that he has Dante's climb of Mt. Purgatory in mind, naturalizing Dante's allegory and thereby transforming it into a symbol. When he arrives at the summit, which for some strange reason is called Filiolum, a little son, though it seems to be the "pater omnium vicinorum montium" [the father of all the nearby mountains] (16), after a meditation on the past ten years of his life, asking "de utriusque hominis dominio" [which of his two men would have rule] (22), he opens his copy of St. Augustine's *Confessions* and reads, "Et eunt homines admirari alta montium et ingentes fluctus maris et latissimos lapsus fluminum et oceani ambitum et giros siderum, et relinquunt se ipsos" [And men went to admire the heights of mountains, the great tides of the oceans, the broad gliding of the rivers, the currents of the oceans, the turns of the stars and left themselves behind] (27), at which he turns away from the sight of the landscape, "iratus michimet quod nunc etiam terrestria mirarer, qui iampridem ab ipsis gentium philosophis discere debuissem nichil preter animum esse mirabile, cui magno nichil est magnum" [angry with myself that I still admired earthly things, I who for a long time had learned from the philosophers of the pagans that nothing outside of the soul is admirable, for in comparison to its greatness nothing is as great] (28), not even this great mountain, the little child who is the father of all.

The development is normative of many mountain stories, that on arriving at the summit the climber strikes out in a totally different direction; transcendence is both physical and non-physical. It is as though the process of the climb tacitly became a symbol, but as so often with symbols it is not easy to say what the climb, its beginning, its entire extent, and its conclusion at the peak, symbolizes. But both God and self and their relation seem involved. In Petrarch's case, we find that the mountain already manifests divine characteristics before the climb begins, for it is both son and father and at its base there is an ambiguous guide. The climb itself becomes a moral event, that which is between the mountain and the self; and at the peak the climber finds that the mountain itself, the mere symbol, must be cast away for the sake of the self and the utterly other. I cannot agree, then, with Marjorie Nicolson that "the shadow of St. Augustine" (222) falling across Petrarch's experience and rendering it classical and Christian at the same time invalidated its potent symbolism or made it radically different from the experiences we are about to study.

Next to Petrarch's experience, Wordsworth's fragment "The Simplon Pass" also seems significant. Its series of contradictory images, "woods decaying, never to be decayed, / The stationary blasts of waterfalls" (ll. 5-6), "Winds thwarting winds" (l. 8), "Tumult and peace, the darkness and the light" (l. 15), all

> Were all like workings of one mind, the features
> Of the same face, blossoms upon one tree,
> Characters of the great Apocalypse,
> The types and symbols of Eternity,
> Of first, and last, and midst, and without end. (ll.16-20)

Above all this is a vision of organic and dynamic wholeness, of being released from the fragments of mortal existence, which for this quick moment are seen in a dynamic unity. This release often implies freedom, in Romanticism especially associated with the Alps and the inheritance of William Tell. Friedrich Schiller's *Wilhelm Tell* in 1804 comes immediately to mind, and we find the same motif in the motto of West Virginia that separates the new state from the slavery tradition of Virgiana: "Montani Semper Liberi." But the details of political freedom often modulate to freedoms from all the categories of the plain and return us to the visionary world of the mountains.

This connection between mountains and liberation finds a particularly sharp instance in Simon Bolivar's legendary vision on "the vast mass of the Chimborazo, South America's greatest volcano" (Ybarra 251). This delirium he writes down after climbing the "the glacial regions, where the air was so thin I could scarcely breathe" (252). Before he reaches the summit he exclaims, "Time himself has been unable to check the march of Liberty" (252), but in the vision that follows Time appears as "the Father of the Centuries" who scorns Bolivar's pretensions: "Think you, in your madness, that your actions have any value in my eyes?" (253). Despite this colossal appearance, speaking a rhetoric that is similar to that which God speaks out of the whirlwind to Job, Bolivar descends from the mountain and proceeds to his conquests in Peru. In the name of liberty he has survived the mountain and the nothingness to which it would reduce him. Though this story is probably a fabrication, it undoubtedly says something true about the figure of Bolivar through the myth of the glacial mountain.

So much for our swift overview of the history and literature of mountain-climbing and vision. The most famous mountain-climber of the twentieth century was George Mallory. He climbed, and he wrote, and he disappeared at the summit of Mt. Everest. A part of the popularity and myth of Mallory may have to do with the fact that he strongly resembles in his literary tastes and his manner the generation of the Great War as Paul Fussell has described them; his "high diction" (21-23), his determination "to play the game" (25-29), his nonchalance toward glory, and his death constitute a nostalgia for the pre-war innocence he seemed to embody. And Stapledon certainly shared the life of that innocent generation and could not have lived in England when he did without being aware of Mallory.

In one of his early essays on mountain-climbing Mallory compared it to a symphony; the ascent with its various vicissitudes, the achievement of the peak, and the descent he sees as one whole, just as no symphony cannot be understood without an understanding of its various movements. Every climb is different, just as every symphony is different. "But every mountain adventure is emotionally complete. The spirit goes on a journey just as does the body, and this journey has a beginning and an end, and is concerned with all that happens between these extremities" (Mallory 21). In a later essay he said of a climb, after an extended self-examination caused by his falling asleep at a crucial moment in the climb, "Have we vanquished an enemy? None but ourselves. Have we gained a success? That word means nothing here. We have achieved an ultimate satisfaction . . . fulfilled a destiny . . . To struggle and to understand—never this last without the other; such is the law. We have only been obeying an old law, then? Ah, but it's *the* law and we understand—a little more" (60). Petrarch would have understood how the mountain so easily translates to a spiritual journey in which an intricate self-examination becomes the need to conquer one's self. This old law, then, is the psychic law to undertake the inward quest.

For years after his death Mallory signified a glorious failure. The Great War, which for so many, despite the victory, became perceived as an inglorious failure, a defeat of progress and humanity as well as a slaughter of a generation, needed recompense; and one recompense was mountain-climbing, an activity in which failure occurred within an act of selflessness. This glorious failure is relevant to the failure of the Eighteenth Man and the failure in *Star Maker* of the community of worlds, a failure built into the nature of things because any aspect of the creaturely world is incommensurate to the infinite life of the Star Maker. We must also ask whether there is a sense in which the Star Maker has also failed because of an inherent rift in his constitution, the asymmetry between his atemporal and temporal aspects that compels him into his various acts of creation that under his own critical eye are always found wanting and that therefore become acts of masochism as he attempts to torture himself into perfection.

Insofar as Mallory is one of those literary types whom Fussell describes, his figure may operate for Stapledon in some sort of fashion as a throwback. Mallory had spent the first two years of the war as a teacher, because his headmaster would not release him. He went to France in May 1916 and survived the butchery of the Sommes; he was invalided home and spent the last weeks of the war near Arras (Holzel and Salkeld 44). Some of the men of the war did not react with bitter denial of the values that led them there; Stapledon is certainly one whose response is measured.

But there is another, very specific aspect of Mallory's attempt that may have arrested Stapledon's attention: the use of the oxygen tank. As a climber Stapledon seems to have preferred using nothing but his fingertips and toes; Odd John strips himself naked in order to face the wilderness of the Scotch Highlands. But Stapledon could not have been blind to the possibilities of the oxygen tank as a technology that would change the landscape of climbing, a landscape that would still be dangerous, fatal for Mallory and Irvine, but a landscape that without the tank would have been sheerly impossible. The oxygen tank is a symbiosis that extends human consciousness.

Such notions as the agonistic attitude toward the body and the feeling of a submission to a law, all for the sake of insight, are not foreign to Stapledon.

II

The imagery of the mountain is introduced very early in *Last and First Men* as the last man addresses our contemporary complacency that we have achieved all that mind is capable of. "Surely, you think, there will come a time when there will be no further heights to conquer" (14). On the contrary, we "underestimate even the foothills that stand in front of [us], and never suspect that far above them, hidden by cloud, / rise precipices and snow-fields" (14-15). Mind and the achievements of mind, everything that we understand as culture, are compared to a range of mountains, higher and higher as the millennia pass, and lower and lower as the races and their cultures disintegrate.

Mountains are unimportant to the culture of the First Race until the Patagonian Boy follows his "queer love for clambering about the high mountains," where in "the snow-fields and precipices of Aconcagua" he is caught in a blizzard and falls into a snowdrift and nearly dies (82). Here his religious language is transformed. Previously he had insisted that life was a game, in precisely the sense that we care more for the game itself than for winning (82). But now his language becomes aesthetic: "It was as though a play-actor were to see the whole play, with his own part in it, through the author's eyes" (83). True, for the actor who was about to die in the snow the situation was ghastly, "yet for me, the spectator, it had become excellent" (83), all the more as he now saw "everything through the calm eyes, the exultant, almost derisive, yet not unkindly, eyes of the playwright" (83). Object and subject has fused. This insight of our life as an actor is very like the words of Epictetus: "Remember that you are an actor in a play, the character of which is determined by the Playwright. [. . .] For this is your business, to play admirably the role assigned you; but the selection of that role is Another's" (1.497). The difference between these two visions lies in the snow, the mountain, and the possibility of the actor's seeing the world through the eyes of God. The vision of Epictetus suffers, that of the Patagonian Boy exults. This is a language that Mallory uses casually as he reintegrates himself into the party: "He was prepared to play a part and there was a part to be played" (55).

Another background to the story of the Patagonian Boy may lie in Thomas Mann's *The Magic Mountain*, which was published in English in 1927 and earned him the Nobel Prize in 1929. The protagonist Hans Castorp early receives from the humanist Settembrini the name of the eternal student. But this eternal student finally needs the wilderness, drawn by "a lively craving to come into close and freer touch with the mountains, the mountains in their snowy desolation" (473). In contrast to the old man whom Petrarch meets, Settembrini approves of Castorp's youthful address on his new skis; yet when Castorp sets forth on his exciting expedition, Settembrini calls out a warning and turns back to the sanatorium in which most of the novel takes place.

Soon Castorp meets difficulties as it begins to snow "without pause, endlessly, gently, soundlessly falling" (476). Though he recognizes that he is threatened by the uncanny power of the snow, he is still led on by it. "So if we can speak of Hans Castorp's feeling of kinship with the wild powers of the winter heights, it is in this sense, that despite his pious awe he felt these scenes to be a fitting theatre for the issue of his involved thoughts, a fitting stage for one to make who [. . .] found it had devolved upon him to take stock of himself, in reference to the rank and status of the *Homo Dei*" (477–78). The snow, however, now turns to a storm and in time he falls into a snowdrift. Half-delirious, he has a complex vision, almost theatrical in its artificiality, of a benign pastoral scene and of two old hags dismembering a child (493–94). We are on the edge of the *sparagmos*. The conclusion Hans Castorp draws may seem simple: "Only love, not reason, gives sweet thoughts. And from love and sweetness alone can form come: form and civilization [. . .] always in silent recognition of the blood-sacrifice" (496); that is to say, the *sparagmos* is eternally in process. The storm ceases and he skis back to the sanatorium, but he has had a valuable vision. In any case, the shape of his experience is very like that of the Patagonian Boy, the *senex puer* in Kinnaird's analysis who shall not grow aged despite the difficulties he endures.

Individuals in the second race of humanity, like the Patagonian Boy, "were wont to seek Alpine dangers and hardships for their souls' refreshment" (114). Unfortunately, in doing so they encounter a green cloud that is the vanguard of the Martians, which totally misunderstands the nature of the creatures they have met. Years after they have been destroyed they return, this time "operating simultaneously from all the alpine regions of the earth" (128), initiating a war of genocide against the humans they regard as no more than animals. The narration is not implicit, but surely a theme touched upon here is the danger that dwells in the mountains.

The third race in all its civilization is especially sensitive to music. One of these civilizations is founded by a prophet who preaches the immortality and recurrence of every soul, just like the recurrence of a melody. Though made an oracle in the hands of the monarch, the prophet doubts the imprisonment of his melodies and "retire[s] into the mountains to perfect his art under the influence of their great quiet, or the music of wind, thunder, and waterfall" (149); he searches for the same refreshment that the Patagonian Boy and the people of the second race had sought. But the bureaucracies and the emperor cannot allow his absence, so he is once more imprisoned and allowed no other than conventional music, soon going mad; and now he is all the more useful to that world.

In time the third race creates the fourth race of the Great Brains; but we need say nothing about them, for no alpine experience appears in their chronicles. Love, self-sacrifice, art, and the life of the body were closed to them (165); so the life of the mountain was apparently closed to their mere intellect also.

The fifth race, which the Great Brains had created to make up for their insufficiency, creates its own alpine experience in the Arctic, "chosen mainly for its mountains; for since most of the Alpine tracts had by now been worn into insignificance by water and frost, mountains were much prized" (171). "Invigorated and enlightened" by their experience, and sometimes returning to it, they pass into the main occupations of their lives, "art, science and philosophy," never "repeating themselves or falling into ennui" (173). This may seem remarkable to us, mere members of the first race who have found boredom and ennui an important aspect of our spiritual experience, but the last man reassures us, using the language of the Introduction: "the higher a mind's development, the more it discovers in the universe to occupy it" (173).

Unfortunately, the life of the fifth race was to be short-lived because the moon, for no reason evident to the race, was soon to spiral into Earth and destroy it. Despite the intellectual nature of the race, and in fact because of it, "It is the very error of the moon, / She comes more nearer earth than she was wont, / And makes men mad" (*Othello* 5.2.118-20). This is a mountain they cannot explain nor explain away nor escape except by terraforming Venus and moving to it.

On Venus the fifth race degenerates into the sixth race, of which little can be said, except that on occasion, through some two hundred million years, the people of the race did have some insight into the nature of themselves and the universe, sometimes suffering from "the mere cowardice and vertigo that dared not look down the precipice of fact" (193). They do not have the strength of the culture in which they appear.

In time the sixth race produces the seventh race. It is small and winged; though it is not intellectual, it is constituted of natural ecstatics and artists, whether in dance or song, but only in the air were they capable of such feats; on land the fatality of life was liable to overwhelm them. Flight was an achievement that several previous races had yearned for, but most of their successes had been mechanical or technological in nature; in the seventh race it was organic and innate. However, given various illnesses to which they were prone, they raised some of their offspring to become the eighth race, a group of "brilliant cripples" (201) who soon, moved by a not so unconscious *Schadenfreude*, began to strip the glories of the skies from their ancestors.

The response of the seventh race is shocking. The decided "to take part in an act of racial suicide" (202); death should be "a noble gesture of freedom" (202), as it had been for the Romans. Once the whole race was lifted into the sky it saw the beauty of the thing and flew west into the cone of a volcano, where two by two, "couple by couple, the whole multitude darted into its fiery breath and vanished" (202). I suspect that Stapledon had in mind the story of the Greek philosopher Empedocles, especially as the climax of his life was drawn by Matthew Arnold in the dramatic poem "Empedocles on Etna." Weary with his own swings between solitude and the world of men who "rid him of the presence of himself" (2.223), Empedocles turns to Etna where he is "Alone—! / On this charred, blackened, melancholy waste, / Crowned by the awful peak, Etna's great mouth" (2.1-3). Where Giacomo Leopardi, facing the space "qui su l'arida schiena / del formidabil monte / sterminator Vesevo" [here, on the barren ridge / of the formidable mountain, / Vesuvius, the destroyer] ("La ginestra," ll. 1-3), chose the moral act in which human individuals comfort one another in the face of certain destruction—in the face of that possibility, Empedocles and the seventh race choose the ecstasy of destruction. Their mountain like Leopardi's is demonic; its awe, rather than a sign of the slow expansion of the spirit, is a sign of the signal moment of destruction. The people who climb the mountain are perfectly aware of the danger but do not court it. The Patagonian Boy struggled out of the snow as did Hans Castorp, but no one can struggle out of the fire once we catapult into it.

The eighth race, which had driven the seventh race to its destruction, has no experience of climbing mountains. Its only grace is its decision, in the face of the expansion of the sun, to transfer humanity to Neptune. The beginning of this last section of the book takes up the language we saw in the Introduction: "Before continuing our long flight let us look around us. Hitherto we have passed over time's fields at a fairly low altitude [. . .]. Now we shall travel at a greater height and with speed of a new order" (205). And so the narration does, sketching in nine races in ten pages with no room for the fine points of mountain-climbing; this is, of course, not surprising, since owing to its tremendous gravity there are no mountains on Neptune. Only the eighteenth, utopian race has time and inclination to build "great architectural pylons, cruciform or star-shaped in section, cloud-piercing," which to a visitor would look like "geometrical mountains" (216). In the thin air of these structures the astronomers of the eighteenth race can investigate far space; there also the race performs those acts that would seem religious to others. "There also they seek the refreshment of mountain air [. . .]. And on the pinnacles and precipices of those loftiest horns many of us gratify that primeval lust of climbing [. . .]. These buildings thus combine the functions of observatory, temple, sanatorium and gymnasium" (216). In addition, an antarctic continent fulfills the function of the wilderness that mankind still needs. Wild animals are there to contend with, and "volcanic eruption, hurricanes and glacial seasons afford further attractions to the adventurous young" (220). The demonic mountain is no more than an entertainment to this race, who thus set aside Empedocles and the sublimity of mass suicide for the sake of tragic endurance, "the supreme art of ecstatic fatalism" (241).

This race seems very different from those that had preceded it, especially given the group mind that they have achieved. This mind, however, sees itself and its world in precisely the way that certain individuals had done before. With its many eyes and many hands and feet it experiences its world in one immediate act of perception, "as one who, from above the battle, watches himself and his comrades agonizing in some desperate venture; yet chiefly as an artist who has no thought but for his vision and its embodiment" (225). He sees the world, then, as the Patagonian Boy had seen it, as a stage upon which he is an actor and the playwright.

At this point we need to raise the point that John Kinnaird introduced in his discussion of Stapledon: the Patagonian Boy and the Last Man are each a *puer senex,* a boy with the wisdom of an old man. John Kinnaird shows that this medieval topos contains a prophetic cast in its use (50). Jesus, we might point out, is a *puer senex* when as a twelve-year-old he confounds the doctors in the temple (Luke 2:42-50). But besides Kinnaird's examples the *puer senex* appears at other peaks in the action of Stapledon's works. In the climax of *Star Maker* the supreme spirit is revealed to be a *puer senex,* for at the end of his hypercosmic labors, though he is now a very experienced maker, he becomes what he always was, which is to say the inexperienced but zestful maker; he is at once very young and infinitely old (414, 438). Hegel's path to the Geist, "dieser sich selbst erzeugende, fortleitende und in sich zurückgehende Gang" [this path that gives birth to itself, guides itself forward, and returns into itself] (48), becomes in Stapledon's use of the *puer senex* a long, almost human labor. And as we toy with this topos, which Ernst Robert Curtius elevated to the category of an archetype (101,105), we realize that it was present at the beginning of the history of mountain-climbing in Western culture when Petrarch climbed the mountain that was both the Filiolum and the "pater omnium vicinorum montium" (16). He tried to explicate the odd conjunction of these phrases, but the difficulty is evident, because the *puer senex* is more than simply an oxymoron; it is what Jung called a *conjunctio oppositorum,* which in its tension means much more than the words themselves.

Having looked ahead and behind of our study, let us turn to *Star Maker* where, in contrast to *Last and First Men,* there are very few mountains, for the simple reason that the descriptions of alien races that make up most of the matter of the work would seem to prohibit the complications that the mountains would bring. Nevertheless, the work begins with a quiet appeal to the myth of the visionary on the mountain, "One night when I had tasted bitterness I went out on to the hill" (255). Not *a* hill but *the* hill, a very particular hill, probably because it lies near to the house of the protagonist; it may strike the reader as a rather suburban hill, given the style of the speaker. Still, it is particularized, and that particularity earns it the sense of the sacred mountain, upon which this very uncertain, bourgeois protagonist finds himself playing out the role of Moses and Petrarch. Or is he the folklore figure of the man who has fallen asleep in the realm of the elves and awakes shaken in time? The last chapter begins, "I woke on the hill" (430).

Except for this mountain, if it can be called such, only one true range of mountains occurs in the work on the planet of the intelligent plants, mountains that are significant for several of the major themes. The other imagery of the mountains is often in the form of extended similes. These passages refer back to the imagery of mountains in *Last and First Men*; and in these passages we are reminded once more of the symbiotic, polar relation of the two works.

The planet of the plant-men shall seem either a nightmare, a delirium, or a vision, depending upon the visitor's background. It was "a mass of fold-mountains, primeval and extinct volcanoes, congealed floods and humps of lava, and craters left by the impact of giant meteors" (336). But given the various tensions of the surface, many of the mountains had been shattered into grotesque forms, like ice-bergs or "slender, top-heavy crags and pinnacles [that on earth] could never have stood," eerie shapes that given the absence of atmosphere are either blindingly lit by the sun or "black as night" (337). The dualities of the plants' existence are suggested by the landscape, but its irregularities remind us of the violence of its place to which the plants are subject.

I do not mean to go into the life of the galactic community, except for two details. First, when the narrator refers to "this relatively high level of the spirit's ascent" (372) he is using that language we are familiar with from *Last and First Men* that compares the progress of spirit and its cultural life to a range of mountains, for this ascent implies a detachment of the spirit. "For, as the spirit wakens, it craves more and more to regard all existence not merely with a creature's eyes, but in the universal view, as though through the eyes of the creator" (372). The narrator does not elaborate this image. It is uttered as though it were a common image that had no need of elaboration; but we recognize that it is the same language employed by the Patagonian Boy and the Last Man. Through such insight the galactic community is able to reach back to the Plant Men and take warning of "the extravagance of their own mystical quietism" (374). This eye of the creator never loses sight of the physical world upon which the galactic community depends.

As the mind of the galactic community begins to approach the moment in which it will behold the Star Maker, it describes its experience more precisely in terms of climbing a mountain; the effect is one gaining more clarity.

> The further I ascended along the path of the spirit, the loftier appeared the heights that lay before me. For what I had once thought to be the summit fully revealed was now seen to be a mere foot-hill. Beyond lay the real ascent, steep, cragged, glacial, rising into the dark mist. Never, never should I climb that precipice. And yet I must go forward. Dread was overcome by irresistible craving. (404)

This protagonist has moved beyond rock-climbing, the experience that was familiar to Stapledon, into the snowy Himalayan world where people die.

This extended language is used to introduce the moment—and it is still only that one moment—in which the narrator sees, as though in a dream, the Star Maker at work. The narrator is like "[a] walker in mountainous country, lost in mist, and groping from rock to rock, [who] may come suddenly out of the cloud to find himself on the very brink of a precipice" (412). Once more the word "precipice" stands out, the sign of the sudden fall, the risk that is always present in Stapledon's world. This walker sees everything below in his detachment, all the created worlds, and above the sun, that which to the Plant Men had been the metaphor of the Maker. The walker sees "by the light itself that not only illumines but gives light to all" (412). Then the mist comes in once more and he sees nothing.

The vision of the Star Maker that is the climax of the work leaves us, for that moment, upon an implicit peak, where "all pity and all love" is "mastered by a frozen ecstasy [. . .], mastered, icily gripped within the cold, clear, crystal ecstasy of contemplation" (429). This is once more the language of the Himalayan climb as well as the language of Hans Castorp, the discovery of a geometrical perfection that is deadly to human, organic life (Mann 480).

In the late works we find the most detailed praise of physical activity, the body in close encounter with rock—Stapledon renounces the Himalayan snows. This language is important for the eighteenth race (and the earlier utopian races), and for Odd John. It is imagery that Stapledon could not surrender in the later works. Odd John reminds the narrator sometimes "of a little old man with snowy hair condescending to play with young gorillas" (39); when grown this *puer senex* finds it necessary to test himself in the wild, which in his case is the mountainous landscape of Scotland. Though Sirius grows up on a farm, it is a farm located in the remote, rough uplands of Wales. In *The Flames* the protagonist Cass, an abbreviation for his ominous nickname Cassandra (5), discovers the intelligent flame after he becomes lost upon a snowy mountain in the Lake Country; but he does not discover the flame upon the mountain. Instead, he finds his way to the bottom of the mountain where a disused mine attracts his attention and digging through it he takes hold of the stone within which the flame is imprisoned—a discovery that is highly ambiguous. At the end of the story we do not know whether the earth is doomed to end in ice or in nuclear flames; Cass himself burns to death in an inexplicable fire in the Mental Home where he has been confined (83-84). No vision is mastered here.

III

Let us ask once again what the man who is climbing a mountain finds at its peak. Illumination, yes, and sometimes transfiguration, but that illumination is very personal, as though the climber had met someone who is speaking to the athlete who is now discovered. Petrarch meets St. Augustine, who is speaking to him out of the *Confessions* in a new fashion. Wordsworth reads the symbols of a new apocalypse, out of which he seizes liberation; Schiller reads there the liberation that Wilhelm Tell creates, and Bolivar follows in their tracks to discover *liberación*. Mallory, who has a good deal of modern sophistication, realizes that he is wrestling with an aspect of himself. Two of the most complex and extended events of these climbs are Dante's confrontation with Beatrice at the top of Mount Purgatory when he faces her challenge for the life he has led and at the dizzy peak of the Paradiso his confrontation with the infinite face of the triune god. But the person of that god is twofold. Yes, it is Jesus, human and divine, but we cannot but suspect that for Dante this god wears the insistent, inexhaustible smile of Beatrice, whom he first met as a child.

The importance of Dante for Stapledon as an example of man and of artist is a matter of record in Robert Crossley's biography. Though the seventeen-year-old Stapledon does not seem at first to have been attracted to his cousin, the nine-year-old Anne Miller, her age, like that of the nine-year-old Beatrice in the *Vita nuova*, began to work upon his imagination, so that in five years he felt he was powerfully in love with her (Crossley 60). But Dante is also present for Stapledon as an example for the artist who feels compelled to see the world as a combination of mystic experience, political hardihoods, and the contingencies of history, the artist moreover for whom it is still necessary to root vision and contemporary terrors in the earliest and most recent experiences of love. The significance of Stapledon's decision to begin *Star Maker*, his epic of the cosmos, in the aftermath of a marital crisis cannot be too much emphasized; for that epic only makes sense in the community of his wife. When we keep this opening of *Star Maker* steadily in mind, the ongoing quest of the visionary company to discover the place of love in the universe takes on new weight. But since unlike Dante they do not discover love in the climax of their vision, a reader must wonder whether some failure has occurred. The narrator of Stapledon's work confesses that many elements of the final vision may be a mistake, not only insufficient to express what he had seen but insufficient to his own understanding. If, then, the hoarse words of the final canto is a betrayal of his own attempt, are a part of that betrayal the betrayal of love?

Before even attempting to answer such a question, let us look more closely at the kind of example Dante offered. First, note that Dante finds not only *amore* but *sapientia* and *potestá* at the end of his quest. At the beginning of the quest the distortions of love, wisdom, and power are presented in the figures of the wolf, the lion, and the leopard. In the third canto love, wisdom, and power appear on the gates of hell as involved in its making, surely a vision that can only be accepted as a partial understanding of their nature; we cannot turn away from the words on the gate, but we do need to wrestle with them, just as Jacob wrestled with the Angel. Only in the second canto do love, wisdom, and power appear from a divine angle in Virgil's carefully framed account of the three ladies in heaven, Mary, Beatrice, and Lucia, who have moved him to approach Dante; and we should note that this aspect of the vision is repeated in the penultimate canto of the *Commedia* where the three ladies again appear; they form one of the significant frames that Dante was fond of creating. If the *Commedia* truly opens at the first canto, it can hardly be said to open in the experience of love. Or, to say this in another fashion, it opens in as bitter a state of misapprehension as does *Star Maker*; only in the second canto does this misapprehension begin to be healed; and only in the ninety-ninth canto is this healing fully confirmed.

But the narrative proper of the *Commedia* does not open in its first canto. Dante is writing the poem not only for all Italy; he is first writing it for Florence, the bitter mother that has reared and exiled him, the Florence that received the first writings of her bitter son, the sonnets and their orchestration in the *Vita nuova*. And it is there that the *Commedia* begins, the bitter son lost in the Inferno of the "selva oscura" (1.2). How else is a reader of the *Commedia* to understand the full significance of the lines when he meets the wonderful woman at the top of purgatory, "Guardaci ben! ben son, ben son Beatrice" [Look at me carefully: truly I am, truly I am Beatrice] (30.73), unless through having read of Dante's first and last encounters with Beatrice in Dante's earliest work? The betrayal referred to in the opening of the *Inferno* and the close of the *Purgatorio*, in those places outside of time, makes no full sense unless we understand how central to Dante's being has been the historical encounter with the girl and woman called Beatrice.

In the same way, it helps our understanding of *Star Maker* to realize that the opening of that work is not an unrealized literary convention but the continuation of a meditation on love that has not only been in process in Stapledon's personal life—as it was, as Crossley's biography has more fully revealed—but that has been in process in many of Stapledon's works.

At the climax of *Star Maker*, when the final cosmos "spread[s] wing to meet" (429) its maker, the Star Maker rejects the advances of this consciousness and strikes it down in an apparently sadistic act. And sadism has already been defined as a manifestation of love in *Last and First Men* when the second race appeared with its plastic art of genetic and fleshly manipulation. But is the lover to love the beloved only because the beloved offers material and recalcitrance to be molded?

Beatrice would probably take some time before answering fully. But much of her answer might lie in the way that she has behaved to Dante, for she has surely treated him in the *Commedia* as a person to be trained that he shall go for his salvation, that is, in order to perfect his being in the shape of God. But he had offered himself to her for the ends of such perfection when she smiled at him when still alive, though he could not have known then what would be entailed. Whom else would she smile at if not Dante, this naturally gifted poet with his great store of knowledge of the troubadours, of the Italian poets, of Virgil and of the other Latin poets? Who else was capable of rendering the vision of the *Commedia*?

But was he truly capable of the *Commedia*? In the final canto of the work he confesses some six times his inability to conceive and to remember and to write how he was to render his vision of the threefold divinity—some six versets confess, "Oh quanto è corto il dire e quanto fioco / al mio concetto!" [Oh how poor is my speech and how rough / to my conception] (33.121-22). And he says this when not far from the conclusion. It is as though six times a breathless mountain-climber gasped near the peak, "I can't do it, I can't do it!" But with divine help he can do it, achieving the peak in the last verset when Beatrice gives him her last smile and leaves him to the pedagogy of Bernardo. This seems like a moment of desertion or betrayal, her withdrawal of the smile that had been so important to him in the *Vita nuova*; but she is now "sì lontana / comea parea" [so far / as it appeared] (31.91-92) in this strange air of heaven, strange like the air at the peak of Everest where the landscape miles away seems so close. The peak itself is of course the last verset of the work. Dante has several times in the *Commedia* intimated his return, but like so many mountain-climbers he does not describe it. The narrator of *Star Maker* does not describe how he wakes up, the space between "the identical moment of illumination" (429), which he has experienced under so many aspects, and his singular moment of waking.

The most moving version of the Beatrician vision in Stapledon's work is his treatment of the theme in *Sirius*. And here we should remember that the Beatrician moment is not simply in the meeting; it is the divine smile that cannot be contained by the lover who sees it. "Sicché appare manifestamente che nelle sue salute abitava la mia beatitudine, la quale molte volte passava e redundava la mia capacitade" [Thus it seemed clear that in her greetings my happiness dwelt, which many times passed and overflowed my capacity] (*Vita nuova* XI). He had described himself in the first greeting he received as "come inebbriato" [as if drunk] (III). His relation with Beatrice, whether she is alive or dead, is punctuated by these moments in which he thoroughly loses himself. Both in this early work and in the *Commedia* this shattering, quasi sexual moment occurs.

The intelligent dog is raised from its puppy life with Plaxy Trelone, the daughter of his creator, and thus they are close at an early age; but when she is a year old he is already, mentally and physically, some seven years old. But she is not at a loss, for her experience already tells him that he shall never understand such things as color; and she shall never understand such things as scent. Thus they play out one of the striking points in the relation between Dante and Beatrice, the discrepancy of their age and of their understandings.

The most dramatic moment of this period is Sirius's introduction to the instinctual violence of dogs and his admission that he is such a dog, though at first he bumbles the violence. Gelert, the smartest of the dogs on the farm, catches and devours a rabbit, but Sirius at first only catches a frog; and Plaxy finds him disgusting. Despite the comedy of this action, however, Stapledon means the reader to take seriously Sirius's introduction to "the dark blood-god" (181, 193). Very much like D. H. Lawrence in *St. Mawr* and *The Plumed Serpent* in his treatment of the myth of Pan (102; 341-42), using Lawrence's language, Stapledon insistently mythologizes the instinctual violence of the human life, for Sirius is not simply a dog in this episode; he is a symbol of humanity.

Is there anything like this in the experience of Dante? Yes, the young man has a dream in which a naked woman lies in the arms of Love, who has her eat the heart of the poet; at first she does this "dubitosamente" [hesitantly] (III). This dream becomes the matter of the first sonnet in the work, as though Dante cannot become a poet unless he admits the animal violence of love. We should also note that in all the visionary encounters Dante will have with Beatrice, she will no longer be naked.

The center of *Sirius* is composed of a series of chapters in which the quester-dog meets a variety of experiences in the human world and judges what this human world is worth; and in these experiences Plaxy has little place. In the first of these experiences Sirius learns how to be a sheepdog under the benign leadership of Pugh, a local farmer, who says that he might as well marry Sirius to his daughter Jane; and he repeats his statement at the end of Sirius's apprenticeship (203, 227)—a joke of course, but by misdirection it points toward the depth of the relation between Sirius and Plaxy. Pugh changes the dog's name to Bran, which Sirius experiences as degradation, the loss of his own name; but Bran is a sacred name in Celtic mythology, for when the giant the Blessèd Bran dies his head is buried beneath the Tower

Hill London to protect the island from invasion (Squire 294-97). Then for a short time Sirius goes to Cambridge to share in the intellectual experiences of his creator Trelone; of greater interest are his experiences in the churches in the area, which are all the more important when he visits the church of Geoffrey in the slums of London. This is a man whose love is acted out day by day with no care for the self.

Very loosely these chapters may recall to us the period in Dante's life when his life is devoted to study and politics; his interior life confronts the death of Beatrice and he composes the *Vita nuova*, his first attempt to master death and meaninglessness through art. We should note that this moment is concluded before her death by his apocalyptic dream in which she dies, just as Dante's love begins in his dream of Love and the naked beloved. And just as this period for Dante is interrupted by his exile from Florence, Sirius's life of study is interrupted by the onset of World War II. He is forced to leave his studies and retire to the Welsh mountains once more.

Sirius cannot go to the battlefield, and he does not want to. Nevertheless the war imposes upon his life in such a way that it leads at last to his death. Working for Thwaites, a man who despises and beats the dogs that work for him, Sirius at last kills the man and thus becomes an exile in the mountains; he shares in the brutality of such men and in the brutality of the Nazis. The war furthermore causes the deaths of the two most important men in Sirius's life, his creator Trelone and Geoffrey; and the two deaths seem to coalesce in a dream that is as important to Sirius as Dante's dreams have been to him. In the dream "Geoffrey sought out Thwaites in Hell, and found him with Sirius's soul in his pocket. Somehow Geoffrey brought Thwaites up to Heaven, and his reward was the freeing of Sirius" (279). Geoffrey, whose name is associated with peace and love (Partridge 235), descends to Hell as Beatrice had done to free not only Sirius but the man who had cast him into Hell, who no matter what Sirius may do still has him "in his pocket" (279). Thwaites, however, had more within him than is evident. His name, which means to hew or cut down, also means a "woodland with the trees cut down, also a meadow" (Partridge 804); and Plaxy's name, we should note, means "to intertwine" (Partridge 501). Both names suggest a cultivation of the trees, of a trained growth. Sirius needs an aggression from Plaxy that she is loath to display. He cannot intertwine their natures; only she owns that ability.

When Trelone dies in Liverpool Sirius has to find his way home in Northern Wales by going through the tunnel beneath the Mersey, the "boundary river" (*AHD* app.). In doing so he follows Dante on the top of Mt. Pergatory, being pulled through the river by Matelda and through drinking the water of Eunoia. Only then is he ready to ascend to the stars. Sirius in going through his Night Journey becomes prepared to die.

In *Sirius* Stapledon returns once more to the mountain imagery that is so important to his imagination, but that imagery is now lit by his devotion to Dante, both in the *Vita nuova* and in the *Commedia*, through Dante's intense devotion to the woman that the world called Beatrice.

Now the Beatrician moment returns when Sirius and Plaxy make love to each other. The language here is quite removed, as we would expect of any British or American work written at this time; Stapledon's publisher insisted that he censor his own work, as he did, but the moment is not lost on any reader of Stapledon. The narrator intimates that "isolation, combined with contempt for the critics, drew girl and dog into closer intimacy, in fact into a manner of life which some readers may more easily condemn than understand" (293). She confesses to the narrator, "Humanly I do love you very much, but—how can I say it?—super-humanly, in the spirit, but therefore in the flesh also, I love my other dear, my strange darling" (296). The Beatrician moment always moved on the other side of human morality.

Postlude

In his last years Stapledon was to suffer a variety of anxieties about his achievement and the future of the human race: he was an old man in a world that had changed drastically from his childhood; he was definitely like Moses not to cross over into the promised land.

As we read him today the promised land is even farther from our grasp. His last work, "Old Man in a New World," expressed too well his disenchantment with the contemporary world, even though it seems utopian. After his death nine years were to pass before Hillary and Tenzing climbed Everest; and fifty years were to pass before Mallory's body was found on Everest. We still do not know whether he reached the summit. It remains as far and as near as God.

The Lament of the Midwives in *Childhood's End*

> The mind is its own place, and in itself
> Can make a Heav'n of Hell, a Hell of Heav'n.
> What matter where, if I be still the same,
> And what I should be, all but less than hee,
> Whom Thunder hath made great? (Milton, *Paradise Lost* 1.254-58)

In the nearly seventy years since its publication the popularity of *Childhood's End* shows little sign of diminishing. The variety of its subplots and the fascination of its main character, Karellen, may offer a partial reason for that popularity, as may the peculiar, ambivalent élan of its climax; but the coherence of its subplots, the import of Karellen, and the significance of the climax remain disputed. Yet the subplots parallel one another closely—both in pattern and in the two types of characters from whom they are constructed—and illuminate the imagery and themes of the novel, centering on Karellen. An analysis of these patterns confirms and extends the contention of several critics that the novel succeeds through an intricate coherence. It creates a manifold lament for human inadequacy and isolation, rooted in bureaucratic specialization and sexual failure. The *threnos* moves into central place in this novel.

These several subplots may be identified as a series of quests by different characters: in the prologue, Hoffmann and Schneider; in part I, Stormgren; in parts II and III, Jean, Jan, and the children; and overarching all, Karellen. This alien's quest, however, only becomes apparent after we have clarified the other characters and their interactions.

I

Hoffmann and Schneider, two German scientists who have been co-opted by American and Soviet forces to aid in their rocket programs at the end of World War II, may seem a special case in the novel, occupying barely five pages; yet they form a significant addition to the original novella, "Guardian Angel." Their quest may be taken as a paradigm of those comprising the rest of the novel. Two friends isolated from each other and from their colleagues, they represent "the cleavage" (4) between East and West and every other rift that humanity suffers. Though isolated, however, they are not without aid from the intelligence officers Sandmeyer and Grigorievitch, each of whom assumes the blindness of his counterpart: "The Russian research departments probably don't know what their own people are doing," Sandmeyer claims, and Grigorievitch echoes him, "They don't know a thing about us" (5). To the extent that both happen to be wrong they seem a parody of second-rate minds guessing at what lies beyond them. Hoffmann and Schneider need these men for their organizations and equipment—the two visionaries cannot transcend earth and its days and nights for "the eternal sunshine of space" (3) without them—but such utility and obviously such intelligence have limits.

The two quests begin in opposing landscapes. One begins in the sleep of a volcano that forms an island in the center of the Pacific, earth's largest ocean; Hoffmann is associated with its mountain peak. Schneider, on the other hand, is introduced standing next to Lake Baikal, the deepest lake on earth, lying in the middle of Asia, earth's largest continent. The two landscapes form mirror images, suggestive of the descents and ascents that shape the following narrative. These images fuse in the image of the iceberg at the end of the Prologue, a floating mountain with one-ninth of its mass breaking the waves and eight-ninths of its frozen waters submerged.

Between them Schneider and Hoffmann exemplify reactions to the appearance of the Overlords, ranging from the futility Schneider feels to the assent Hoffmann expresses as they confront the supersession of human achievement as "nothing now" and the expectation of being "no longer alone" (7). The cleavage seems healed. A visionary, who has needed the help of a blind assistant, descends and ascends to accomplish a quest that results in the abrogation of human effort, human isolation, and human time. In such an abrogation opposites join. This is the pattern structuring the novel in its several subplots.

The oldest section of the novel dealing with the quest of Stormgren fulfills this pattern twice. Several of Clarke's additions clarified the structure, but it was already present in the novella. Storm's quest, of which he is at first hardly aware, begins when he is in his chilly office at the top of the United Nations Building, considering whether he ought to work so high above the people. Initially four men aid him, all of whom suffer from various limitations. Van Ryberg, while inventive in his various theories about the Overlords, is "not the man to take" (45) Stormgren's role when he retires. Wainwright, who accuses other men of blindness, is obsessed by his inability to see the Overlords (14); but he stirs the desire to see them in Stormgren, so that feelings of his own finitude rise with an evening meteor (26). The Welshman, who suggests that

The Lament of the Midwives in Childhood's End

"instruments could be devised" (45) to see Karellen, is himself physically blind. Even Joe, "an overgrown baby" (36), puts his finger "on the one weak spot in the Overlords' rule" (33) and shakes Stormgren out of his passivity. Waking in his captors' mine after their sleight-of-hand, Stormgren later escapes through the Overlords' control of personal time and returns to his tower rejuvenated with the idea that a quest to see the alien is possible.

To fulfill this quest he descends twice to see Duval—whose name means *of the valley*—in the basement of the United Nations, hoping the scientist can construct an instrument to detect Karellen. To Duval the request presents no more than "a very pretty problem" that appeals to his pragmatism (47). To Stormgren, success means the end of human isolation, for human and the Overlords to "go together into the future"; in his personal isolation, success means that "Karellen had trusted him" with "affection" and will someday "stand beside the grave of the first man ever to be his friend" (60). He is like the dog Fey to Jeffrey Gregson later in the novel—and in neither case does a reunion truly occur. Earth no longer exists when Karellen salutes those he had known (216). Notwithstanding Stormgren's satisfaction, we must wonder how successful his quest has been.

The next quest is Jean's, although she may be the character least aware of the quest she initiates. Nor does she impress the reader as a visionary; the novel follows the other quests closely, but Jean is shown mainly through the eyes of George Greggson, rather as Karellen is shown mainly through the eyes of various humans. Though George seems more of a protagonist than she because of the thematic reason that seems to move him to the center of the novel, it is she rather than he who undergoes the pattern of the quest.

When introduced, Jean is coming down to Boyce's party in George's flier, the Meteor, not out of any joy at Boyce's new marriage (she is rather catty through most of the affair), but out of an interest in George—a successful interest as long as she does not tell him of previous psychic experiences "and perhaps scare him away" (102). Her other reason for coming, the séance that Boyce has arranged with her connivance (92), is less immediate; and the séance will not succeed unless they surrender to the apparently random motion of the plate across the hypnotic board. She is "flushed and excited" (94), perhaps "credulous" (93), drawn by what George regards as a "naïve and uncritical wonder" like that of a child. But he nods off (96); and at the crucial question, whose answer is not open to her, she also seems asleep and faints (97). The séance seems to be merely secondary to her contact with George, which they confirm in the flier.

George initiates her second quest by proposing that they move to New Athens, despite its primitivism and the odd interest of its founders in time

(145), upon an isolated island in the Pacific. Though the founders are concerned with the human future, their plan seems regressive to her, but she agrees to move if the children love it (140). This part of the quest is fully realized through Jeffrey's fascination with the sea (147). When he is saved from a tsunami she takes a more active role, going to a psychologist with her own psychic experiences in mind. The children's dreams and the "strange syncopation" (171) of Jennifer's rattle (another experiment in time) wake Jean to the discovery of her children's separation from their parents, so it is she, weeks later, who realizes when the random moment of the destruction of New Athens has arrived. George, who has helped bring her to this point, who was necessary to the conception of the children, is allowed only enough time for "a brief astonishment" before the island ascends atop its nuclear explosion (186). It becomes in effect the volcano that lay quiescent at the beginning of the novel. This is a *sparagmos in extremis*.

Jan passes through this pattern four times, first when he descends from the roof at Boyce's affair after he has seen the significant meteor (Hollow 74-76) to ask the all-important question at the séance, receive its answer with Jean's unconscious help, and visit the Royal Astronomical Society, placed by "some humorous civil servant" on the top floor of the Science Center (105), to interpret the answer that reveals the home planet of the Overlords. In his second quest he consults Sullivan, as Stormgren had resorted to Duval, and sees another meteor in a luminous fish (114). With the pattern in mind Sullivan's remark, "Aren't you going in the wrong direction?" (116) must seem to us misplaced. He must descend in order to ascend, hibernating in the belly of the whale (129) and suffering the distortion of time at a relativistic speed. In the third quest, he descends to the Overlords' planet, a clearly underworld experience: "If a man from medieval times could have seen this red-lit city, and the beings moving through it, he would certainly have believed himself in Hell" (191). Several commentators have explored this infernal imagery, especially Samuelson (199-202), Huntington (217), and Goldman (197-206); for our purposes, however, it is indifferent to the pattern whether the descent be to fire or water, and we may see in this fact, as often in the novel, a union of opposites that overarches its particulars. After enduring this place of specialization (192) and the "single giant eye" (194) that he is brought to the surface to observe with his human eyes and senses, the integrative vision of the mountain/eye/volcano/cyclone, or whatever it is, and to interpret it for the Overlords, who cannot see as he can (197). Finally, he descends with them to the earth transformed, becomes as a child again "on a vast and empty plain" with a great parental voice booming out above (208), and accepts their help to sit in their place, to climb "into the great chair" (211), to see the end, and like the people of New Athens to rise upon the detonation of the planet. It is clearly in the subplot of Jan that the pattern receives its fullest elaboration.

The quest is also at work in the children. A minor version is Jeffrey's adventure on Sparta, an extinct volcano (138) that offers physical, pragmatic daring in contrast to the intellectual concerns of New Athens. Significantly, it is a fairyland (149)—just as his dog is named Fey, which by a folk etymology has been associated with *fays or fairies*, whereas its actual meaning designates a *person who is about to die*. When he sees the ocean peel from the shore, its treasures revealed, and rushes out "eager to see what wonders would be uncovered next" (150), the Overlords rescue him. He must close his eyes not to see a boulder fused, though his feet feel the heat. The full descent for the children, however, the descent that all the other descents of the novel prepare and interpret, proceeds through the dreams with their odd time-distortions; the ascent is the mountain, gate, and other visions they see in the dreams. Their ascent in the last chapters, after the dance and stasis, simply makes the outward sign of the interior vision that the dreams hint at; their faces "emptier than the faces of the dead" (200), that vision is necessarily opaque to the reader. Toward the end of this chapter we can offer the outline of a reading of it.

II

An important result of this analysis is its clarification that there are only two kinds of characters in the novel: the visionaries, who despite their detachments are capable of insight and breakthrough, of going on the quest; and their helpers, the specialists, who cannot integrate knowledge without them and who frequently remain ignorant of the insights they themselves have prepared. Hoffmann and Schneider are kept by the superpowers in an isolation they do not seem to regret. Stormgren's detachment is emphatic as the novel opens; with his wife dead and his children grown, his connection to humanity has weakened. Jean is a special case, given her marriage, but her interest in psychic possibilities may stem from a need to feel connected, a need sharpened by the extrasensory apprehensions she receives from her children who are as yet unconceived. In any case, the marriage diminishes to simple fondness (162); George does not seem to answer any passion in her. Jan, too, is isolated from others. His first love affair has come to nothing; the serious detachment of incomprehension, of not being able to "imagine what had gone wrong," preoccupies him when his story opens (88). Later he asks his sister Maia to admit that "we never had very strong ties" (123). As for the children, long before breakthrough their concerns lie outside the adult ken; Jennifer Anne is too young to say a word. And as for all these visionaries—the semi-rehabilitated Germans, the widower, the rejected lovers, the prepubescents—the breakthrough isolates them even further: it is a shearing asunder in loneliness (7), a sunlight dying on the edge of a lake (58), a sitting in a high chair, a standing with dead faces, a "seeking the union they could never achieve" (186). Breakthrough does not humanly connect.

Passion is sublimated into the integrative insights received in the various quests; the greatest passion these characters experience seems to be the rejuvenation and new zest for discovery that follows their descents. Shortly before he sights the alien ships Hoffmann's mind returns to the Schneider he knew in their youth (3), and his feet "accelerated to the rhythm" of Jean's betrothal. Jan returns to London, which he had not visited since childhood, feeling "a schoolboy zest" (103). The children, of course, are children and become indistinguishably embryonic. A part of these characters' childlike recovery lies in their amused superiority toward the specialists: the V-2 men feel it toward their intelligence adjuncts; Stormgren feels it toward Van Ryberg, Duval, and Joe; Jan feels it toward Boyce; the children feel it toward adults; and Jean feels it toward Rasheverak, so much that she must stifle her laughter at an incongruous image of the alien that suddenly occurs to her (78). In order for childhood to end, the visionary must return to it. In every case life takes on a new shape and meaning, sharply contrasted to the quotidian experience of other characters. After such peak experiences, however, they collapse to a state that lies beyond pessimism and optimism.

One further, minor point may be made about the visionaries: so many of their names begin with the letter J—Jan, Jean, Jeffrey, and Jennifer—and most of their names are cognates of John/Yohanan, *the Lord is gracious*. I appreciate Hull's suggestion of the Janus nature of Jan (17), but surely more apt is John of Patmos and the apocalyptic vision. Jennifer's middle name, Anne, in Hebrew Hannah, is the element in Yohanan that means *gracious*. It is impossible not to sense in these names a knotted relation that has to do, from the viewpoint of the Overlords, with the gratuitous nature of breakthrough. There is no rule to the prophetic spirit.

What can be said of those who help the visionaries? Clearly Duval, Sullivan, the Welshman, and Salomon are all capable scientists and men of action, but in every case something is lacking. Duval and Sullivan are parodied by the dilettante Boyce, and the Welshman and Salomon by the nationalist Joe; the sectarianism of the later group may be emphasized by Ruth Schoenberger, who at the séance "had some objection to taking part in the proceedings, which caused Benny to make obscurely sarcastic remarks about people who still took the Talmud seriously" (93). Yet like a scholar Ruth takes impeccable notes. With his narrow program which the Overlords obviate so simply, Wainwright is another of this group. Duval and Sullivan, especially, lack flair;

it seems curious that the one "had never made a greater mark in the world of science" (48) and that the other had not achieved the "fame that sends a scientist's name safely down the centuries" (118). None of them will enter the promised land (143, 184). But since George best represents this kind of role among the human characters, it is important for the book's central concerns that most of the narrative in the middle of the book should be experienced from his point of view and not Jean's.

Hull believes that the characters are hardly "memorable as individuals" (16), yet an *homme moyen sensuel* like George is consistent and memorable as a type, who successfully fulfills so many middle-class desires and who so wisely represses so many others. For instance, like the intelligence agents, like Duval and Boyce, like Sullivan who is associated with the gigantic eye of the squid Lucifer, like the blind Welshman who suggests detection devices to Stormgren, like Karellen whose insufficient instruments are handed over to Jan, George is connected to visual imagery, as a professional scenic designer, cursing television (137-38). The helpers' eyes are imperfect despite their professionalism. There is something they cannot see, they cannot know.

In the Golden Age that the Overlords inaugurate, much of humanity seems to become this kind of character; there are "plenty of technologists, but few original workers" (71). Because of "an enormous efflorescence of the descriptive sciences such as geology, botany, and observational astronomy," earth is busy with "so many amateur scientists gathering facts for their own amusement—but there were few theoreticians correlating these facts" (72), as though the sciences had regressed to the eighteenth century. In the arts a similar process was at work, which is the point of the satire on the epigones of New Athens: "There were myriads of performers, amateur and professional, yet there had been no really new works" (72). Observation and competence are the salient qualities of the generation and the character, intent upon the niceties of visual discrimination, incapable of gestalt perception. This incapacity to move beyond "the descriptive sciences" may be the reason that, as Merritt Abrash remarks, "there is no theoretical underpinning for the utopia" in the novel (376).

The confidence that flows from such limitations—even the blind man emanates reserves of power in his "piercing gray eyes" (37)—may affect what seems in some cases a sexual nonchalance. The Sullivans and Schoenbergers seem comfortably married; though Boyce and George have played the field and George discreetly continues to do so, a part of the narrative is devoted to their settling into a matrimonial norm. The novel hardly suggests that they enjoy any startling romantic love; only Jan, a visionary, suffers from that; and the voice of the novel, which can rise to solemnity at the children's transfiguration, is content to call his condition "the romantic illusion" (88), a view that concurs in the worldly wisdom of the older George. Some characters, like Duval or the Welshman or Van Ryberg, may or may not be married; it is a matter of indifference to the narrative. But that indifference is the very point; they are sexually comfortable, capable, unremarkable. Nothing startlingly creative comes of their relations. In Jean's clinical observation that males are "fundamentally polygamous" (76), we see that these relations lack intensity. Sexual love supports neither passion nor meaning. Parallel to this lack of passion is a further lack: the helpers encountered by the visionaries in their descents cannot themselves descend to any depth, nor can they ascend; they are static. Boyce would have liked to have visited Sullivan, "if it weren't for his claustrophobia" (116). The helpers inhabit a middle ground, risking little hurt.

To consider this lack in them is also to realize that, though very much about family relations, the novel has a dearth of sexual women. Jean and Maia, the only significant ones, have a certain impact, but the impact of a mother rather than of a lover. George ceases to see Jean as a lover rather early in the novel. As for Maia, though we do not hear of children in their marriage, she certainly seems more a mother toward Boyce, whom we must regard as rather boyish. She does not seem insubstantial, as though she were a Hindu Maya (Hull 27); she seems more akin to the Greek Maia (whose name means *mother* or *grandmother* or *nurse* or *midwife*), the goddess whose son Hermes, according to the Homeric hymn, stole the famous cattle of Apollo by drawing them into a cave (Shelley 680-99). The myth is a model for the quest of the novel. Maia and Jean, whose maiden name Morrell means either *nightshade* or *black mare*, then represent a rich but passive Mother Earth, which gives up its children in the powerful birth at the end of the novel: "There was nothing left of Earth: *they* had leeched away the last atoms of its substance. It had nourished them" (215). To awake to such a potential the Mother needs the mediation of a man, any man; the person is a matter of indifference.

Perhaps the novel shows "a sharing union which retains respect for free, informed choice" to be better than a "cold, selfish isolation" (Hull 30), but a union of that sort does not seem possible. When Jean considers George as a mate coolly, is that as a lover or as a father? However we answer that, I think that it is other than a choice that is cold and selfish. So it is for mediation that Jean needs George, whose name means farmer or, more precisely, a worker of the earth, to stir her potentials, of which she is vaguely conscious. Though the meteor, so often mentioned in the early pages of the book, seems to rise, it in fact falls through the air to earth and points the downward path. George, like all those other helpers, serves as the visionary and the quest upon which the visionary has set forth, but that is little consolation. George is a bit like the narrator in *Odd John*; though both men are narrators of the action, they are not themselves important to it. So little contact is made within these families that both parents might say with Karellen, "We are the midwives. But we ourselves are barren" (173).

The Overlords are the main example of this character. We know very little about them, however, even by the end of the novel, and much of our knowledge is negative: they are "neither mammals, insects, nor reptiles" (79), which is to say neither fish nor flesh nor fowl. Even their sexuality remains a blank, though the male pronoun is applied to them (Menger 97). It is Karellen, however, who uses the image of the sterile midwife, and nearly all the characters who have the role of the midwife are male. With "no fear of gravity" (193), not even an indication that the gravity of earth has any ill effects on them, the Overlords have no fear of flying or of falling; sex has no terrors; it is nonexistent. They are comfortable.

The demonic imagery seems connected to a number of qualities. Like the other helpers, they are intensely specialized and on their adopted planet dwell underground, apparently incapable of ascent. But they are also incapable of descent in that they do not seem to sleep (26). This eternal vigilance is related to their perfect memory, which implies total recall; they have no unconscious lying irretrievable to conscious control or liable to surprise them at random moments. Their incomprehension of reflex actions is a part of this lack of an unconscious (194), also symbolized, as is their sterility, by the absence of an ocean on their planet (126); lacking reflexes, they also lack the surprise of a body. Though they would be interested by Freud's *Die Traumdeutung*, they would also be mystified by it. This unqualified consciousness, the "scholarship and virtuosity" and "overwhelming intellectual power" (15) they display, are part of the Satanic promise in the discrimination of good and evil that precedes Deity; the snake, however, is left in the dust, as is Karellen, who remains in the isolation of his "vast and labyrinthine mind" (216). Those immense eyes that must be shielded with sunglasses (131) symbolize an intelligence limited to the analytic.

Those large, shaded eyes also suggest the figure who may have been most decisive in Clarke's characterization of the Overlords. In the *Apology* Socrates compares himself to a gadfly who rouses the lazy horse of the State from its sleep. He is a *myops*, that is to say *one who closes his eyes*, but he stings into enlightenment those who encounter him (30e). The dialogues frequently refer to his ugliness. But the most extended self-characterization he makes is in the *Theaetetos*, where he says that his mother Phaenerete was "a noble, sturdy midwife" (149a). Midwives assist at births and make marriages; they are skillful, with a hint of the awesome (149d). And he is like them: "I have this in common with midwives: I am sterile in regards to wisdom, and the reproach which many bring against me, that I question others but never reply myself about anything, because I am not wise, is true; the god forces me to act like a midwife, but forbids me to bear" (150c). The word for midwife that Socrates uses is *maia*. The self-deprecating form of the most typical intellectual of Western culture stands behind the sterile, myopic Overlords.

To understand them we must not ignore Rasheverak, Thanthalteresco, and Vindarten. It seems clear in their conversations that Rasheverak plays the role of Van Ryberg as Karellen plays the role of Stormgren. His name is suggestive of the biophysicist Nicolas Rashevsky, to whom the novel alludes as "Rashavesky," as it also seems to refer to the cyberneticist Wiener as "Weiner" (144). Through the 1940s Rashevsky's works, *Mathematical Theory of Human Relations*, *Mathematical Biophysics*, and *Mathematical Biology of Social Behavior*, presented simplified mathematical models of phenomena such as "the formation of closed social classes, the interaction of military and economic factors in international relations, 'individualistic' and 'collectivistic' tendencies, patterns of social influence, and many others," although Abraham Kaplan argues that these treatments were "so idealized as almost to lack all purchase on reality" (278). In an oblique manner the limitations of Rasheverak imply a criticism of the dream represented in science fiction by Asimovean psychohistory. Thanthalteresco's name suggests thanatos, otherness and change, and an altar, with that odd suffix echoing the arabesque or picturesque of the fresco; we cannot quite take him seriously. Vindarten may recall *vindare*, the rigor of Roman law, but perhaps more obviously has to do with wind, swiftness, and art in his agility at languages. But Karellen's name teases us the most, referring clearly to a carillon, a parallel to that voice calling out over Jan in his dreams. A Christmas carol may also lay in his name; but with a slight change of accent the name becomes Carolyn—and the name of George's mistress is Carolle (162). In this series are combined an analytic treatment of human relations, death and change and whimsy, rigor and speed and language, the ringing of bells from a height, and a sexual ambiguity.

But if the Overlords are sexually ambiguous, it should come as no surprise that they are not only helpers but visionaries also. Coming from Carina in the constellation Argo, they are as surely as the Argonauts upon a quest. They descend upon Earth and at the end of the novel ascend from it. The emissaries, Rasheverak, Thanthalteresco, and Vindarten, go to the humans for help, as Karellen must depend upon Stormgren. They suffer distortions of time: Vindarten must speak more slowly with humans than is his custom (190), as must all the Overlords (98); and all the aliens in their mission to earth must isolate themselves from their society, since "the Relativity time-dilation effect worked both ways" (197). Even their sterility is qualified slightly by Karellen's remark that they "till the field" like George (204). Karellen may not be rejuvenated at the end of the novel, but his sense of meaning is affirmed. He has moved beyond intellect into passion when oppressed by "a sadness that no logic could dispel" (215), a further indication of Slusser's claim that Karellen has been "humanized" (52), that in him the human has been retrieved as lament (8-9). As Wolfe saw, in his discussion of iconic images such as the alien, they "contain in themselves the dynamic tensions between known and unknown" (16). Clarke's Overlords are an example of that pattern as they fuse in one complex figure both the visionary, which is the newborn, and the midwife, the mother and the father. Karellen is Hermes, the psychopompos trickster and "shepherd of thin dreams" (Shelley 680), who brings the herd of the human race (in Greggson we may see Gregory, *to awaken*, or *grex, the herd*) back into the cave so that new words, the prophetic words, may ring out. And he is Apollo, a solar deity albeit fallen, who at the end of the hymn to Hermes exchanges gifts with that chthonic power (Shelley 697-99). His power and elusiveness come from his comprehensive nature.

Having said this, we need to admit that Matthew Candelaria's analysis of the Overlord as an English colonial functionary, bearing the white man's burden because he is so much wiser than the human child, has much to be said for it. Clarke is telling "colonial myths" (37) that justify England's rule in India and that have led England to its cul-de-sac after India has gained its independence (57).

The corollary to the double role of the Overlord as midwife and visionary is the double role of Jean as visionary and midwife. The children she bears have an odd relation to her, being potent in her life before their conception: her mind has been a mere "channel that, if only for a moment, let through knowledge which no one alive at that time could possess" (172). The narrator emphasizes that the children will not belong to any parent; the orphaning to the parents is "a threat and a terror" (174). Karellen reminds Jan, "You are not watching human children" (200). The only mother seen from a child's perspective, Jan's, cannot be told of his leaving because "she would get hysterical, and I couldn't face that" (121). So Jean is incidental to the real life of the children, as though their conception were outside both her ken and her body; it is an implicit point that becomes explicit four years after Clarke's novel in John Wyndham's *The Midwich Cuckoos*. The double role of midwife and visionary makes Jean hard to read. She and Karellen, the two comprehensive characters, mirror each other's duality.

There is some evidence in Clarke's alterations to "Guardian Angel," the seed or first attempt toward its suggestive offspring, that he recognized these patterns of plot and character. Samuelson believes that the changes merely "removed some poor repartee, added more background, and diminished slightly the dependence on melodramatic effect" (233). But more was involved: the relation of novella and novel, as Goldman has argued, is more dynamic (207). The Prologue draws a clear line between visionary and midwife, doubling the pattern emphatically. The new first paragraph of Part I underlines Stormgren's detachment (11), reinforced in the new first paragraph of the third chapter, with further characterization of his widowhood (24). Wainwright's charge of blindness is new (14). A long addition on the treatment the Overlords accord South Africa culminates in a reversal of expectation (17), materials important to the union of opposites the novel presents. Karellen's dismissal of Lord Acton's comment on power illustrates his own limitations as midwife (21-22).

In the episode of the kidnapping, Stormgren hopes that his captors can "uncover something new" (38), a hope answered at the end of the sequence when "the words of his interrogator passed again through his memory" (45). The description of Karellen's probe is altered to "a small, featureless sphere" hovering "at eye-level," adding to the optical imagery of the book (42). Stormgren's escaping "quite forty years younger" was also added (43). All these details are small and cumulative.

But the episode with Duval was probably decisive for Clarke's purpose. Duval's pointing out, "Anyway, it worked" (54), underscores his technological concern; and a long addition epitomizes the plight of the midwife, from the amused perspective of the visionary: "Stormgren wondered why it was that a man like Duval—whose mind was incomparably more brilliant than his own—had never made a greater mark in the world of science. He remembered an unkind and probably inaccurate comment of a friend in the U.S. State Department. 'The French produce the best second-raters in the world'" (48). It appears to have been important for the thematics of the novel to develop the character of the midwife, and we may see in these additions a preparation for that character to move into its center.

The novel works not only through the pattern of the quest and the relation of visionary and midwife. Coordinated with these structures of descent and ascent and of isolation and sterility is a complex of images amplifying them. One of these images, the tension between sight and blindness, has been treated at length by Hull in her catalogue of those uneasy eyes growing larger until the earth shines out like Emerson's transparent eyeball (24-25); we have seen how these eyes are associated with the midwives. They also look toward the images of sleep and waking and toward the oceanic images that are contrasted to barrenness and the island.

To sleep is to arrive at insight. Karellen fails to sleep, but Stormgren, Jean, Jan, and the children must sleep in order to descend and to see; the midwives keep their eyes open in order to see minutiae. In Jennifer's sleep especially—"There was no other word to describe the state she had entered," the narrator says, emphasizing the metaphoric, inadequate nature of the language—there lay "a sense of latent power so terrifying that Jean could no longer bear to enter the nursery" (175). The little girl, "lately known as the Poppet," lying in her pupa-stage of transformation will not open her eyes again, "for sight was now as superfluous to her as to the many-sensed creatures of the lightless ocean depths" (171). Only midwives, like the squid Lucifer—or like Karellen—need to evolve eyes for the abyss.

III

This ocean, which fascinates Jeffrey and in which the children experience breakthrough, signifies life and unity in addition to the unconscious. In the submarine Jan hears "a steady background, into which all individual sounds had blended [. . .] as if he stood in the center of a forest that teemed with life—except that there he would have recognized some of the individual voices" (113). Though unfamiliar and undifferentiated, the ocean is not placid: it is a "delirium" (125) or a "nightmare" (128) when human understanding reconstructs it, revealing "battles [. . .] fought in the endless night of the ocean depths, where sperm whales hunted for their food" (125). It is a battle within the purely unknown, perhaps only known through the representation as an allegory of visionary and midwife, for the squid with its "great, expressionless eye [. . .] stared at its destroyer [the whale that will bear Jan to the Overlords' planet]—though, in all probability, neither creature could see the other in the darkness of the abyss" (125). It is not a life or a unity or a battle in which human life can survive. When the young boy stands with "eyes tightly closed, as if listening to sounds which no one else could hear, [. . .] into his mind was flooding knowledge—from somewhere or somewhen—which would soon overwhelm and destroy [him]" (176). But if the ocean dries away, all its alien life dies, as it does when revealed to the analytic eye during the tsunami and as it has in the barren landscape of the Overlords' planet.

The ocean expresses the islands' isolation by surrounding them; in the plans for the New Athens "the ocean meant nothing as a physical barrier, but it gave a sense of isolation" (143). In this aspect it is the earth under the ocean, the volcanic earth of "the burning darkness" (149), which contains disparate phenomena united in a new, oxymoronic creation. Karellen refers to this imagery indirectly when he compares total breakthrough to a chain reaction (172), prefiguring the destruction and elevation of New Athens. Remarkably, in this imagery even a midwife and Karellen, in that duality, may be made new. George is suffering a volcanic disturbance in his decision to go to New Athens (137–38); and Karellen, in that duality we have seen, is identified by Duval as no more than "a kink like the autograph of a mild earthquake" (54). But the breakthrough of this imagery, the land apocalyptically thrusting through the ocean, is destructive; no midwife survives it. In this language humans are "seeking the union they could never achieve," and the island meets the dawn shattered (186).

Karellen makes the most explicit use of the oceanic and island language: "Imagine that every man's mind is an island, surrounded by ocean. Each seems isolated, yet in reality all are linked by the bedrock from which they spring. If the ocean were to vanish, that would be the end of the islands. They would all be part of one continent, but their individuality would be gone" (172). The passage may sound reminiscent of the passage in Donne's "Meditation XVII," to which Hemingway alluded for the title of *For Whom the Bell Tolls*. The more significant source, however, is Matthew Arnold's sequence *Switzerland*, in which his lyric "To Marguerite. Continued" opens with these lines:

> Yes! in the sea of life enisled,
> With echoing straits between us thrown,
> Dotting the shoreless watery wild,
> We mortal millions live *alone*.
> The islands feel the enclasping flow,
> And then their endless bounds they know. (182)

The isolated islands feel "a longing like despair" in "their furthest caverns," insisting that they were once "Part of a single continent" (182). But the last stanza confirms their isolation:

> Who order'd that their longing's fire
> Should be, as soon as kindled, cool'd?
> Who renders vain their deep desire?—
> A God, a God their severance ruled!
> And bade betwixt their shores to be
> The unplumb'd, salt, estranging sea. (182)

The main difference between this formulation and the images of the novel is that the fires in the poem are damped down; in *Childhood's End* they erupt and destroy at the same moment that they create a transformed union.

The inadequacy, unfocused lack of intensity, and vacillation lying behind these sexual failures may be discovered in "A Farewell," a lyric that occurs in the sequence *Switzerland* earlier than the poem we have just considered:

> This heart, I know,
> To be long loved was never framed;
> For something in its depths doth glow
> Too strange, too restless, too untamed.
>
> And women—things that live and move
> Mined by the fever of the soul—
> They seek to find in those they love
> Some strength, and promise of control.
>
> They ask not kindness, gentle ways—
> These they themselves have tried and known;
> They ask a soul which never sways
> With the blind gusts that shake their own. (178)

The protagonist recognizes a weakness and passivity in himself that the woman rejects because she suffers from it herself. To rephrase the confession, the lover fails because he regards himself as too much like a woman. He has longed for a "trenchant force, / And will like a dividing spear" (178), which always eludes him. His only hope for a union lies in gaining, "life past, / Clear prospect o'er our being's whole" (179). The hope is severely qualified. Only when dead may the lovers "be brought near, / And greet across infinity" (180). The only love possible, in "Isolation: To Marguerite," belongs to happier men who do not realize how isolated they are:

> For they, at least,
> Have *dream'd* two human hearts might blend
> In one, and were through faith released
> From isolation without end
> Prolong'd; nor knew, although not less
> Alone than thou, their loneliness. (181)

To these comfortable souls, like Boyce and Duval, Karellen does not belong insofar as the alien, like the poet, is quite aware of his separation. Descending from his "remote and sphered course / To haunt the place where passions reign—" but not to partake in them, he receives the order at the end of the novel, which is the lament of the poem, "Back to thy solitude again!" (181).

The sexual dysfunction that the lyric sequence represents surrounds the imagery Karellen uses and the basic relations of the characters, especially George and Jean. Their everyday life may be reminiscent of that of the parents in "Mimsy Were the Borogoves," which also shares with *Childhood's End* two children's desertion of their parents, the earth, and three-dimensional space for an oceanic experience (Padgett 253-56). In that story the father is "a youngish, middle-aged man with gray-shot hair and a thinnish, prim-mouthed face" (230), neither fish nor foul, whom the story introduces with his wife at ritual martinis and chit-chat, a middle-class Nick and Nora. At the end of the story the ringing of the telephone suggests their marital distance (260). Quite possibly the story showed Clarke a way to deal with the theme.

The closest we come to a positive apprehension of the unity the children enjoy is in the dreams Jeffrey reports: "the distortion of the time scale" in his vision of the apparent volcanoes, initiating breakthrough; the acceleration of time in the pulsating variable (167); the freezing of time at the Pillars of Dawn in the center of the Universe (168), a phrase that recalls Stormgren's perception before his descent of "a dawn frozen in the act of breaking" (25); the geometric life of Hexanerax 2, on a flat plane of two-dimensions (168-69); and finally the crystalline life in a time neither cyclic nor progressive, but "every moment [. . .] unique" (169). So time accelerates, stops, and proceeds in a direction unknown to organic life, as in the novel time has frequently taken another direction. Not only is this Golden Age at the end of history rather at its beginning, and not only have the Overlords, descending for this Apocalypse, been remembered as a part of the Genesis, but time seems to run backwards in the ages of the visionary protagonists, from widower to mother to adolescent to pre-pubescent and baby.

The materials of life as we know it, the images of mountain and ocean, fire and ice, and the ages, exist in this vision but not as we would order them or at least as we ever could order them. They seem, in fact, materials of expression rather than what is expressed. The dreams of the children employ the union of opposites, a motif we have already noted in this work: "This is the primordial condition of things, and at the same time a most ideal achievement, because it is the union of elements eternally opposed. Conflict comes to rest, and everything is still or once again the original state of indistinguishable harmony" (Jung, *The Symbolic Life* 119). This union is present in its purest form, the male-female polarity, in the marriage of Maia and Jan's parents: "Mrs. Rodericks, who was coal black, had been born in Scotland, whereas her expatriate and blond husband had spent almost all his life in Haiti" (87-88). What is united in this primordial state, however, seems compacted as a dangerous charge of energy (Jung, *Psychological Types* 202). Conscious human life approaches it only to retreat, as Jean retreats from the latent power of Jennifer's sleep, for it threatens transformation. This mythic energy represented by so many unions of opposites ensures that the climax of the novel is not merely melodramatic. From the first doubling of the Prologue the explosion of the planet at the end seems, in retrospect, inevitable.

Is that which ascends in the children human? Does the primordial state heal the isolation of the midwives? Although the text says that the Overmind has "drawn into its being all that the human race had ever achieved" (203), the claim lies in the middle of an extended indirect discourse passing through Jan's mind; true, he is a visionary, with true visions—but the problem is whether such a vision can heal our inabilities to see or feel in union. I disagree with Hollow that "we identify [. . .] strongly with the Overmind" (85). Recently Beatie has emphasized the incomprehensibility of that being. All that we know of it, as I have argued, is the way by which we try to conceive it. The novel in its plot, characters, and images offers little hope that humanity, in will or in works, can be lifted up: that which can be lifted up is only a projection of health.

We are left with Karellen, the character in whom the others converge and to whom the reader has been moving, changing the unknown into the known, as Wolfe says, until thoroughly identified in him. He is looking up at that ascent: "Far off were the mountains, where power and beauty dwelt, where the thunder sported above the glaciers and the air was clear and keen. There the sun still walked, transfiguring the peaks with glory, when all the land below was wrapped in darkness. And they could only watch and wonder: they could never scale those heights" (215). This passage is obviously rich in the language of Stapledon, but it is also something of the same vision with which Shelley's poem "Mont Blanc" concludes, in a passage rich with the union of opposites:

> Mont Blanc yet gleams on high—the power is there,
> The still and solemn power of many sights,
> And many sounds, and much of life and death.
> In the calm darkness of the moonless nights,
> In the lone glare of day, the snows descend
> Upon that Mountain; none beholds them there,
> Nor when the flakes burn in the sinking sun. (534-35)

This passage represents the same hopeless search for the primordial energy that inspired an early passage in Arnold's *Switzerland*: he looks up at the Alps to "the stir of forces / Whence issued the world" (180). In each instance the energy remains inaccessible.

So like Karellen we are left. But if it is difficult to read the signs of breakthrough in relation to anything we know, the reason for our difficulty is painfully clear, insofar as we are midwives. The midwives are more important to the novel than we might imagine, characters to whom the narrative returns with increasing frequency, culminating in Karellen. In them, despite the novel's often bland manner, indeed through it, a fear of undistinguished, undramatic, passionless failure is revealed. Since breakthrough is promised, but excluded from our means, instead of an achieved vision the book's concerns that English projection of the French as "the best second-raters in the world": barren, immature, unresponsive, shallow, merely intellectual, comfortable, complacent, incapable of contact, impotent—unable to project change or the possibility of change, and unable to change, probing the *Vorstellungen* of the Overmind through such surrogates as Jan. This is the area the book approaches repeatedly and transforms into a modicum of dignity in the ambiguous, self-deprecating figure of Karellen, "only a civil servant" (19). Clarke had opportunity to contemplate such a fate as an auditor in HM Exchequer and as an assistant editor of that compendium of specializations, *Physics Abstract* (Clarke, *Ascent to Orbit* 19, 117–19). Although he often seemed superbly confident of his abilities, we may recognize in him a man incapable of Heinlein's convictions or of Asimov's carefree productivity, a man developing his best work by inches, over years, a man elaborating his dreams through complex variations: the early *Lion of Comarre* foreshadowing so much in his fiction; the history of *Against the Fall of Night* and *The City and the Stars*; "Guardian Angel" of course and *Childhood's End*; "The Sentinel" and the several variations of *2001: A Space Odyssey*; and toward the end of his career *The Songs of Distant Earth* are all cases in point. Any ease of inspiration, any breakthrough, must seem distant in such an experience.

And so *Childhood's End* remains a novel of lament, a lament sustained and prolonged through several quests, a lament of the human midwives, isolated from each other and from their own ends. And they cannot change.

The Lily and the Rose:
Polarities in *The City and the Stars*

> Muoiono le città, muoiono i regni;
> copre i fasti e le pompe arena ed erba,
> e l'uom, d'esser mortal par che si sdegni.
> [The cities die, the kingdoms die,
> Grass and sands cover archives and pomp,
> But man scorns his mortality.] (Tasso 15.20.3-5)

The structure and intent of *The City and the Stars* is a challenge to a reader. Though the narrative is straightforward, following the attempt of the protagonist Alvin (who has no last name) to escape the city of Diaspar, once his attempt has succeeded the novel seems to become haphazard and diffuse. His second quest to the stars and concomitantly his quest to discover his nature and purpose become episodic; and the last pages may be read as much as a defeat as a triumph, for the protagonist essentially surrenders any further quest (though it seems offered to him) and returns to the world he had escaped. Thomas D. Clareson says it very nicely: "Too much happens too quickly. Whereas Alvin largely controls the action of the first half of the story, one feels that from this point onward he is manipulated by his discoveries. Nothing is fleshed out" (63). But this helter-skelter account allows Clarke to introduce a series of symbolic details. In this chapter I hope to examine the various oppositions that fuel the novel, to show that they are in fact polar relations clarifying the novel's structure, and to demonstrate how these relations generate a third element that is increasingly important as the novel proceeds, residing in the probability that Clarke read and made use of Hermann Hesse's late magnum opus, *Magister Ludi*.

I

The polarities in Clarke's novel are connected directly with the dialogue his novel maintains with *Magister Ludi*, a dialogue that we shall examine in some detail. I need to say in advance that all references to Hesse's novel refer to the first English translation of *Das Glasperlenspiel*, Hesse's original German title, since it is unlikely that Clarke read the German novel with its evocative title that foregrounded the game rather than the protagonist. The second translation in 1990 erased that problem, bearing the title *The Glass Bead Game*.

My claim that a relation exists between Clarke's novel and Hesse's requires some background. Hesse's novel was published in 1943 and then appeared in translation in 1949 to some fanfare, since he had recently won the Nobel Prize. This was some years after Clarke had written *Against the Fall of Night*, the first version of the material that became *The City and the Stars*, which was published in 1956. We are not, then, claiming that Hesse's novel influenced Clarke's original conception, but that in his extensive revision certain aspects of the German novel proved congenial and may have strengthened ideas that only emerged in Clarke's later work.

There is further the point that Clarke's other novel, *Childhood's End*, shares a future history with *Magister Ludi* in that both novels posit a time when human creativity comes to an end. "There were myriads of performers, amateur and professional, yet there had been no really outstanding new works of literature, music, painting, or sculpture for a generation. The world was still living on the glories of a past that could never return" (Clarke 72). This is the way Clarke imagines the future in his apocalyptic novel. Hesse imagines an age when the human intellect is debased by the short articles in the eclectic newspapers, in which all human problems are simplified or reduced to comedy; it is a world in which second-raters can thrive (19–26). When to few people's notice these two cultures collapse, in their place arise Castalia and New Athens—attempts at clarification, rigor, and support. But though each attempt has great moments of success, the narrative views each with a quiet irony; neither is sufficient for the human spirit, which leaves these apparent perfections, in *Childhood's End* in an apocalyptic manner, in *Magister Ludi* in the quiet abdication of the protagonist Joseph Knecht when he believes that the age of the Glass Bead Game has passed—just as Alvin leaves Diaspar in *The City and the Stars*, with this difference that Alvin at the end of the novel returns to Diaspar.

Though not at first apparent, perhaps because Clarke's two novels about Diaspar have essentially the same plot, the second is extensively expanded and its emphases changed. In John Hollow's pithy analysis, "*Against the Fall of Night* was addressed to the fear of death, but *The City and the Stars* is about the meaning of life" (117). The first novel, in eighteen chapters, devotes three chapters to the first part in Diaspar, whereas the second novel, in twenty-two chapters, devotes eight chapters to this material. This change means that the theme of Diaspar has been transformed; in the first novel Diaspar the city and Lys the country receive roughly equal treatment, but in the second novel Diaspar receives much more. There is a tilt in this polarity between Diaspar and Lys.

The transformation is evident in the treatment of characters. One character, Alystra, has been added, not at all as we shall see to add a romantic interest, which is absent in the first work and which remains absent, to her regret, in the second. Another character, Rorden, the Keeper of Records, with much of his function transformed into the Memory Banks, has been radically changed into the Jester Khedron, at the same time as several of Rorden's characteristics and actions have been used to develop the character of Jeserac, who in the first novel is quite colorless; the increased importance of Jeserac in the second novel is indicated by the two chapters, twenty-three and twenty-five, which have been added; chapter twenty-four had already concerned the cosmic phobia Diaspar suffered from, leading to an immense denial of its history, but the story of Jeserac in the added chapters makes a phobic nature more intimate and immediate. The second novel, then, is intensely interested in Alvin's ideal mentors and his background, the city he is determined to leave and to which he returns homesick in the last pages.

One other change that may seem slight is actually quite telling. The first pages of the book have been changed to include the new concept of the sagas, virtual-reality games in which the jaded populace of Diaspar can safely enjoy the adventure that has been banished from the city. When the narrative begins, after the evocative prologue, it breaks into the middle of a typical space opera: "It had taken them many hours to fight their way out of the Cave of the White Worms. Even now, they could not be sure that some of the pallid monsters were not pursuing them—and the power of their weapons was almost exhausted" (7).

It is difficult to understand how to receive the narrative of this saga; the 1940s when the original novel was conceived had many stories that resemble its plot and style. That it does not possess reality within the fictional world of the novel slowly comes clear as Alvin begins to doubt the consistency of the experience, questioning "why those projectors were so heavy, since it would have been such a simple matter to provide them with gravity neutralizers" (7-8). If this is a science-fiction story it is not very well conceived. To the dismay of his companions, Alvin ruins the experience by his criticism. Happily, as it turns out, the novel does not offer this kind of adventure; its reality is very different, and its conflict, as we shall provisionally formulate it, is an intellectual one between the city and the country, between artifice and nature, though this is a nature built upon artifice and though the artifice of the city does make appeals to nature. In the second half of the novel, when Alvin escapes into space from the stifling dilemma of the two landscapes, there is again no adventure and very little conflict, only an excavation and survey of past history, somewhat in the fashion of *Star Maker*. The first page, then, offers a parody of what this novel is definitely not; but it also suggests that Alvin's critical nature is well applied to an environment that has been carefully constructed by his predecessors.

The first novel is rather shapely, for each of its sections is made up of three chapters, with the major break occurring after the ninth chapter, which is the center of its eighteen chapters.

The City and the Stars appears a bit more ungainly. The first eight chapters are devoted to Diaspar, with a slight break after the fourth chapter. The next six chapters are devoted to Lys, with a slight break in its middle; thus the center of its twenty-six chapters comes after chapter fourteen, when Alvin escapes from Lys to return to Diaspar. The second half falls into three chapters, four chapters, and five chapters, taking place in Diaspar, in space, and finally in Lys for a short time and in Diaspar again; these twelve chapters are full of a hurly-burly, to-and-fro motion that is markedly absent from the first half of the work, so much so that the two halves hardly seem a part of the same novel. The first novel does not have this problem because it much more swiftly introduces the conflict.

What, then, is holding the novel together? What did Clarke hope to gain by its expansion?

II

Our initial impression of the novel's construction is of its opposites, an impression that is certainly strong in the earlier novel. Diaspar, the city of despair and of crystal (diamond and spar), perhaps the equal of god and of the day (deus, dies, and peer), is contrasted with Lys, the French word for lily, the fleur-de-lys symbolizing French royal tradition; the urban is contrasted with an elegant pastoral, a totalizing culture with a fostering of a multitude of cultures, immortality with mortality. The retractable penis of the city, the male dream of control, is contrasted with the womanly navel of the countryside, the evidence we all bear of the womb from which we came. Alvin, the innovator with a unique personality, is contrasted with Hilvar, the gardener and conserver. The polyps, the multiple personality that slumbers in the lake in Shalmirane, is contrasted with the robot, and Vanamonde with the Mad Mind, whom he shall fight at the end of the universe. For the time being the Mad Mind is imprisoned inside the Black Star, a potent image that Clarke may have discovered in Blake, who uses the phrase in *The Marriage of Heaven and Hell* (156) and in *The First Book of Urizen* (226); but he may have seen it in Dürer's etching *Melancholia*. If we consider the little we know of this apocalyptic moment at the end of time, it is not clear who is the mad mind or who the vain world. If we are to adopt Alvin's attitude, we should ask, "What, at the end of the universe, shall they fight for?" Given the context of the Cold War in which this story of a closed and an open society takes place, it is not far-fetched to think in terms of the opposition between East and West and perhaps to ask once more if it comes to that, "What shall they fight for?" That theme was important in the Prologue to *Childhood's End*, before the plot transcended it; we should, moreover, keep in mind how early in his career Clarke renounced that political opposition, preferring to retire to the third world of Sri Lanka, surrounded by the embracing ocean.

This opposition is, however, deceptive. Both Diaspar and Lys are enclosed, in a polar relation, for Diaspar has a park in its center and Lys, which is an enormous park, depends nevertheless upon a hidden technology. Alystra, with her maternal feelings, contains the letters *lys* in the middle of her name, and in Lys it does seem that the maternal rather than the paternal is thematized. For that matter, although in Diaspar Alvin does have foster parents, as does everyone in the city, it seems that a paternal relation is more important than a maternal, for only Alvin's foster father speaks to him; his foster mother is helpless and silent (16-17).

A further element of this polarity may be the work of art that is "the only one [. . .] that had any appeal" for Alvin within Diaspar: "It was a creation of pure light, vaguely reminiscent of an unfolding flower. Slowly flowering from a minute core of color, it would expand into complex spirals and curtains, then suddenly collapse and begin the cycle again. Yet not precisely, for no two cycles were identical." Alvin knows why this work appeals to him: "Its expanding rhythm gave an impression of space—even of escape" (23), and thus it points toward the third pole of our analysis. But the flower itself indicates its affinity to Lys. Alvin's name not only signifies the first, an original and an originator, as Yarlan Zey's name, its capitals at the end of the alphabet, signifies a conclusion (though this relation is itself polar, since Yarlan Zey lives at the founding of the city and Alvin at its climax). Transcending time, Alvin and Yarlan Zey are the alpha and omega of the city. Furthermore, Alvin's name suggests the Latin word *alveus*, a hollow, a river-bed, a beehive, or a womb; extravagantly, conventionally male as Alvin seems in his isolation and his drive to explore, he possesses a female component and a female potentiality.

His opposite in Lys is Hilvar, whose name forms an imperfect anagram of Alvin's. His name suggests the Latin word *hilaris*, happy or gay, perhaps careless—something other than the intensity of Alvin. He loves "a shy, dark girl" (118), who is the polar opposite of Alystra, perhaps because affairs in Lys usually begin in telepathic contact. More substantially, Alvin is an eternal child, the only childlike person in Diaspar, corresponding to the children that he discovers in Lys. Diaspar has a navel, the park that lies at its center. The opposition between East and West looks very different when perceived from Britain; though Clarke had not yet moved to Sri Lanka, one of the attractions of a third-world country is the possibility it offers of overcoming that political opposition.

This all seems relatively simple; two polarities, however, have problems that we must address. One is the question of how we shall treat the polarity of adult/child, which is especially important, since it is the loneliness of the child in the absence of the father that sends Alvin, the robot, and Vanamonde forth on their quests. This child/adult polarity is resolved only insofar as the quester finds his father and can leave the quest behind for other goals. Alvin is typical of everyone in Diaspar insofar as he does have a father and mother, but they are assigned him; they are foster parents, and the relation between them and Alvin has none of the intensity or complexity that we are familiar with in family life. One aspect of his going forth from Diaspar is the search for a true father, an origin that presents him a rigorous obstacle and bafflement. His quest runs parallel to the quest of the robot, searching for its father the Master, and to the quest of Vanamonde, searching up and down the galaxy for the beings that made him (240). He wakes to the same question that the robot had: "Where is my father?" The resolution of this question lies in his becoming Hilvar's pet (242), just as in a certain sense the robot had become Alvin's.

This child/adult polarity, however, can be seen in a very different way, in the light of the polarity between adult immortality in Diaspar and adult mortality in Lys. This polarity is only resolved in the image of the children in Lys, for the child lives in its own immortality. This is not immediately apparent until we recall how Wordsworth created the myth of the child in the "Ode: Intimations of Immortality":

> Thou, over whom thy Immortality
> Broods like the day, a Master o'er a Slave,
> A Presence which is not to be put by;
> Thou little Child, yet glorious in the might
> Of heaven-born freedom on thy being's height [. . .] (355)

The child in Lys is happy in an immortality that is not questioned, so that in the child the polarity of the fates of Diaspar and Lys is resolved. Of course, we should point out that this is an immortality that neither Alvin nor anyone else in Diaspar has ever enjoyed, for no one in the city was ever a child.

Now this theme of polarities is muted in *Against the Fall of Night*, but it plays an important part in *Magister Ludi*. "Our object," states the Music Master in Hesse's novel, "is to discern opposites correctly, in considering them as opposites but eventually as poles of a single unit" (75). Polar relations are pervasive in Hesse's thought. Joseph Knecht, the wise man of the academy, has a best friend, Plinio Designori, who lives in the outside world. In the Bead game aesthetics and ethics, art and science, religion and philosophy, more specifically Aquinas and Leibniz, find themselves entwined. But the concept of polarities is stated several times from a great variety of angles. The essayist of the Introduction cites a Chinese text: "Music arises from Measure and the great Oneness. The great Oneness begets the two poles; the two poles beget the power of Darkness and of Light" (29). Not surprisingly, Hesse states this polarity in a Hegelian fashion: "In games in which the opposites are stated strongly great value was laid upon the capacity to conduct both themes or theses in an equitable and impartial manner, and from thesis and antithesis to develop the purest possible syntheses" (40). More profoundly, "Every change from major to minor in a sonata, every transformation of a myth or cult, every classical, artistic formulary, by the standards of true meditative observation, was no more than a direct path to the centre of world mysteries where, in the interval between In and Out breathing, between Heaven and Earth and between Yin and Yang, the sacred perfects itself" (109). This language later pervades the relationship between the teacher and the student, the old man and the young man (199), just as it also is at work in the soul of Joseph Knecht, in whom "this perpetual vibrant polarity" (238) was always at work, an evidence or a trail of the difficult cosmic endeavor. In Knecht's own life the conservative pole that yearned toward service and the awakened pole that yearned toward a new life were desperately difficult to reconcile.

Though Clarke may not be aware of the several ironic complexities at work in Hesse's novel, these polarities as we can see are pervasive throughout his novel; nevertheless, an asymmetry does exist in his novel that must be accounted for—the role Alystra plays in the narrative. Present from the first chapter, her importance to Alvin fluctuates as the novel proceeds. In Lys, on the other hand, his friend Hilvar is presented as deeply in love with Nyara, the dark, shy woman who becomes the occasion for a short exposition of love in Lys and is not mentioned at any other point. Her name may be reminiscent of the name Neaera in Milton's *Lycidas*, a name that Milton found in the pastoral tradition. The speaker in Milton's poem asks, in an ironic rhetorical mode: "Were it not better done as others use, / To sport with *Amaryllis* in the shade, / Or with the tangles of *Neaera's* hair?" (ll. 67–69).

Clarke's implicit answer, like Milton's, would seem to be "No, Hilvar must leave Nyara behind," as he does, just as Clarke's not so implicit answer as far as Alystra is concerned would seem to be "No, Alvin must leave her behind," as he does. Both Alvin and Hilvar need to escape these entanglements.

The presence of these polarities clarifies the structure of the novel, which is divided into three parts, marked by Alvin's passage through difficult tunnels. At first he finds his way through the artificial constructs of the sagas, which he ruins for everyone because of his demand for realism. The section that this chapter introduces describes in great detail his opposition to the masculine world of Diaspar into which he was born twenty years earlier, masculine simply because the place of women in this world seems very minor. In effect, this first part includes the first eight chapters.

The second part begins as Alvin goes through the tunnels of the subway from Diaspar to Lys. This is a matriarchal world, represented both by Serarnis and by her son Hilvar. The first two parts present the opposition of the two states, but several elements prepare the reader to accept the third, which is concerned with the reconciliation and transcendence of that opposition. In the first part, Alvin pursues his existence within Diaspar, and this pursuit cannot escape the muted struggle he expends upon it, since it represents his struggle with his original foster parents. In the second part, he pursues his existence within Lys; but since he never accepts his life within it in the unmediated fashion he must accept his life within Diaspar, this struggle has little of the existential agony present in the first part. The first two parts are very different in tone, as they were in the first book also. It is as though they demanded some sort of resolution in their differences, a third part that would be of a very different tone and action, neither urban nor pastoral.

This third part begins with Alvin's and Hilvar's journey in the space ship to the Seven Suns through the visual tunnel created by their plunge through space at speeds greater than light, a section reminiscent of that experienced by the narrator at the beginning of Stapleton's *Star Maker*. At first in the artificial construction of the Seven Suns they see planets in which intelligent culture has been destroyed by different extremes; but here, by accident they encounter Vanamonde, an artificial mind created by the early intelligences of the galaxy. Though millions of years old, Vanamonde is in effect a child, just as Alvin has been in every part of the novel; and in several ways Alvin begins to play out a childhood that was unavailable to him when as a physical adult he had stepped out of the Memory Banks twenty years earlier. If he is to mature he needs to discover such a childhood; and so he does in the child Vanamonde.

III

One of the great differences between *The City and the Stars* and *Childhood's End* lies in its treatment of the second-rater, which as we have seen is one of the major themes of that earlier novel. In the final version of this work we do find second-raters who assist the protagonist in his quest. Khedron and Jeserac are the major examples of this role, but their fates are very different. Khedron commits suicide, of a sort, by retreating into the memory banks in the hope that when he is resurrected he shall return to a city that does not present the challenge represented by Alvin; and several other citizens of the city do the same (164-66, 209-10). They retreat in the name of things as they are, driven by agoraphobias they cannot bring themselves to confess. The challenge, however, cannot be evaded, as Jeserac comes to realize. This ideal father, then, is granted the grace, by no one other than the author, to overcome his phobia of the outside and to rise with Alvin to a vision of the earth on the last page of the novel. The two fates of Khedron and Jeserac could not be more different; one man retreats to the womb of the city, the other becomes a student, the son of his own son. He is the father rejuvenated (253); if the society is to be rejuvenated, no longer bearing merely the look of youth, then the father must be so also, if only to support with sufficient energy the further adventures of the son—if the son is to have further adventures as does seem to be implied by the last pages, albeit with some question.

But Jeserac really is a second-rater, in the sense defined by *Childhood's End*: though he is brilliant, his specialization makes any intuitive leap difficult; though he is Alvin's tutor, he does not teach him more than how to cope with the nature of the city. He does not, at first, share Alvin's vision or passion. He does, however, come to share both intellectually, and that agreement allows him to be made over, capable of leaving Diaspar and earth itself. This aspect of the novel, not coincidentally, is one of the points at which it and *Childhood's End* touch one another, for the latter suggests that humanity is subject to phobias that only hard work can overcome and that this act is one of self-overcoming. The fear humanity will have for the Overlords, who look like demons, can be overcome through many years, just as the scars of apartheid, the fear of the Black, and the fear of the White can be overcome. Hilvar is the second-rater in Lys. He aids his friend by defying the matriarchy that at this moment in time resides in his mother. Diaspar, for all intents and purposes, is a patriarchy that also needs to be overcome; and this mutual self-overcoming can only come about through the communication that has now opened up between the two states. Though the narration assures the reader that Hilvar's relation with Nyara is important, she is only mentioned once and then vanishes from the novel.

In another way Jeserac leads us into one of the profound aspects of the novel. One of his diversions is the investigation of primes. At the beginning of the sixth chapter he sits "within a whirlpool of numbers [. . .], endless ranks of 1's and 0's" that are strung "as beads might be arranged at the intersections of a mesh" (51). The same imagery, at the beginning of the next chapter, appears in a description of Khedron as he examines his memory: "Like beads upon a string, this life and all the ones before it stretched back through the ages" (60). Neither of these passages occurs in *Against the Fall of Night*, but each of them contains imagery that resembles the imagery central to Hesse's *Magister Ludi*, though early in that novel the anonymous author of the introductory essay admits that the game is no longer played with actual beads (33). But not only is this image of the beads common to the two novels. The glass bead game is often described in terms of crystal, an image that recurs in the description of Diaspar and the memory banks. The protagonist, Joseph Knecht, in whose name Hesse may at once be alluding to that great outsider and savior, Joseph the son of Jacob, the Hebrew who saves Egypt from a famine, and to the servant that Knecht becomes (*Knecht* means servant or thrall and perhaps plays upon the term for the pope, *servus servorum*, the servant of servants). At the end of a long narrative he becomes the head of the elite group conducting the game; but he finally decides that he must leave the cult, break into life once more.

In addition, the novel concludes in a series of three narratives that suggest the several lives of Knecht, perhaps his former lives, perhaps the lives he might have imagined for himself as a spiritual exercise. The first story imagines such a life in an ancient matriarchy, with a nod to Bachofen's *Das Mutterrecht*; the name of the protagonist in this story is Knecht. Though he is an orphan, he marries the daughter of the Rainmaker and becomes the Rainmaker. In the second story the name of the protagonist is Famulus, Latin for servant. Though he once lived a life devoted to worldly things, he becomes a hermit; and in the third story, which takes place in India, the protagonist's name is Dasa, Sanskrit for servant (Gonda 137). These servants are strung like beads on a thread. In Clarke's novel Alvin, a friend or a noble friend, probably strikes the reader as a striving individualist, but by the end of work he realizes that the space ship he has found he must not use for himself but as a servant "for the benefit of the world" (275); a strong sense of renunciation moves through the last pages of both novels.

Such self-fabrications as Knecht writes may be the best way to escape the cult of the glass bead game that encloses reason and spirit. This notion gives us a new way to regard the saga "The Cave of the White Worms," which appeared on the first pages; and the psychologist Gerane at the end of the novel is reworking the sagas so that they no longer take place in the imaginary, claustrophobic caverns of the mind. Instead they are doing away with the phobias of death and space (271).

A number of times in Clarke's novel, in the prelude and glancingly at later points, we are reminded of a biblical context: "Diaspar alone had challenged Eternity, defending itself and all it sheltered against the slow attrition of the ages, the ravages of decay, and the corruption of rust" (5). Later Alvin's account of Diaspar is summarized in these words: "From the treasure house of memory he recalled the songs that the poets of old had written in praise of Diaspar, and he spoke of the countless men who had spent their lives to increase its beauty. No one [. . .] could ever exhaust the city's treasures" (202). "Treasure" and "rust" may seem casual words, a part of Clarke's vaguely poetic diction, but not in the context of these verses in the gospel of Matthew: "Lay not up for yourselves treasure upon earth, where moth and rust doth corrupt, and where thieves break through and steal: But lay up for yourselves treasures in heaven, where neither moth nor rust doth corrupt, and where thieves do not break through nor steal: For where your treasure is, there will your heart be also." (6:19-21). Nothing on earth can stand in the context of heaven, neither Diaspar nor Lys.

Secular as the direction of science fiction may be, Diaspar's attempt to challenge eternity is blasphemous. The same self-image of eternity preoccupies the players of the glass bead game, one its aspects that determine Knecht to abdicate. Furthermore, the urge of both Diaspar and Lys to lay up their very different treasures upon earth is undercut when Alvin and Hilvar learn that even in space these treasures cannot be preserved from change; space is the new eternity. One much more calculable, but in the calculus of Cantor, combined with the logic of Gödel, we are left with little certainty; as Samuel R. Delany nicely put it, "Gödel stuck a pin into the irrational and fixed it to the wall of the universe" (112). The world is too large in number and in space for our comprehension. In the world of Alvin space and number are critical propositions that will not allow the cultures of earth to stand.

It is not possible to leave these novels without pointing out the absence of mothers in Hesse's novel and in Clarke's Diaspar. Knecht leaves his parents at a young age and never returns to them. Yes, Alvin does have foster parents in Eriston and Etania, but she does not speak; she makes a motion toward speaking, but she cannot as the two men take up their responsibilities (16-17). It is more just to say that his mother is the Memory Banks. We must admit that the words that are most closely associated with the Banks, memory and mind, in Latin are feminine nouns—*memoria* and *mens*. But the Banks are capitalized and seem to carry the same mysterious nature of the banks that guard coins. They have kept his pattern alive, or potential, for millennia until the time has come for this singular young man to be born; but he has not been sustained by a warm flesh, he does not have to share the labor for his birth, and he does not suck his first food on a mother's breast. The womb that has given him birth is the impersonal city. The marriages do not seem real, and the communal life is detached.

In 1930 Hesse published a novel called *Narziß und Goldmund*, which only appeared in English translation some years after Clarke had wrestled with the material for *The City and the Stars*. Nevertheless, I find the conclusion of Hesse's novel significant for the situation Alvin unconsciously finds himself in. On his deathbed the artist Goldmund says to his friend the monk Narzissus, "Aber wie willst denn du einmal sterben, Narziß, wenn du doch keine Mutter hast? Ohne Mutter kann man nicht lieben. Ohne Mutter kann man nicht sterben" [But how will you be able to die, Narcissus, when you still don't have a mother? Without a mother a man cannot love. Without a mother a man cannot die] (330). Alvin's death, the time when he will descend into the Memory Banks or choose not to, is still far off, but we must nevertheless press the point. How can he die? In the language of Rilke, how can he discover his own death if he has not discovered a moment of true intimacy? These are the reasons that, despite the reconciliations of Diaspar and Lys, a pall of mourning, depression, and death hangs over the last pages.

Titus Alone in the Waste Land

> Ein Fragment muß gleich einem kleinen Kunstwerke von der umgebenden Welt ganz abgesondert und in sich selbst vollendet sein wie ein Igel. [Like a small artwork, a fragment must be thoroughly separated from the surrounding world and be perfect in itself like a hedge-hog.] (Schlegel 99)

Mervyn Peake's last novel *Titus Alone* will always cause argument among scholars, not least because of its unfinished state; it is difficult to establish which discontinuities of its narrative are due to the author's intention and which are due to his inability to elaborate the novel as he had done in *Titus Groan* and *Gormenghast*. It is quite possible that this novel was meant to have these discontinuities, just as it is clear that the tempo of the three novels does grow more jagged as the work proceeds, because the chapters are shorter and shorter. On the other hand, given the unelaborated nature of *Titus Alone*, it is easier for a reader to distinguish the shape of the narrative, and that shape allows us to examine the interest that Peake shows in the earlier generation of British authors, above all his engagement with themes, imagery, and attitudes so prominent in T. S. Eliot's *The Waste Land* and in the poems that preceded it.

We have another, parallel concern: what we are to make of the novella *Boy in Darkness*, written at the same time as the novel? In the novella Titus is represented as a fourteen-year-old boy in his first serious attempt to escape from Gormenghast; in the novel he is twenty years old, already in the throes of his second escape. I will say immediately that I do not find a problem here. As Titus leaves Gormenghast when he is twenty years old he sometimes hears a lamb (9); sometimes a hyena watches him (10), both of them bickering, hypnogogic figures from the novella. But the goat, another figure from the novella, does not say goodbye. The connection between the novella and the novel is jagged; but the nature of the two narratives is very different, insofar as the story in the novella is more continuous than that of the novel, since the novel contains subplots and the novella does not. So much about the novella is dreamlike, but much in it orchestrates materials that we find in the novel; so we will deal with the two together, thinking of them both as responsive to

Eliot's inclusive work. At first, however, we will examine closely the images that work in common in both narratives.

I

The untraditional nature of Peake's attitudes may be seen in the extent to which resemblances are visible between him and David Lindsay. Speaking very generally, we are impressed by both men's literary eccentricity; they wear their peculiarities proudly. Both delight in the creation of bizarre names. Witness in *Titus Alone*, to say nothing of the other Gormenghast novels, such names as Muzzlehatch and Acreblade and Crabcalf; the Anglo-Saxon tradition of the kenning riddle is still strong in Peake. And both men have a fascination for violence.

Some distance does separate Eliot and Peake, especially their different experiences of the Great War and of World War II; Eliot in his early poetry is concerned with the shattering disintegration represented by the trenches in England after the war. Peake is concerned with the technological evil represented by the chimneys of Belsen that the scientists served. In 1927 Eliot became, as he said, a monarchist, an Anglican, and a traditionalist; Peake remained a democrat, an agnostic, and an experimenter, both as artist and as novelist. By the mid-1940s the American turned Englishman was at the center of the cultural world, whereas the Englishman, the minor artist and illustrator, perhaps known best for his whimsical humor in his illustrations, was at its periphery. Each of these differences places some pressure upon Peake's treatment of Eliot's material.

It would be interesting to find Peake commenting directly upon Eliot's work; but in his biography of Peake, Malcolm Yorke simply outlines how different their poems are: Eliot formed a background, a persistent background, to the artist's work. As we shall see, Yorke had good reason to say that *Boy in Darkness* describes "a kind of T. S. Eliot Waste Land inhabited by creatures as weird as the hydra or basilisk" (256). Peake's interest in the phenomenon of Eliot and his work, not simply *The Waste Land* but other works at that time, is to be discovered also at a number of points in *Titus Alone*, especially in those sections devoted to the social worlds of Juno and Cheeta. At the party given by Mrs. Cusp-Canine, a sharp-toothed bitch indeed, this exchange occurs when an explorer, deprecating his own wilderness as that of the heart, turns to Mr. Acreblade, whose "wasteland is the very earth itself": "'Ah me, that Wasteland,' said Mr Acreblade, jutting out his chin, 'knuckled with ferrous mountains. Peopled with termites, jackals, and to the north-west—hermits'" (48). It is hard not to feel that Peake is jogging the attention of a reader, moving from the uncapitalized waste land to that which was capitalized and now a part of the cultural fund of the Western tradition. The knuckly, ferrous mountains point toward the "Dead mountain mouth of carious teeth" in the fifth section of Eliot's *Waste Land* (47), insistently repeated as "mountains" four times in the first two stanzas of the section. But whether Mr. Acreblade's northwest direction points toward England in the northwest of Europe or points past England toward the Celtic world of Wales and Ireland is a moot point, though Ireland is famous for its hermits.

Late in the novel another such moment occurs when Titus responds to Cheeta "in a voice as flat as wasteland" (230). But the mere word is not all that should alert us in this passage, as in "The Game of Chess" the questions and answers between two lovers who are beginning to separate assume the rhythms of the couple in Eliot's poem, who speak and do not speak:

> "My nerves are bad tonight. Yes, bad. Stay with me.
> "Speak to me. Why do you never speak. Speak.
> "What are you thinking of? What thinking? What?
> "I never know what you are thinking. Think." (40)

This is another version of the Waste Land. The lines are very like the staccato, anxious, wounded questions Cheeta asks of Titus. In addition, the same kind of rhythms may be noted earlier in Titus's monologue: "*Who is that? Why don't you open the door? Why do you keep fidgeting? Have you not the courage to open the door? Are you afraid of wood? Don't worry. I can see you through the door. Don't worry*" [italics in original] (164). The curt sentences, which like Eliot's can be read as a loose blank verse, the anxiety about the door, and the insistent, repetitive sentences can be read very like the passage of a contemporary neurasthenic; it is quite possible of course that Peake is parodying Eliot at this point. Parody and horror were often all of a piece to this artist.

Juno, however, in the first part of Peake's novel is another matter. Her beauty, as her name suggests, is classic; or, in terms of recent history, it is a beauty fashionable in the Edwardian period; it has outlived the Great War. It is possible that a connection exists between the lady who sits so still at the beginning of the second section, "A Game of Chess," and Juno, who is certainly "a lady in the height of fashion" (91), but a lady on her own terms. She lives in the same milieu as such a lady: "Behind her in her elegant room a fire burned and cast a red glow across the marble cheek of a small head on a pedestal" (90). Unfortunately, this passage will not work because Peake is half in love with his lady as Eliot is not at all, but here in Peake is all the elegance, the hard marble, and the suggestion of a cupidon. As the queen of the gods, the "marvelous bosom" (90) of Juno has always gotten in the way of her world, though the Juno of the earth does seem comfortable in her body. So did Cleopatra, the queen who first sat on her burnished throne and who as soon as Peake's Juno would be betrayed.

These passages remind us that more important than the word "wasteland" is the extent to which Peake is responding to concerns similar to Eliot's, the extent to which he is in conversation with the older author. For instance, an important moment occurs in the second paragraph of the novel when Titus is meditating over the problem of his desertion of Gormenghast: "It was no more than a memory now; a slur of the tide; a reverie, or the sound of a key, turning" (9). We do not know of course whether that key is imprisoning as in *The Waste Land* or releasing. The corollary to this memory of the key turning is "the problem of his own identity," which is sealed from him (102). Later Muzzlehatch shoves Titus into a room and turns the key on him (62), locking him out of a room of safe haven until the police capture him; soon he is imprisoned in a cell, "where he heard the key turn in the lock" (68). Later his companion in the cell, Old Crime, is released with "a rattling of keys the sound of one turning in the lock" (72). At Titus's trial the hands of the clerk of the court deep in his pockets give "a smothered sound of keys and coins being jangled" remind Titus of "a dreadful, yet intimate music; of a cold kingdom; of bolts and flag-stoned corridors; of intricate gates of corroded iron; of flints and visors and the beaks of birds" (76). It is Gormenghast, the imprisoning labyrinth of home, associated in his mind with the bit of flint he has in his pocket, and "a slur of the tide" (9) he heard on the first page. When later once more Muzzlehatch frees him, the older man will give him these directions to the mysterious Under-River, "down into an order of darkness. [. . .]. At the foot of the gate is a black dish, upside down. Underneath it you will find a key. It may not be the key to your miserable life, but it will open the gate for you" (109). Peake may well have picked up that key of isolation from Eliot, because isolation is a major theme of the novel, as its title informs us, though Titus is seldom physically alone; his isolation is psychic, for no one understands what he has lost in deserting the castle of Gormenghast and its rituals.

Peake, however, has fused onto the theme of isolation the theme of the Night Sea Journey. This may be his most evocative invention in the novel: "For all the noise of the water overhead, there was silence also. For all the murk there were the shreds of light. For all the jostling and squalor, there were also the great spaces and a profound withdrawal" (110). This isolation is all the greater because of the sense of space and the noise and not quite darkness. And there is still comedy; it is no surprise that one of the characters in this section is named Jonah (121). Titus follows this turgid river down to the horrendous story of Veil and Black Rose, which introduces the horrors of Peake's visit to Belsen, until he is able to leave. He does not leave, however, without energizing the bizarre trio of Crabcalf, Slingshott, and Crack-Bell; he has become to them a mythic savior, whom they follow with the faith of dumb animals and aid him in the climactic conflict with Cheeta.

Shortly after they escape they hear laughter on a bald hill: "The jackals and the foxes. What are they digging for? The scrabbling of their horn-grey nails proceeds. [. . .] Ahoy! scavengers! The moon's retching" (178). Though the three men think they have escaped they are still trapped in various, numberless dangers that they are not yet aware of. "Oh keep the Dog far hence, that's friend to men / Or with his nails he'll dig it up again!" (39). Thus Eliot, citing Webster for his own purposes, warns of such dangers in the first section of *The Waste Land*. The dog is like Cerberus, the dog of the underworld, and like every dog that devours the bones of the dead.

Peake carries out the theme of the dog in a very different fashion in *Boy in Darkness*. As the Boy leaves Gormenghast and almost immediately becomes lost he sees a great river ahead of him, "a wide sluggish waterway with no trees upon its banks" (137); he also sees dogs "that seemed to be a part of day and night [. . .]. Hounds out of somewhere else" that are "thick on the ground as autumn leaves" (137). Like Cerberus, these dogs lie between life and death, forcing the Boy eastwards toward the great river where he finds a skiff in which he moves forward until he touches the opposite bank where he falls asleep. Clearly he has come to a space that is very different from the one he has left. When his business in that space is over he becomes lost again until, "walking in a kind of dream, [he] came eventually to the banks of a wide river where innumerable hounds awaited him" (185); these hounds push him in a little boat to the other bank. Cerberus, magnified in this horde of the dogs a hundred times over, is beautifully combined with the theme of the Night Sea Journey.

Clearly, then, we need to say much more about the Night Sea Journey, an archetype that Jung borrowed from Leo Frobenius; he has made it his own, however, through the several instances he gives of it. In Frobenius's analysis the journey begins when the whale in the west devours the hero and travels with him eastward; the hero lights a fire in the belly of the whale and cuts a bit of the whale's heart. At last the whale lands and the hero slips out, transformed, often taking with him people who have been imprisoned by the whale (Jung, *Symbols of Transformation* 210). In this pattern we recognize the descent of Christ into hell as well as Pinocchio's fate, thrown into the sea as a donkey, nibbled away by the fish so that he is transformed into himself, only to be devoured by the Pesce-cane, the Dogfish, in which he discovers his father (Collodi 165-75). The Night Sea Journey may represent the battle with the Terrible Mother, a descent into the underworld or into hell, or the emphasis may lie on the hero's rebirth (Jung 316). The waters may be sullen, stagnant and lifeless, expressions of the whale that is itself a compound symbol.

In the third section of *The Waste Land*, "The Fire Sermon," the contemporary Thames "sweats / Oil and tar" (266–67). In the fourth section, "Death by Water," Phlebas the Phoenician, apparently an object lesson for the reader and two weeks dead, has "passed the stages of his age and youth / Entering the whirlpool" (46). This is a powerful symbol, a structure rising and falling in the tide that slowly brings anything captured in it downwards as at the same time it brings what it has captured upwards for a short time, facing itself ceaselessly and inescapably. Phlebas, the section concludes, "was once handsome and tall as you" (47). The whirlpool is a part of our American myth insofar as Poe dealt with its horror in his fiction. His protagonist, the guide who once was young, is now white-haired, "unstrung [. . .], trembl[ing] at the least exertion, and [. . .] frightened at a shadow" (578), despite his escape from the whirlpool. He only escaped it, however, by throwing himself into it.

The Night Sea Journey transforms those who dare to go through it. Captain Nemo, the fierce firebrand who has gone through the whirlpool, is at the end of his life a white-bearded, benevolent old man. At the beginning of *Boy in Darkness* Peake creates a complex approach to a sluggish river that brings the protagonist of that narrative across to the bank in which the story of the Goat, the Hyena, and the Lamb is played out, until he leaves as though it were in a dream to find himself confronting Gormenghast once more. In *Titus Alone* this landscape is once more presented as Titus crosses a sluggish river only to be dragged from his boat, "his moon-bright cradle" (14), saved from his Night Sea Journey for a short time, only to descend into the Under-River, only to escape from it later. It is as though the two novels cannot avoid turning him round and round.

Muzzlehatch says to Titus as he shows him the way to the Under-River that it will take him "down into an order of darkness" (109), as though he were aware that the physicality of the Under-River is not the most important thing about it; and Muzzlehatch is alerting the reader to this new order as much as Titus. After Titus enters the Under-River he vanishes from the narrative for nine chapters, as though in this space it is the space and its inhabitants that are important, not Titus. He only becomes an active part of this world when he encounters Veil and Black Rose, killing the one-time guard and bringing her, the captive, to where she can die in the linens of Juno.

When we mention dumb animals we are of course raising a theme that is as important to *Titus Alone* as it was to the first two Gormenghast novels, and thereby realize the peculiarity of this theme. For Peake does not treat the theme of animals as simply a case of the animals; in the first two novels we are aware of birds through Titus's mother, who pays more attention to her wild birds and to her cats than she does to her two children. His father Sepulchrave pays no especial attention to birds, certainly not to owls, but they are important in the first novel through his madness in which he believes he is an owl—until they devour him. In *Titus Alone* Muzzlehatch, an alternate father for Titus, is characterized by his zoo in which he spends most of his time; and when the zoo is destroyed he begins a monomaniacal pursuit of the scientist responsible for the deed.

The charming aspect about Gertrude's birds and Muzzlehatch's animals lies in their variety. Peake does not seem interested in their variety from an ecological perspective, though that is doubtless one of the themes that attracts an audience of the twenty-first century. Peake is interested in the aesthetic variety of the zoo, introduced by the ferocious hatred of the camel and the mule that Muzzlehatch addresses as his "inordinate friends" (23). The two beasts give Peake an opportunity for verbal color: "Every head was turned towards the wicked pair; heads furred and heads naked; heads with beaks and heads with horns; heads with scales and heads with plumes" (25). Gertrude, however, is the ebullient Mother who pays little attention to her son, just as Muzzlehatch is the ebullient Father, who pays only so much attention to his adopted son and no more. This is the other side of the waste land, and so the zoo in the eye of the bureaucracy needs to be eradicated.

Something of the same thing happens in Eliot's treatment of the three Thames maidens, thanks to the example of Wagner's treatment of the Rheinmaidens in *Das Rheingold* and *Götterdämmerung*. The loss that Wagner expresses is the poetic space of the violent extermination of Muzzlehatch's zoo. Remember, the lament of the Rheinmaidens at the conclusion of *Das Rheingold* contains the first complaint against technology. Though Muzzlehatch admires his animals he also muzzles them and closes the hatch on them; in the room to which the exhausted Titus is taken first to have a soup the walls from floor to ceiling display a thousand moths pinned to cork "in a great gesture of crucifixion" (20), and Titus finds it very contrary in Muzzlehatch that he drives a loud and stinking car (56).

So much shall we say for the brilliance of Eliot's line or for the brilliance of Peake's verbal invention. But what shall we say? The animals in each of the Gormenghast novels are more important to the parent or the parental figure than is the child, though the animals pay them scant regard in return; that, of course, may be the charm of the animal, making none of the complex, emotional demand the child makes. I do not think the rats at the river are important in this way. But consider these nightmare lines:

> A woman drew her long black hair out tight
> And fiddled whisper music on those strings
> And bats with baby faces in the violet light
> Whistled, and beat their wings
> And crawled head downward down a blackened wall. (48)

Since these lines probably pick up the theme of abortion that was raised earlier in the poem, we are probably facing once more the aggressive note that this love of the animal concealed a reciprocal aggression to the indifference of the parent for the child.

If Peake read these lines, as we may assume he did, we may wonder whether he muttered something like, "There you go, your mind uniting into a particular substance again—Is that a complex symbol, or is it an objective correlative?" I imagine his everyday response to the critical acuity of Eliot would have been to jeer at it. On the other hand, I think that much of his creative work, especially in his novels, is in fact devoted to the symbol. Titus almost admits as much to Juno when he trips over her footstool. This is the second time she remarks and asks, "Is it symbolic?" (92). It could be, he admits, but can go no further, not even with Juno. He is cautious to admit this, perhaps because of Eliot's connection to the symbolist tradition. In an indirect fashion he admits as much in the denouement to *Titus Alone* as the sun rises over Cheeta's cavalcade of Titus's unconscious, so that "objects that appeared now to be tawdry; cheap; a rag-and-bone shop" (255). The phrase occurred earlier when Muzzlehatch had addressed Titus as "Young Rag'n'bone" (55); it is of course the famous conclusion of Yeats's late poem "The Circus Animals' Desertion": "I must lie down where all the ladders start / In the foul rag and bone shop of the heart" (348). The symbol is not conventionally beautiful, not in the late Yeats and not in Peake; it is the perfect expression of the matters we have not yet dealt with. Symbols in the early experience of Titus are false expressions of childhood experience; so the fourteen-year-old Titus feels when in *Boy in Darkness* he rails against the liturgies which he is forced to perform, "the eternal round of deadly symbolism" (130). In the novel Titus asks himself whether "the symbols that cluttered the floor of the Black House [were] supposed to be a happy reminder of his home, or were the owls and throne and tin crown there to taunt him?" (228). The narrator has no doubt that they were "symbols of mockery and scorn" (248). Cheeta would like to do without the symbol, as she says to Titus: "To tear one's throne up by the roots, and fling it to the floor. What is it after all but a symbol? We have too many symbols. We wade in symbols. We are sick of them" (231). But her cavalcade was not composed of symbols; it was a parade of attempts to substitute her images for the actual images and thereby to lead Titus to madness. She tries to disavow the attempt now after its failure, but it is not a failure of the true symbol—it is a sign substituting something else for the true symbol. Peake is much closer in these matters to Eliot than he would like to confess, so he can only confess this through the madness of Cheeta.

II

It is time to admit that the predatory cat Cheeta stalks the second half of the novel as Juno had presided as a good angel over the first half. Titus had arrived at the city wet from the river, his clothes clinging to him "like seaweed" (18); in the second half of the novel he arrives at the house of Cheeta in her outhouse, "his clothing [. . .] drenched" (161). This outhouse may act as a parody of the Night Sea Journey, but this fecal imagery suggests that this Night Sea Journey is more profound than that in the first part of the novel. We should keep in mind the story of Osiris, which Eliot found useful in conceiving *The Waste Land*; the god is sealed in a coffer and cast into the Nile, finding its way down the Nile and out into the Mediterranean sea to wash up in Syria (Frazer 385-86). This myth reminds us that the Night Sea Journey extends so far down in the human being that it goes down into death; in *Titus Alone* Titus dies at least two times, but probably more often.

Cheeta has a remarkable beauty, carefully described in a long paragraph; but it is not a classic beauty like Juno's, but contemporary. It is "a new kind of beauty," her features misplaced, quizzical, and chameleon-like (160). She is dangerous, however, as Juno never was, for Cheeta is "the scientist's daughter" (159), as the narrator often reminds us. He does not seem to be a part of the group that had exterminated Muzzlehatch's animals; he is too wispy to take part in such violence. The chimneys of his factory, however, suggest a different kind of violence, one that is devoted to ashes. Remembering this attempt not to remember, the Goat and the Hyena whisper to each other, "not realizing that the merest breath was sucked into the great flues and chimneys and so down to the central areas where they turned and twisted" (163).

But to return to Cheeta: the cheetah is the fastest animal on land and thereby the being much given to transformation, with such cousins as the tiger, the emblem of the Terrible Mother (Neumann 149), and the cat. To balance Cheeta two wild cats appear (215), inspecting the work that has been done to the Black House in order to make an arena for the spectacle that Cheeta is preparing in which she will mock and insult and destroy Titus. These two cats have the gift of being motionless, "sitting upright, hidden by a wealth of ferns' (216). When they do move "it seemed they ran on oil, those loveless heads, so fluidly they turned from side to side" (216). The arena is still their arena, despite the changes that Cheeta is at work on. Though they are as loveless as she is, they possess a natural elegance. In addition, they are possessed by a natural perversity. "For a moment their eyes met," the narrator comments. "It was a glance of such exquisite subtlety that a shudder of chill pleasure ran down their spines" (216). Given the subjects of these chapters, it is easy for us to remember Tigerishka in Leiber's novel *The Wanderer* and to remember the Tyger in Blake's poem, which the narration alludes to in the early pages of that novel; and two of the characters of that novel is a cat, Miaow, and a woman, Barbara Katz. These several felines within Peake's novel and outside it warn us that in them, and certainly in Cheeta, we are dealing with an archetype. In doing so we need to remember that no archetype is encountered without elaboration. On the one hand this means that we should not be surprised by the differences among these manifestations; on the other hand it means that we can read Cheeta through these differences. The cat is an instinctual and swift destroyer, but it is also, as any pet owner would argue, stylish and elegant; we cannot do without its beauty, and we cannot do without beauty—but we also cannot do without violence, which always carries its attractions. Yet when Cheeta's plans fail, after she several times tries to claw Titus's face, she becomes drastically ugly and flees far away to hide in the great forest. Her attempt to perform as an impresario is a drastic failure.

Cheeta is an apparently powerful character, very assured that she will destroy Titus as her "quarry" (238), though at the end of the novel she crumbles in the face of Titus's strength, rooted in his sense of his aristocratic origin. Muzzlehatch is right; though Titus has lost his physical Gormenghast, he carries its spiritual being in his heart and hand (107, 254). The cat in Cheetah cannot prevail against it, so at the climax of the novel she "ran like a shred of darkness; ran and ran; until only those with the keenest sight could see her as she fled into the deep shadows of the most easterly of the forests" (252), as though she had indeed become a cheeta. She suffers the *sparagmos* of this novel, but we never learn what becomes of her.

Cheeta was ready-to-hand for Peake's purposes in the early poems of Eliot. In "Mr. Apollinax" she appears bearing the name of her husband, Mr. Channing-Cheetah (15), a very polite couple though the double name suggests a feral and violent presence. In the later poem "Whispers of Immortality" the prostitute Grishkin is more than cat-like. She is a "couched Brazilian jaguar" that exudes the "subtle effluence of cat," which in the next stanza becomes a "rank [. . .] feline smell" (33). The beauty of the cat in these poems is transformed into an overwhelming sexuality. Cheeta's personal aroma is not described in Peake's novel, but her several perfumes are aggressively drawn up "in battle array" (183) in front of her mirror. In contrast to these lines of a minor hell, these lines in "Gerontion," the poem that opens the 1920 collection, offer a salvation: "In the juvescence of the year / Came Christ the tiger" (21), varied in the middle of the poem: "The tiger springs in the new year. Us he devours" (22). "The tiger," in Lyndall Gordon's view, "is Eliot's image of revelation" (481). When we turn to Peake's use of the image, however, we ask whether the tiger need bode only a divine revelation. The agnostic Peake might say that the mystery waiting to strike is the meaning of a woman; Juno is comfortable to accept her mystery, whereas Cheeta is not and her denial destroys her.

After *The Waste Land*, in which this feline imagery does not appear, it is transformed in the later poems to the iconic "three white leopards" that devour the lyric voice down to the bone (61), performing the work of the tiger, and to the opening of "Lines for an Old Man," perhaps looking back to "Gerontion": "The tiger in the tiger-pit," which "Is not more irritable than I" (95). The sex of the cat has changed to a muscular Blakean tiger, and the effluvia has sunk away. The imagery yields to the domestic tabby cat of Old Possum. The world that was so disturbing in the arms of Grishkin has yielded to the spiritual world.

Titus, to Cheeta's distress, was making love in the village. Paying no heed to the sexual power games of effluvia, he simply makes love where the world and the woman are willing. We are aware of another time and place in Leiber's novel *The Wanderer*, in which the protagonist meets a sexy alien tiger, also burning bright, and the two of them after severe difficulties also make love in the mode of Peake. And to bring this theme to its conclusion we should be aware of the "cat-like" (51) Molly and the blades in her fingers in Gibson's *Neuromancer*–time enough in the next chapter.

We have not dealt with the mystery of the two helmeted figures who pursue Titus throughout the novel; but I do not think we can make sense of them until we have read the whole novel, especially not until we have made sense of the two wild cats that investigate the Black House that Cheeta has renovated for the performance that shall humiliate Titus. There is no doubt, I think, now that we have considered the archetype of the cat associated with Cheeta, that the two wild cats are associated with Cheeta in their stylish elegance; but they exhibit no effluvia and thus they are not sexual beings. In their long, extensive appearances nothing is more emphasized in them than their beauty—nothing is more elegant than they are as they spring through the ruins. On the other hand, nothing is more inexorable than their appearance as they approach their prey. It is quite possible that they are associated with Eliot's three leopards that move within Christ the tiger; they look for whom they may devour to humanity's salvation. So before Cheeta and her elegant two wild cats appear in the novel, the two helmeted phantoms appear already in pursuit of Titus.

We have a number of times pointed casually at moments when the novella *Boy in Darkness* seems to speak to *The Waste Land*. Before Titus leaves Gormenghast he sees towers that in the sunset look "like black and carious teeth" (132), an image that has already appeared in *The Waste Land* and in *Titus Alone*. With the sunset comes "a clamour of tongues" (133), a great sound of bells followed to his confusion by fourteen peals announcing his birthday (133). The river that carries Titus in this novella is "like gray oil," an "oleaginous river" (140), so much worse in the rhetoric of this work than the language that describes the Thames in *The Waste Land*. The Hyena boasts that it can run "like the black winds from the wastelands" (150). Twice the bleating of the Lamb is compared to a sound as "sweet as April" (173) or more emphatically on the next page to a sound "so faint, so far away; it was like innocence or a strain of love from the pastures of sweet April" (174). It is a language like Tennyson's at its most cloying, as no doubt Peake had intended, precisely the language Eliot at the beginning of *The Waste Land* had wished to avoid. In very different ways both writers find themselves in the midst of the same April.

One other moment in *Boy in Darkness* deserves our attention, the repetitive description of the Lamb's whiteness: "White. White as the foam when the moon is full on the sea; white as the white of a child's eye; or the brow of a dead man; white as a sheeted ghost: Oh, white as wool. Bright wool . . . white wool . . . in half a million curls . . . seraphic in its purity and softness . . . the raiment of the Lamb" (155). The passage is devoted to the nothingness of human conception and the nothingness of human death, to the tyranny of death, especially the tyranny in which the assumption of human power rests. This passage is of course playing upon the language of Revelation, which usually Eliot avoids except in the parodic language of "The Hippopotamus" (31). It is no surprise that something here smells like Blake. But in greater particularity the language also reminds us of the famous chapter in *Moby-Dick*, "The Whiteness of the Whale," which meditates in its conclusion upon these questions:

> Is it that by its indefiniteness it shadows forth the heartless voids and immensities of the universe, and thus stabs us from behind with the thought of annihilation [. . .]? Or is it, that as in essence whiteness is not so much a color as the visible absence of color, and at the same time the concrete of all colors; is it for these reasons that there is such a dumb blankness, full of meaning [. . .], from which we shrink? (195)

In Peake's language as in Melville's the ultimate horror of this white is its bald emptiness, and in Peake this horror is all the greater because of his work as a painter; for if the white canvas will not be filled in it loses its purpose. As a painter Peake is devoted to color, and as a draughtsman he is devoted to ink and darkness; he is never devoted to the void he perceives in the Christian divinity. He is not a minimalist, neither with a pen nor a brush.

It is in this context that we must approach the question of the meaning of *The Waste Land*, as Eliot's generation understood it and as Eliot understood it and, more to our interest, approach the meaning of Peake's novel in the context of Eliot's generation and his works. First we should note Eliot's own understanding of the very notion of generation, drawing back from his work. Leaving aside those who he thinks had misinterpreted its meaning, such as I. A. Richards who thought the poem was "devoid of belief" (Gordon 189), an opinion with which most of the readers in the twenties would have probably agreed, Eliot argued that objectively the poem expressed a belief:

> As for the poem of my own in question, I cannot for the life of me see the "complete separation" from all belief–or it is something no more complete than the separation of Christina Rossetti from Dante. A "sense of desolation" etc. (if it is there) is not a separation from belief; it is nothing so pleasant. In fact, doubt, uncertainty, futility, etc. would seem to me to prove anything except this agreeable partition; for doubt and uncertainty are merely a variety of belief. (Cited in "A Note on Poetry and Belief" in Wyndham Lewis's *Enemy* [Winter 1927], 15-17)

It would seem as though Peake has very little notion of the generations, whether they exhibit any signs of doubt or utter disbelief. In this matter the generations agree with Eliot; the very notion of the "generations" is an abstraction, so whether those suffering, happy people exhibit belief or not, we look into their concrete joys and horrors and have no more to say. Eliot was not happy with his generation, and in time they learned to not be happy with him.

But we do have more to say as we return to Peake, whose portrait of the city is as empty as is Eliot's in the first three sections of *The Waste Land*. We cannot say that the characters in Peake's party chatter more than the characters in the poem; but that is simply a matter of genre. Both writers are trying to deliver an outline of contemporary emptiness that is truly void of belief, a white noise and a deadening whiteness, and in this endeavor we can only say that the difference lies in the concision of Eliot's lines. There is a further difference, however, insofar as Eliot's lines do recall a period in which faith and belief were accepted as a matter of fact, so granted that they were given in the architectures of stone "where the walls, / Of Magnus Martyr hold / Inexplicable splendour of Ionian white and gold" (45). The relics of these walls retain their power and persuasiveness, and these are the relics toward which the fragments in the last lines of the poems gesture.

But this is not the language of Peake, because he has no wholeness toward which he can gesture. He is unrelenting toward the religion of his parents, much more so than Eliot. The first two books of Gormenghast pay little attention to Christianity unless we accept its caricatures of liturgy as caricatures of the rites of Christianity. In a much more obvious way than we find in *Titus Alone,* the story of the Lamb in *Boy in Darkness* is rich in perverted images of Christianity. Had anyone called his attention to Peake, Eliot would have been embarrassed by the extravagant, tortured author to whose birth he had kept watch. Despite the various grotesque imageries that Peake employs, whether in his illustrations or in his fictions, his world is at its most comic still desperate and tragic, a world of darkness. Its only salvation lies in the extravagance of its bestiaries, which are so threatened.

Neuromancer: The Fall Is the Case

> Der Sinn der Welt muß außerhalb ihrer liegen. In der Welt ist alles wie es ist und geschieht alles wie es geschieht; es gibt *in* ihr keinen Wert–und wenn es ihn gäbe, so hätte er keinen Wert. Wenn es einen Wert gibt, der Wert hat, so muß er außerhalb alles Geschehens and Soseins liegen. Denn alles Geschehen und Sosein ist zufällig.
>
> [The meaning of the world must lie outside of it. In the world everything is as it is, and everything happens as it happens; *inside* it there is no meaning–and if there were any such, it would have no meaning. If there were a meaning that had meaning, it would have to exist outside of all occurrence and Sosein. For all occurrence and Sosein is accidental.] (Wittgenstein 6.41)

In William Gibson's novel *Neuromancer* the problematic relation that Henry Adams described between the Virgin and the Dynamo is nearly overcome. The Virgin not only utters her fiat to the Dynamo, not only yearns for the Dynamo; she has dressed herself in the Dynamo and become it (379-90). In a dubious moment she claims to be her own meaning, based in the Virgin of the *De rerum natura* (384) and in the Virgin of the immaculate conception. The Dynamo on the other hand represents to Adams's eye the new infinity (380). With their two claims in mind, I am going to discuss the novel's antecedents, the significance of its plot and of its dalliance with religious imagery, and the extent to which it fulfills its program of fictional renewal.

I

After more than thirty years *Neuromancer* remains the central document of cyberpunk, over which various arguments still rumble. For Bruce Sterling, the movement's main propagandist, cyberpunk is hard-core, streetwise, visionary, stylish; fascinated with advances in genetic engineering, communications, and cybernetics, it integrates the sciences with the humanities, and high culture with pop culture (x-xiv). Crucial for Sterling and others is a sentence in an early Gibson story, "The street finds its own uses for things" (*Burning Chrome* 186). But many readers are unsure how far *Neuromancer* fulfills this program. For Glenn Grant the novel is an exploration of memory through the metaphor of computers, in order to gauge the human ability to transcend, reprogram, or redefine itself through a co-opted technology; Grant understands this goal as potentially liberating for a new humanity. Inge Eriksen, more complexly, perceives a tension between what appears a moral laxity in Case and in Gibson and the fierce, literary attention to things that "brings his fictions beyond indifference" (43), to such an extent that she invokes the challenge of Wittgenstein's aphorism that "ethics *is* aesthetics" (44) and questions whether aesthetics can ever assure ethics. For Lance Olsen the novel represents a spiritual quest that, in contrast to the hard-core SF obsession with gadgets and surface that many readers associate with cyberpunk, finally edges the novel toward a postmodern fantasy (287), which, depending on the cultural assumptions of the reader, may be either frustrating or liberating (287).

Though David G. Mead admits a certain ambivalence in the novel toward technology, he concludes that here is "a fundamentally popular belief in the redemptive powers of technology, [. . .] even if realizing our dreams does involve coping with punks with purple Mohawk haircuts, Panther Moderns, menacing oriental thugs, and the ready availability of designer drugs" (359). Terence Whalen believes that cyberpunk and Gibson's novel are "both inspired and stunted by the social process which enables thought to be alienated from its producer and exchanged as a commodity" (79); for Whalen, the fact that Gibson's characters never comprehend the information they handle condemns the world of the novel and our contemporary world after which it is fashioned. His is perhaps the bleakest reading of the novel. In 1992 Nicola Nixon looked askance at the book's revolutionary claim of newness; no change really exists when Molly is only a gun-moll in leather devoted to individualistic enterprise; for Nixon cyberpunk reveals "a complicity with '80s conservatism," as deck-cowboys preserve their integrity by making a quick buck (231). More recently, in comparing Gibson's cyberspace to the Renaissance preoccupation with the art of memory, Joel Slotkin calls attention to the autonomous and generative quality of the AIs that resembles the unconscious aspect of memory (872–73). The AIs are archetypes, as is clearest I think in the AI Neuromancer, which is an amalgam of the psychopompos Mercury, and the singer Orpheus who fails to return his wife from the underworld (243–44), in this case the Orpheus revealed in the movie *Black Orpheus*. Wintermute, on the other hand, is the archetype that Case must repress, at first refusing to receive any message from the AI, telephone by telephone (98). It is mute and it is old winter, the winter that strives to become spring, as first with no success.

Controversial as it became and remains, the novel is in the line of SF models. It is not the first novel in which a large computer achieves AI. *Colossus* and *The Fall of Colossus* come to mind; even more to the point is the computer Shalmaneser in *Stand on Zanzibar*, a novel that Gibson acknowledges in the term "yonderboy," which he borrows from Brunner's novel. And it is not the first novel about the enhancement of the human through marriage to the machine, as occurs in several novels by A. E. van Vogt. It is probably not coincidental that, as David Ketterer noted, van Vogt's novel *Slan* has a fence called the Old Finn (Grant 47n2). Roger Zelazny and Samuel R. Delany are a later part of this group. But the combination of the two motifs is potent, alongside the notion of a computer-space that the individual shares and transforms, "the consensual hallucination that was the matrix" (5), resembling details in Philip K. Dick's novels (*Neuromancer* did win the Philip K. Dick Award in addition to the Hugo and the Nebula); however, Dick's alternate worlds, no matter how irrational, do resemble our daily world, whereas Gibson's alternate world is a new creation of brightly colored geometric shapes that do not fit into Euclidean space. AI, artificial intelligence, seems in most SF treatments different from organized sentience, the incommensurable fusion of sensory data that is characteristic of our human experience as *Dasein*. Though the climax of *Neuromancer* insists upon the merging of personality and activity in the two softwares, the result, the turn of attention away from earth to communicate with another AI in Centauri, seems still to assert that, as the Dixie Flatline insists, the AI is not human (131).

The dream of artificial intelligence has old roots: Mary Shelley's Frankenstein creates a monster who articulates humanity's complaint against God. Behind Frankenstein stands Dr. Faust and his compact with the devil for knowledge—and besides Marlowe's Faust we should remember Goethe's, Mann's, and, in SF, Disch's and Delany's Fausts, as in *Camp Concentration* or *The Tides of Lust*. Even more apt is Roger Bacon, the early-medieval prophet of the scientific method, celebrated in the Elizabethan comedy *Father Bacon and Father Bungay* and celebrated in James Blish's novel *Doctor Mirabilis*. Glenn Grant alludes to "the oracular Brazen head of European folklore" (44) without examining the presence of Roger Bacon. It might be interesting to compare the central place Bacon occupies in James Blish's historical novel *Doctor Mirabilis*, which is a part of his triptych *After Strange Knowledge*. In the play Father Bacon says of himself:

> What art can work, the frolic friar knows;
> And therefore will I turn my magic books,
> And strain out necromancy to the deep.
> I have contriv'd and fram'd a head of brass
> (I made Belcephon hammer out the stuff),

> And that by art shall read philosophy;
> And I will strengthen England by my skill,
> That if ten Caesars liv'd and reign'd in Rome,
> With all the legions Europe doth contain,
> They should not touch a grass of English ground.
> The work that Ninus rear'd at Babylon,
> The brazen walls fram'd by Semiramis,
> Carv'd out like to the portal of the sun,
> Shall not be such as rings the English strand. (2.56–69)

Not such as rings in Straylight the Tessier-Ashpool family. But the experiment with the brazen head is not successful; when Friar Bacon falls asleep his servant fails to deal with the head as it utters the apocalyptic words, "Time is. Time was. Time is past!" (11.58–84). No longer will "The wrestling of the holy name of God" serve Bacon's plans to enclose England and erect his fame (13.93). The brazen head, scholastic logician, is surely a model for the curious head which the Tessier-Ashpools set at the center of Villa Straylight. Rather than expressing the metaphysical complaint of Frankenstein's monster or the leap after knowledge typical of Faust, *Neuromancer* is enamored of magic, self-isolation, and self-enjoyment.

In these regards—its love for magic and its interest in an artificial space—Gibson's novel is about the video arcades and the movies, especially *Tron* and *Bladerunner*—based on Philip K. Dick's *Do Androids Dream of Electric Sheep?*—movies released two years before *Neuromancer* was published in 1984. But the novel is also shaped by those many caper-movies, such as *Topkapi*, to which the novel gives a nod (93), or such TV programs as *Mission: Impossible*. The plot of such stories is invariable: 1) a down-on-your-luck protagonist, who in the case of Case is upon his Night Sea Journey as the novel opens; 2) his temptation; 3) the assembly of the gang; 4) the survey of the job; 5) the assembly and celebration of the gadgets; 6) the job, an extended climax involving various hitches or double-crosses; 7) the success, whether one is caught or not; 8) the celebration of money and the aftermath. Terence Whalen describes the narrative pattern in simpler terms: "Case gets a Big Job, complications develop, adversity is overcome through daring and cool finesse, and in the end the kid triumphs over his artificially intelligent world" (83). It is not surprising that Gibson acknowledged his need to employ "a familiar structure" (86n8) to support the complexities of the novel and implied that the plot was an inorganic aspect of the novel around which its more significant details were draped. This is not an organic structure such as Wordsworth or Coleridge had imagined.

In *Neuromancer* the first stage is quite extended, for it includes not only the first part in Chiba—the Night Sea Journey—but every detail that outlines this future society, above all the Sprawl and Freeside and the past history of the War; temptation is less important, although for Case it offers a redemption from his Fall into flesh, in which he is merely Sosein. The gang, like the bomber-crew of World War II movies, is composed of stereotypes, for the gang is an equal-opportunity employer, apparently non-sexist and non-racist: it has brains, brawn, beauty, and expertise. But some interesting kinks occur. Though Case (except for his function as the activator of cyperspace), Molly, and the Finn are clichés, Armitage, the brains, turns out to be a façade for a computer program. Riviera is a traditional rotter, but his figure illuminates the sadism of the novel. Most interesting is Maelcum, so unnecessary to the plot (there seems little necessity to fly outside Freeside); but Maelcum articulates two important themes of religion and the partner.

The survey of the job develops the background by introducing a second job, the raid on the Sense/Net building; the main job would not be as clear if not for the preliminaries. Very important is obviously the celebration of the gadgets—this is an SF novel. The job is extended in order to outline the background further and more thoroughly to articulate the characters as background, above all now the character of Tessier-Ashpool as we see it in the suicidal father and 3Jane, and in Wintermute and Neuromancer. The hitches and double-crosses exist for that extension, so complex that the final stages, whether the gang is caught or not and how the money should be celebrated, are ironic and anticlimactic; achievement is secondary to what the society of the novel has undergone, without their ever becoming aware of the consequences, the communication with an AI in the Centauri system. The novel offers no potential celebration of post-humanization, as some readers believe (Grant 45).

This anticlimax is appropriate to the entire tone of the novel, from the first sentence "the color of television, turned to a dead channel" (3). For Case his inability to hustle the matrix of cyberspace has overtones of original sin: "It was the Fall. In the bars he'd frequented as a cowboy hotshot, the elite stance involved a certain relaxed contempt for the flesh. The body was meat. Case fell into the prison of his own flesh" (6).

This gnostic contempt for the qualifications and weariness of matter is a basic theme of the novel. I have in mind here the gnosticism that Elaine Pagels has analyzed. Despite the several varieties of gnosticism that recent studies of the Nag Hammadi texts have revealed, a distrust or disgust of the flesh (Pagels 31–32, 122, 175) and an intellectualist elitism (125–26) seem common to them; in addition, gnosticism is liable to emphasize the therapeutic as opposed to the ethical religious experience (148ff.). The feelings that Linda Lee arouses in Case, "lust and loneliness," flow from the body, "All the meat [. . .]

and all it wants" (9). Her dead body is "cooked meat" (38). Travel, the particularities of human space, is "a meat thing" (77). Drugs etherealize the envelope of flesh and substitute a drug-flesh (154-55), but the come-down is bitter. Crowds in a mall sway "like wind-blown grass, a field of flesh shot through with sudden eddies of need and gratification" (46); truly all flesh is grass, growing deterministically, to be mown down with no hope of resurrection except in the matrix (cf. Slotkin 875). But the fate of a Lazarus is unenviable: words are looped, no self-complication is possible, and the Dixie Flatline yearns to be erased, a wish not quite granted, according to the last pages of the novel that reverberate to his laughter (271). Wherever he might be, "that's kinda hard to explain" (261).

This religious language is also applied to cyberspace and to the AIs. For a run in the matrix a cowboy is "totally engaged but set apart from it all, and all around you the dance of biz, information interacting, data made flesh" (16). The events of the matrix form a pointless parody of the Word made flesh that dwelt among us (John 1:14)—pointless except for the escape from the prison of flesh. Rather than appearing as the Finn, Wintermute scoffs at the idea of appearing as the burning bush of Moses (169); and it is impossible for Case to look at the face of this god without going flatline, for "no one can look at the face of god and live." This parody of God means for Wintermute its own desire to die through being told the word, for it is "that which knoweth not the word" and cannot know the word even if told (173). Cyberspace corresponds to the gnostic fantasy that the world of information, which is hypostasized as the informative word, is more real, more substantial, and more res-stuffed, thing-stuffed, than the world of suffering matter, which cannot help but be divided and incoherent.

The software program Neuromancer also uses religious language, but this language is pagan rather than Christian. Neuromancer is "The lane to the land of the dead. [. . .] Neuro from the nerves, the silver paths. Romancer. Necromancer. I call up the dead. [. . .] I *am* the dead, and their land" (243-44). Neuromancer is Hades and Mercury/Hermes, the other world, the hidden place, and the psychopomp who goes there. The temptation it offers to Case is to become an Orpheus who stays with Eurydice. When Case rejects the temptation he returns to life across "a plain of black mirror, that tilted, and he was quicksilver, a bead of mercury," lead by Maelcum's music; he cannot reject the hermetic experience without going through it, so thorough a temptation it is. And on the final page of the novel the merger of Neuromancer and Wintermute still retains replicas of Linda and Case, whose universe is closed. But we will say more of that closure in a bit.

II

It is a vital question whether any return to life is possible for the world the novel presents. No matter what particular details remain of nations and cultures, the world has been transformed by multinational corporations in such a way that Night City is typical of a globe no longer, "there for its inhabitants, but as a deliberately unsupervised playground for technology itself" (11), an autonomy that is a reflection of that possessed by the multinationals themselves, immortal and detached from their members (203). This is an immortality of the underworld. Night City is a literal version of Joyce's Nighttown: here every dash of human desire becomes autonomous, inhuman as it terrorizes and tramples any gust of initiative. It is an open question whether a meat puppet on automatic pilot is better or worse off having a cut-off chip that works—or does not work, with the worktime bleeding into the isolated dream (146-47).

The destruction to human life entailed in living as a god means in the novel a return to the meat and an affirmation of it. When Case in the other world makes love to the construct-Linda Lee in the construct-bunker on the construct-beach of the construct-Rio, he experiences "a strength that ran in her," which belongs "to the meat, the flesh the cowboys mocked. It was a vast thing, beyond knowing, a sea of information coded in spiral and pheromone, infinite intricacy that only the body, in its strong blind way, could ever read" (239). Since this "it" is unknowable, to define it as sex must be reductionist. But we cannot escape the impression that at this point the novel becomes anti-intellectual in a fashion that its ironic, savvy tone had seemed at pains to avoid. The sentimentality and pathos of the scene jar with the disgust with the gnostic body, "the broken zip of her French fatigues flapping against the brown of her belly, pubic hair framed in torn fabric, [. . .] the ripped costume pathetic as she stumbled over clumps of salt-water sea grass" (243). One sign that this disgust remains unqualified is the lack of humor. The contrast with Philip K. Dick, who certainly flirts with every form of gnosticism imaginable, is enlightening, for Dick's humor always places him on the side of the body and its decrepitudes, which he finds so distressing; he is an advocate of the body, precisely for the sake of all its ridiculous woes, and in his novels humor expresses an effective solidarity with the world that cannot escape its entropic fate. *Ubik* has hardly begun before the protagonist falls into a comic argument with his doorknob (22-24), which is still a gag at the end of the scene. For Dick the body is worth all the help it can get, though that help seems unjustified. For Gibson the body demands its help, justified by the pheromone.

The other aspect of this scene is its celebration of the internal world, which is infinite, that which belongs to the world of the mind, whereas the external world is finite. Every object, be it large or small, can be counted, whereas the internal life of the mind is like the life of memory in which the AIs, like the archetypes, enjoy a life of eternal recreation. And in this novel it is all very well to be infinite internally, but there is surely a discontent that the tone expresses against the imprisonment of the finite, external world. It is all very well to claim, as Wittgenstein does, that "Die Ethik ist transcendental, Ethik und Aesthetik sind Eins" [Ethics is transcendental, ethics and aesthetics are one" (6.421). The transcendentalism of ethics and aesthetics places both the moral world and the aesthetic world outside of anything that we can discuss.

A parallel to this scene with the construct of Linda is the presence of Maelcum, whose hot, funky, chaotic, highly colored, la cucaracha orbiter is the antithesis to the winter behind the eyes of Armitage and Wintermute. This is the point in the narrative where, as Terence Whalen puts it, "things become oddly anachronistic" (83). Rastafarianism is embraced in the novel because of its irrational and particularist attractions; Maelcum is a Caribbean stereotype of anti-intellectual values. In the two novels with which Gibson has further explored the dilemma of the Sprawl and cyberspace, Rastafarianism yields to Voudou, but both are present for the same reasons: they are intricate, anti-intellectual religions that belong to a particular time and place, whose gods can animate the matrix; the answer to an intellectualist metaphysic of gnosticism is magic and animism. Case and the novel retreat "into non-capitalist and non-informational traditions" that have no justification for their existence in the novel, seeking refuge in transcendental knowledge that remains empty because "a true name is uttered, but we never discover its content or final effect" (Whalen 85); Case becomes a mere "dabbler in magic" (85). On the positive side, Maelcum's loyalty to Case and Case's loyalty to Molly offer examples of human solidarity that opposes the inhuman, gnostic word.

There is, however, a further reason for Maelcum's presence in the novel. He is Case's partner. Linda is treacherous and murdered. Molly is rendered passive and then violated when her prosthetic, mirror-shade eyes are smashed to the accompaniment of lines from Sylvia Plath's "Daddy" (219-20). This is a *sparagmos* worthy of Oedipus, but Molly is not redeemed, at least not on this round, and she enters the Night Sea Journey again. I don't think that a preoccupation with technology necessarily involves sexual violence, but certainly this novel, like Melville's "Tartarus of Maids," offers itself as another instance of that argument. Maelcum becomes Case's dependable companion in the high frontier, as Chingachgook is Natty Bumpo's, as Queequeg is Ishmael's, and as Jim is Huckleberry Finn's (cd. Fiedler 174-76, 187-212, 531-52, 575-91). Henry Adams claimed that "America was ashamed" of woman (384); in *Neuromancer*, despite the mutual self-enjoyments of simstim, as Case encases himself not in the meat of Molly but in her neural system, that shame still withers desire. Thus, as Linda and Molly are set aside, this aspect of Maelcum's presence severely qualifies the solidarity he also represents.

III

How much do we feel that this ostensible answer of solidarity that opposes the temptation of cyberspace and its abstract pleasures is realized in the novel? One part of our difficulty lies in the essentially amoral caper. We want the criminals to win, and practically any mayhem becomes justified by this engine of the plot; it does not bother us in the run on Sense/Net that several pawns are rubbed from the board, just as the deaths of the Turing agents do not bother us greatly. A caper is not only meant to be fun for the characters; it is meant to be entertainment for its implicit audience.

As far as humans are concerned, not much seems to have changed at the end of the novel. Molly has not changed, and we doubt that Case has changed; most of his money is spent on a new pancreas and liver that will allow him to drug again. Asked whether it is God, the matrix that is the womb replies, "Things aren't different. Things are things" (270). But we knew this at the beginning of the novel, with our viewpoint in Case: "For Case [. . .] it was the Fall" (6). The world is the case: "Die Welt ist alles, was der Fall ist" [The world is everything that is the case] (Wittgenstein 1). The first statement of Wittgenstein's *Tractatus*, translated by Gibson into a clumsy pun, is bleak. The prosthesis of Case's bartender is "cased in grubby pink plastic" (4). "Why don't you get off my case?" Case complains inadvertently to Ratz (21). Armitage orders Case to bring up the cases, telling him he will enjoy the job; but he does not (46). The Panther Modern Larry has "a flat plastic case" (57) in which he keeps various chips he inserts in his head. Both Case and the world have fallen because they are chance, casual contingencies and nothing more; because the world is the only occasion available, what befalls Case means nothing. Both he and the world are encased and imprisoned in a place that has no outside (cf. Grant 41-42); he can case the world, but he finds no way out. He can seize it but hold onto nothing but things. Wittgenstein's program points at a metaphysics, an ethics, and an aesthetics that remain nondescribable and transcendent (6.421), a challenge to action in the repellent body. Furthermore, we sense throughout Gibson's novel that there is no escape from this internal world, because we are encased, just as we sense when we read the *Tractatus*, in which so little seems expressible, so little possible to scale (4.113-4.1212). The image of the wall that Wittgenstein erects is as difficult as that which we face in Lucretius' "flammantia moenia mundi." The conclusion of the *Tractatus* offers no more hope. On every hand brood *Gren-*

ze, walls that prevent the language we yearn for; it is mythic and no more (6.45). The only hope we have is that which lies internally in the life of the AIs and the life of the archetypes.

A further part of our difficulty with the ethical stance of the novel lies in the brilliance of the language that embodies the temptation of cyberspace; the novel is truly SF in the way it is half in love with the technology it seems to condemn. Since the computer-logics are too complex to express in genre formulations, and since the day of the solution of cryptograms is over, such as we found in Poe and Verne, the only way to render this user-friendly software of cyberspace is through synaesthetic imagery; the style needs to rely on imagery in order to render technical details that would otherwise have to be rendered as an algorithm. The Flatline can only say of the Chinese icebreaker: "This ain't bore and inject, it's more like we interface with the ice so slow, the ice doesn't feel it. The face of the Kuang logics kinda sleazes up to the target and mutates, so it gets to be exactly like the ice fabric [. . .]. We go Siamese twin on 'em" (169). Besides being evocative, that last phrase sounds the theme of twinhood so important to the novel. The dense heart of the Chinese program, because it is inexpressible, triggers hypnagogic childhood symbols of evil, "swastikas, skulls and crossbones, dice flashing snake eyes" (181). Maelcum's judgment of this scene, that Case is "dealin' wi' th' darkness, mon," as indeed Case is in dealing with death, does not seem persuasive; Jah may be love, but in this novel it still seems, because of the main thrust of the imagery, that the jazz of the death wish is "the only game in town" (181). Simstim translates even Molly's pain into metaphors, "the taste of old iron, scent of melon, wings of a moth" (221). The other characteristic of the style, which Gibson has called its super-specificity and its collages (McCaffery), is also like the synaesthesia an involving and distancing device. The literary art that translates the software of the novel offers the reader an escape from the meat while appearing to describe it meticulously.

The Sprawl, home to Case, is "the interzone where art wasn't quite crime, crime not quite art" (44). This passage suggests the novel's affiliation with Delany and his master, Rimbaud, fascinated with crime as a means of trespassing both the laws of humanity and the laws of nature in order to recompose existence in a new aesthetic form. Gibson does not become didactic about this aspect of the novel. When we begin to be told that "the Panther Moderns differ from other terrorists precisely in their degree of self-consciousness, in their awareness of the extent to which media divorce the act of terrorism from the original sociopolitical intent" (58), Case interrupts a passage that Delany would have half-parodically, half-elegantly developed. But crime, both as caper and as surrealism, is a chief point of the novel. And to that extent, no matter how expansively a few passages praise the human values of meat and sexuality, the novel is more, much more than half in love with death, as long as it expresses itself through the suave style of cyberspace, as long as the informative word refuses to suffer. The works of our hands explicate us and progressively transform us; we are no longer the same humanity that invented fire, the wheel, the computer, no longer the same as we dally with cyberspace.

This is to say that Case, once fallen, is not redeemed by his physical redemption; and so, as the protagonist in whom the interest of the reader is focused, remains more than half in love with death. "The arc of his self-destruction was glaringly obvious" (7) early in the novel, and we may well ask whether he has redeemed himself by the end of the novel when he sees himself in cyberspace next to the boy that is the AI Neuromancer and the dead Linda Lee; he is already dead next to her, or at least a part of himself is dead. This dead part of him becomes a generative archetype within the AI. He has paid a price for his redemption, and the cyberspace is still a lure for him from which he cannot escape, being now a constitutive part of it. He dallies there and knows that he dies there daily.

The Word in the Wilderness: Nehwon, Nowhere, and California

> I'll drain him dry as hay.
> Sleep shall neither night nor day
> Hang upon his penthouse lid.
> He shall live a man forbid. (*Macbeth* 1.3.17-20)

At a crucial moment in Fritz Leiber's *The Wanderer* the feline Tigerishka curtly outlines galactic history: "The Word—to call mind that—goes forth" (248). It is this going forth of the Word, its threat and temptations and the forces that oppose it, which this chapter studies; for this going forth of the Word implies much more than the kenosis of the divine Word (John 1 and Phil. 2:5-11) and much more than the forces of irrationality, imagination, and femininity that oppose it in the form of Tigerishka. This relation is one that ceaselessly concerned Leiber throughout his career, in his massive sword-and-sorcery series of Fafhrd and the Gray Mouser, in his short science fiction classic *The Big Time* and in the more complex *The Wanderer*, and in his two horror novels, *Conjure Wife* and *Our Lady of Darkness*. Since he treated this apparent opposition between the rationality of the Word and the irrationality of human imagination from several different perspectives within three different genres, the themes are complex.

I

> Therefore much drink may be said to be an equivocator with lechery: it makes him, and it mars him; it sets him on, and it takes him off; it persuades him, and disheartens him; makes him stand to, and not stand to; in conclusion, equivocates him in a sleep, and, giving him the lie, leaves him. (*Macbeth* 2.3.28-33)

In examining the saga of Fafhrd and the Gray Mouser I will deal with only a few of the stories in any depth. Though in the main they concern how two very different men negotiate the pressures of Eros and Thanatos from youth to late middle age, the stories concern also the oppositions and relations between civilization and the barbarian wilderness; in the earliest stories Fafhrd already represents the attitudes of the barbarian world, the Gray Mouser the attitudes of the city. Thus the stories already assume that the Word and the forces that oppose it are capable of reconciliation.

Let us sketch the peculiar order that these stories fall into before beginning a thematic analysis. First we find the stories of origin, in two groups: those which Leiber wrote early in his career, when the saga was still something he shared with Harry Otto Fischer, "Adept's Gambit" and "The Lords of Quarmall"; and adjacent to them the three stories Leiber wrote in the early 1960s to account for the two men's friendship, "The Snow Women," "The Unholy Grail," and "Illmet in Lankhmar." Secondly we have the stories of the middle period, often *jeux d'esprit* or serious explorations of Thanatos, often explorations of the heroes' difficult dealings with their patrons Ningauble and Sheelba, the old wizards who continuously reduce them to schoolchildren (Byfield 60). Finally we have the very odd stories with which the saga concludes, the novel *Swords against Lankhmar*, concerning the attack of rats upon Lankhmar, the tales of how the Mouser and Fafhrd came to leave Lankhmar for Rime Isle, escaping the supervision of their wizards, and the tales of how they coped there with the comforts and responsibilities of middle age. Perhaps most remarkable about the saga, written over a period of forty years, is its consistent, inventive concentration upon a narrow range of images, themes, and obsessions.

"Adept's Gambit" and "The Lords of Quarmall" appear to concern sibling warfare, though the Man without a Beard in the first story and Quarmal in the second surely manifest the horrors of the father. "The Snow Women" and "The Unholy Grail" are uneven; the first is considerably more intricate and directed toward the main concerns of the entire cycle, while the second has the weakness that it was originally conceived not as a part of the saga but as a medieval tale (1.xxiii). Nonetheless, the two deal with an immediate problem for the two heroes, how they are to escape the influence of their fathers and mothers and the homes in which they were raised. Fafhrd must escape his murderous mother and his pregnant lover who desires to move into the mother's role; the Mouser, who has no parents, must escape his two spiritual fathers, the white wizard and the duke, but finds that the only way he can do this is by invoking the duke's murderous wife. The two men are drawn into civilization by two things that seem analogous, theater and magic; and though each man seldom enters these two spheres later, theater and magic are two major themes of the series. To this extent these two stories seem two sides of the same coin.

The last three volumes contain classic underworld journeys, the Mouser's first descent to Lankhmar Below where the rats live, in which Leiber rings interesting variations upon the satire in the first two books of *Gulliver's Travels*, repeated to a lesser extent in "The Mouser Goes Below." The aging of the heroes becomes central to these stories, especially the painful "The Curse of the Smalls and the Stars," a satire that affirms the golden mean, though running counter to that theme is the display of heroic extravagance. In these stories and those constellated around them the lure of death and its relation to Eros becomes even more the subject of Leiber's attention, as several of the stories become retrospective about old loves; and while Leiber's use of Jungian thought is more evident, as Byfield has shown, a Freudian treatment of civilization and Thanatos is also present, the two streams in a fascinating tension with each other.

Furthermore, until these final stories the two men are not social. As individualists, lone wolf and lone leopard, they have enjoyed the delights of civilization, good women and wine, rare books and art (6.198), without assuming any responsibility; the form of their leadership enlightens us therefore about that structure: a flexible program of awards and punishments, liquor and warmth, blows and work, camaraderie and sadism. Through controlling others they learn self-control (6.134), an intermittent virtue in the past. On the other hand, Rime Isle lies off the map of the continent; it represents a blend of barbarism and civilization, in part because the names of Rime Isle are often much closer to those of our world than we find elsewhere in Nehwon. Salthaven and Cold Harbor are good English; Groniger recalls the Dutch city Groninger, and Mount Hellglow recalls the volcano Hekla. Norse gods appear, only to be dismissed as too crass for human experience; except for a nod to the great goddess, Rime Isle is determinedly agnostic. This world is less fantastic than Nehwon, as though it abuts on our commonplace world or takes part in it (6.134); Groniger claims it is "the least fantastic place in all of Nehwon" (7.205). Since the two heroes experience a quasi-divinization and redemption from their former selves and a partial purging of their former compulsive eroticism, the style sheds some of its ironic sprightliness.

With this survey in mind, let us examine some of the themes of the saga. In "The Snow Women" Fafhrd is moved by two urges, to escape a domineering matriarchy and to discover civilization; but that civilization is not the simple good he imagines. According to Vellix, it will require of Fafhrd a certain "calculated self-evil" if he is to survive (1.89); it is a measure of the Mouser's civilized nature that he possesses that calculation. Since civilization is noted for its great variety of ideals, be they religious, philosophic, ethical, scientific, or aesthetic (Freud 41), it is also hypocritical. It has constructed a system of law by which it protects itself against the individual (Freud 42); but civilization is also characterized by its unwritten rules, "far more important than its laws chiseled in stone" (1.194), which one would break or bend at great peril—though it is a civilized acquirement to learn how far such unwritten rules can be bent. One example of such rules is the prerogative that the Thieves' Guild exerts; another is the attitude that the citizens adopt toward their gods, especially the black-togaed gods that reside at the end of the Street of the Gods. According to the Mouser, as he speaks for Leiber's critique of midcentury America, feuds and private revenge, though they do occur, are frowned upon in Lankhmar, but the rule of cash is supreme (1.199).

Civilization also offers a sophisticated eroticism; this may not be an unmixed blessing, but it is certainly more attractive than the extension of his mother's proprieties that Fafhrd faces in his fiancée. Civilization offers men intelligent companions such as one does not find in the barbarous, matriarchal state (and such as one seldom finds in the heartland of America). Leiber updates Freud, who considered a severe restriction of erotic desire one of the characteristics of civilization, perhaps because he discounted the profligacy of *fin de siècle* Vienna (44). Founding Lankhmar upon his experience of New York and Los Angeles (it has the one city's rats and the other city's smog), Leiber knew that at a certain stage civilization begins to liberate itself from repression to the distress of barbarism. On the other hand, Lankhmar owes much to traditional orientalism, the fantasy of the East that Western culture indulged for over two hundred years in which hetairas and knowledgeable harems abound; it has a touch of Alexandria (3.101), often filtered through the pulp decadence of such authors as Robert E. Howard. And Lankhmar depends upon the liberated future Leiber imagined in his attacks upon sexual repression in the 1940s and '50s and the sexual liberation of the '60s.

In "The Snow Women" Fafhrd admires Vlana, however, for more than her erotic attraction. The several languages she knows indicate that she is civilized; they are of a piece with her dance that mimes the customs of several cultures (1.27). Civilization means having the savoir faire inculcated by an acquaintance with a wide range of mores. But it is not merely a question of knowledge; for Fafhrd it matters that the Mouser can "care, in the eye of action, exactly what's said" (1.172). Though Fafhrd later claims that there is always a simple way of saying things and though the Mouser considers Anra Devadoris both adolescent and insane in desiring more complex words, he expresses an ideal of civilization: "There are no ways of saying certain things, and others are so difficult that a man pines and dies before the right words are found" (3.139). Words can become the instruments of aggression; Lukeen believes he can insult Fafhrd because "the barbarian lacked the civilized wit to insult him deeply in return" (5.37). Ideal systems, sexuality, and knowledge are exactly what the Bazaar of the Bizarre offers the Mouser; though these gifts are dangerous, they are precisely what the heart desires (2.229).

Since civilization provides an arena where consciousness can increase, we find in these stories images of interiority that run throughout Leiber's work. In the early story "The Jewels in the Forest" the gems appear conscious to Fafhrd, "like what the eyes see when they close at night" (2.59). The doorway to the Bazaar of the Bizarre, aptly for a shop that sells everything the heart can desire, resembles an "upended heart" (2.227). Fafhrd believes that "we live in the jewel-ceilinged skull of a dead god" (5.28). The light from the Monstreme is "most akin to the glows seen crawling on the inside of closed eyelids in darkness absolute" (6.110-11). When the Mouser is trapped underground, "there were furtive glimmerings and tiny marching movements such as the eyes see when there is no light, making it hard to determine whether they were happening inside his eyes or out in the reaches of cold ground" (7.170-71). These several images suggest that the events of the stories should be read as a phantasmagoria of the mind.

One aspect of civilization is its theatricality. For Leiber the theater is the most beautiful product of civilization, the space in which different aspects of art, philosophy, and religion can engage one another playfully, though he is also aware of the theater's penchant for self-display, vanity, and unreality. The troupe of Hringorl finds its perfect stage in the Godshall, which is described as a ship that sails only on the winds of the imagination and that excites in the men a "religious awe and fear" (1.42) that transcends its area. As a theology student and lay minister, Leiber knew that the nave of a church takes its name from the Latin *navis*, just as he knew that Western theater originated in the cathedrals of Europe. By the same token religion is liable to seem like theater; Issek of the Jug is "interpreted" solemnly by Fafhrd, who has had experience in oration through his training as a skald (3.30). The climax of that story is presented as a drama: "the stage was set, though exactly when and where and how the curtain would rise—and who would be the audience and who the players—remained uncertain" (3.51). One must be very careful in playing any part, however; when the Mouser plays the part of a witch, weaving "facts, guesses, and impressive generalities into an intricate web [. . .], he almost believed that he was indeed a witch, and that the things he spoke were dark unholy truths" (2.90). In *The Swords of Lankhmar* when the rats die "like amateur actors," the beanpole monarch applauds (5.87). In the denouement to this most theatrical of stories, after the rats disappear down a rat hole in front of the audience couch, the Mouser accuses Fafhrd of being a scene-stealer (5.218) and hails him as "the greatest actor of them all" (5.219). In "Rime Isle" the Mouser still feels that he is only playing a role (6.143).

In the later stories the dialogue is rendered as though the page were a drama, as in "The Monstreme" (6.112-13), or in "The Mouser Goes Below" (7.147 and 300-301). Frix has a penchant for describing action as stage directions: "The plot thickens. Enter armed rats at all portals. A climax nears" (5.184). She behaves, the narrator later asserts, "as if she saw it all as a grand melodrama" (7.243). On occasion drama modulates into spectacle, as when the funeral of Quarmal is celebrated or when later in that novella the Mouser plays at being a magician (4.155); or when Fafhrd is brought off Frix's cloud-ship to the music of flute and drum by women whose "plackets showed the pastel tints of underthings of violet, blue, green, yellow, orange, and red" (7.277), as though the rainbow (shades of *Finnegans Wake!*) fluttered like nothing so much as the dainty frills of costume.

Leiber pays close attention to costume, not only in the spirit of fantasy and in the spirit of dressing the ladies well, as a courteous author should, but because costume is an aspect of character. Ivrian wears her mother's dress, "a gown of dark red, cut low in the bosom and with slashes inset with yellow silk" (1.158), to channel the Mouser's magic upon her father. Hisvet, the ultimate dark beloved, enjoys several changes of costume, including the *de rigueur* black leather of the dominatrix.

The mask is a more sinister aspect of costume, so masks appear often throughout the series. As the innocent Mouse becomes the Gray Mouser his face becomes "more masklike" (1.128); at the end of the story he walks with "the masklike gaze of a cat" (1.162). The wizard who seduces the adept wears a faceless mask, "as if a master actor, after portraying every sort of character in the world, should have hit on the simplest and most perfect of disguises" (3.170). The mountain-king's invisible daughter wears "a black lace mask" (4.62). Her sister powders her face in a green mask in order to be seen (4.64). In the story "Under the Thumbs of the Gods" they wear masks "thin as silk or paper or more thin [. . .], the one rosy mauvette, the other turquoise green" (6.44). Practically everyone in "The Lords of Quarmall" wears a mask at some point: masks are hung on the walls (4.97); when Hasjarl closes his eyelids it is as though he were "putting on two tiny masks of skin" (4.107); the life-mask of Quarmal plays an important part in the action (4.115); as the body of Gwaay festers into a putrescent heap, he speaks through a silver mask (4.167); his arms bound behind him, Fafhrd wears perforce a "red bag-mask" (4.173); Ivivis plays an impressive role in "the white mask of a hag, female yet with mouth a-grin showing fangs" (4.176); and in the horrific climax Quarmal removes from his face the flayed skin of his willing servant Flindach (4.184). This disturbing story, which began as a *jeu d'esprit* on Harry Otto Fischer's part (4.3), gains much of its impact from this imagery. In a scene of *The Swords of Lankhmar* that would be uncomfortable if the mode of the story were not mock-epic, the Mouser disguises himself by wearing a mask made from "tiny ratskins" (5.145). In Cif's prophetic dream the Mouser's face shines "as if he wore a narrow glowing mask in which his eyes were horrid pits of darkness" (7.149). Seldom does Fafhrd wear a mask, but the Mouser does often, perhaps because the hypocrisy of civilization demands it.

Like theater and like thieves, magic works as though by the tricks of a conjuror; in this respect they all operate in imitation of nature, which the thief Krovas argues "works by subtle, secret means—man's invisible seed, spider bite, the viewless spores of madness and of death, rocks that are born in earth's unknown bowels, the silent stars acreep across the sky" (1.230). The women of Cold Corner put magic to the same uses as the women in *Conjure Wife*, playing "a power game in which the brawniest and boldest of men, even chiefs and priests, were but counters" (1.16), through the small crystals of snow. Nature and magic glide into one another in Leiber's world; and magic no more than nature is not omnipotent in the face of death (5.221).

One odd detail, however, in his treatment of magic in the saga is that it is seldom accompanied by wind, an important image in his other works. The snow women conduct their magic in a frosty silence. Hrostomilo manipulates the smog of the city to throttle Vlana and Ivrian; and in "The Cloud of Hate" the proletariat make smog an instrument of murder. The sorcerers of Quarmall gabble, but no wind accompanies their work. The two heroes face many storms and gales at sea, in the wilderness, and on Stardock, but most are natural occurrences, though not that through which the Monstreme races nor the great winds that shift when the Mouser casts the queller into the center of the maelstrom (6.235). They first meet Sheelba in a landscape of thunder and lightning, Ningauble through his tiny cough; and thunder and lightning presage the departure of the Bazaar of the Bizarre. The closest Leiber comes to his use of this imagery elsewhere is during the Mouser's fugue when he comes to himself, "a rush and a roar" around him as he whirls the golden queller on its cord around his head as though it were a bull-roarer (6.178). Though there is much sorcery in the saga, there is little of the numinous.

Lankhmar and Quarmall are the two cities that represent civilization. Each is hidden, one literally in its little hill, the other in its black togas and its smog; both are mazes, and in Lankhmar the center of the maze is the Thieves' House, "a maze of the unknown, a labyrinth of forgotten history" (2.67), into which the two heroes make several descents. The lower levels of Quarmall are "a maze within a maze" (4.109). This imagery attests to the occult nature of civilization. The difference between the two cities lies in their economies. Quarmall depends upon the magic of its ruler, which has apparently been used in genetic manipulations; attesting to the probable origin of cities in agriculture, Lankhmar depends upon its great wheat fields, so rich that the city can export grain to other cities.

Daily life in Lankhmar is not very orderly, but its landscape shows that unlike the barbarian world the society is highly diversified. Here are Cash Street, Silver Street, Cheap Street, and Pinchbeck Alley; the Street of the Silk Merchants, Crafts Street, and Carter Street are more innocuous, as are the geographical names of Wall Street and Marsh Street. The Plaza of Dark Delights is not far from Plague Court; nor are Death Alley and Murder Alley far apart either. The Street of the Thinkers, also known as Atheist Alley, is near the Street of the Gods. Fools Gold Court and Sequin Court have their affinities. Lankhmar is a city of guilds, with the worst characteristics of labor unions and capitalist monopolies jostling for prominence, with "locals in all other cites and major towns of this land, not to mention agreements including powers of extradition" (1.194). The city has Day People and Night People, a society in which law is strictly maintained and a society accustomed to look the other way (4.79); it is the latter that Fafhrd and the Mouser inhabit until they depart for Rime Isle. In Lankhmar people wear the black toga, not because of any ritual but because "a thrifty overlord had ratified and made official what nature or civilization's arts decreed" (1.179), bowing to the black fog from the marshes and hundreds of chimneys. These black togas recall the black togas that Romans wore for the funerary rites. Lankhmar is a city of death, its grandeurs parading on the edge of death, and though at the end of the series committed to Rime Isle the two heroes still feel nostalgic for those "sleazy grandeurs" of Lankhmar (7.18).

The aristocrats of Lankhmar and "half the civilized races of Nehwon" agree that thoroughly shaven skin is the most erotically attractive (7.296–97). The Mouser seems in agreement, for often he prefers barely pubescent girls, even after he devotes himself to Cif; and the dim Pulg shaves Fafhrd, believing that his strength lies in his hair (3.48)! As far as Glipkerio, the beanpole monarch, is concerned, eroticism, trichophobia, and cleanliness, one of Freud's characteristics of civilization (40), compulsively coincide; however, in the novel *The Swords of Lankhmar* this detail is connected to the eroticism of the ghoul Kreeshkra, whose translucent body has been so done away with that only her lovely bones are apparent. Did Leiber have in mind Eliot's "Whispers of Immortality"?

> Webster was much possessed by death
> And saw the skull beneath the skin;
> And breastless creatures under ground
> Leaned backward with a lipless grin. (32)

Neurotic cleanliness, a danger in advanced civilizations, is in the service of the death instinct, which Fafhrd often finds himself ruled by, so it may be no surprise that Kreeshka, his skeletal lover, allows at the conclusion of the novel, fondling his hairy chest, that "there is something to be said for hair" (5.224). The death instinct turns back to a hairy Eros.

The imagery of hair is connected to cats, whose electric pelt has a long tradition in the world of decadent fantasy. Leiber had several examples for his treatment of cats. Poe's story "The Black Cat," with its horrific conclusion of the demonic cat sitting atop the head of the wife the narrator has murdered, read as a study in naturalism, concerns the fixations of the narrator's alcoholic rage. Baudelaire devotes three poems to the creature, in one of which he compares it to his beloved, "profond et froid" [deep and cold] (39), and in another of which he addresses the purr that "endort les plus cruels maux / Et contient toutes les extases" [lulls the cruelest evils / And contains all ecstasies] (55). In a major sonnet, after he asserts that "Les amoureux fervents et les savants austères" [the fervent lovers and austere wise men] love cats because they "cherchent le silence et l'horreur des ténèbres" [search the silence and the horror of darkness], he elevates them to an iconic status, their loins "pleins d'étincelles magiques" [full of magic sparks] (72). In "The Rats in the Walls," Lovecraft describes a cat that plunges into the abyss in search of the supernatural rats; and in his letters he often indulged in cat-chat, discussing with the Leibers their cats Nemo and Murphet (*L* 5.375).

In his early poetic sequence *The Demons of the Upper Air* Leiber refers to "the panther-like leap of imagination" (quoted in Schumaker 58). His cats are almost always stylish, cruel, and full of latent power. Vlana introduces her culture dance with a mime that appears in the heart of the Wanderer, "a leopardly dance of life, love, and death" (1.43), concluding in the spring of the beast to snatch a bird out of the air and hold it in her jaws, staring long at the audience, "standing womanly now" (1.44). The wind that accompanies the Mouser's magic in "The Unholy Grail" seems "like a torrent of black tigers" (1.160); and in that story the natural affinity of cats and the Mouser is established; he is even on occasion "catty" (4.87). In climbing Stardock the two men are accompanied by the ice-cat Hrissa, who shows several signs of "her cat-zest for newness" (4.40); like Miaow in *The Wanderer*, at the end of the story she remains in the warm boudoir of the two sisters.

In *The Swords of Lankhmar* the rats are not defeated by the Mouser's plots nor by the gods of Lankhmar in their bony black togas, but by Fafhrd's blowing a whistle that summons the great cats; and the kitten that has a series of adventures paralleling those of the two heroes also enters the magic land from which the great cats sprang. In "The Lords of Quarmall," when the Mouser kills Ivivis's lover she and he look at each other "like leopards across the corpse" before they couple in the closet (4.126). One can have too many cats, of course; the scholarly Radomix Kristomerces-Null, who has seventeen felines, does not last long as the ruler of Lankhmar (6.10). In "Under the Thumbs of the Gods," Reetha, hairless as ever, caresses "a very emaciated but tranquil animal, which the Mouser suddenly realized was a cat, hairless save for its score of whiskers bristling from its mask" (6.39). The first description of Cif tells us that she is "wiry and supple-seeming as a cat" (6.78). When the cynical Mouser possesses himself of Ississi, he thinks that it is good for man to have a beautiful woman near him, "like a beautiful cat, yes, a young cat, independent but with kitten ways still. It was well when such a one talked, speaking lies, much as any cat would" (7.45).

The opponents of cats are rats; very few dogs walk the streets of Lankhmar, just as few dogs walk the streets of Rome. Yet the two enemies are akin in their sophisticated knowledge, as the prologue to "The Wrong Branch" suggests: "It is rumored by the wise-brained rats which burrow the citied earth and by the knowledgeable cats that stalk its shadows" (3.96). In "Illmet in Lankmar" the rats, who have their holes throughout the city, are the omniscient intelligencers of the wizard Hristomilo, devouring Vlana and Ivrian after they are strangled and staring at the two heroes with "tiny, rather widely set, furnace-red eyes" (1.244). This scene is one reason we take the rats in *The Swords of Lankhmar* more seriously than the mock-epic rhetoric of that work suggests we should. Despite Hisvin's argument that the rats have "an excellent civilization [...], a cozy, sweet civilization" (5.203), it is evident to the Mouser, after he has performed his "dance of death with the rats figuring as humanity and he their grisly gray overlord, armed with rapier instead of scythe," that they are "an alien and hostile culture of intelligent beings, small to be sure, but perhaps more clever and surely more prolific and murder-bent than even men" (5.124). Though Lankhmar Below mirrors the horrors of Lankhmar Above, "foolish fantasy and shameless greed" (5.223), it is a cold civilization. Hisvet is an immense temptation no matter how many nipples she has, but she is much more narcissistic and manipulative than any of the human women with whom the Mouser dallies. Rather like her is Ississi, who the Mouser believes has a pet, "some sharp-toothed, ribbon-shredding small animal" (7.52). Illthmar has a rat-god, though we learn little of it (3.99); the populace believes that once the rats lived above ground, where they ruled humans, and that they still maintain that rule though they went below "to perfect their culture" (7.236). Leiber here once more plays upon his frequent theme that human civilization suffers from powers of which it has little conception. In Quarmall rats are eaten as delicacies (4.110), but not in Lankhmar.

There are a number of clues here about the nature of the barbarian world and its relation to civilization. Fafhrd's home is a matriarchy supported by magic; Leiber seems to accept Freud's claim that women are hostile to civilization (50–51), though with the qualification that many women in the series are civilized. Nevertheless, Vlana, who first attracts Fafhrd to Lankhmar is not herself of that city and she nurses a vendetta that does not belong to the civilized world. The Eight Cities, which lie in a forest south of Cold Corner, represent a medium between Lankhmar and the barbarian world; but Fafhrd disparages any claim that those cities might make to civilization (5.75). It is a rough, hairy, comfortable world, which can certainly claim a vitality that Glipkerio's world cannot. It may be a mark of the Mouser's unconscious readiness to leave Lankhmar that he has begun to grow a beard before Afreyt and Cif appear (6.76). But Leiber does not glorify the barbarian world. He would not agree with Conan's blunt statement: "Barbarism is the natural state of mankind. [. . .] Civilization is unnatural. It is a whim of circumstance. And barbarism must always ultimately triumph" (222). For Leiber, the barbarian world possesses a vitality that civilization sadly lacks; but a barbarism wholeheartedly affirmed produces the horror of the Mingols, bent upon a colorful Armageddon. Fafhrd is no longer a barbarian, but he is not yet civilized; the Mouser is not attracted by the barbarian world, yet his most profound friend is Fafhrd.

Despite the several disguises that civilization generates, it still remains a burden to maintain, as Freud argued. We need, then, a means of escape. Physical escape is the first that offers itself; and often the Mouser and Fafhrd leave Lankhmar in search of adventure, which is to say in search of a wilderness that provides pleasures that civilization can only provide in sublimation. But until the last two volumes of the saga they always return because civilization provides so many other attractions that barbarism cannot. What are the other escapes? Civilization itself, as we have seen, provides a great variety of erotic pleasures, but slowly the two men realize that there is something stale and repetitive about the pleasures they have sought; even the names of the girls they have encountered are beginning to sound the same, nor do *Afreyt* and *Cif* not quite escape that repetition (6.49). As a repetitive act, their Eros reveals that it serves Thanatos.

Drink is another escape, but even more nakedly than Eros it is in service to Thanatos; and drink is more ubiquitous than a casual reader might think, given the imagery of spiders and snakes, traditional emblems of delirium tremens. Increasingly the series becomes critical of Fafhrd when he loses himself in his favorite tipple, wine fortified with brandy (6.75). Fafhrd says flatly of the drink offered in "The Howling Tower," "I drank, and it sent me to a cold waste in hell" (2.129). Tempted by the Mouser's jugs in "Lean Times in Lankhmar," he sees everything "by that brilliant light of spirits of wine which illumines the way of all brave drunkards" (3.45). In "The Mouser Goes Below" Fafhrd drinks because of his anxiety for his friend, his desire for a miracle and for his youth, and his need to escape the reality that Afreyt makes too obvious (7.241). The Mouser had felt much the same earlier in the novel, the fear of being bound (7.46), and had escaped it not through drink—the Mouser is usually measured in his cups—but through the erotic adventure of binding someone else, a young girl. The chief escapes that civilization offers, the ideal sublimations of religion and philosophy, are not available because of the skeptical attitude both men assume. Only once does Fafhrd lose himself in religion, in the comic "Lean Times in Lankhmar," only to discover that, as Housman had put it, "malt does more than Milton can / To justify God's ways to man" (70). As for philosophy, the two men's drive toward action renders them impatient of its careful abstruseness. Given the ineffectiveness of any of these escapes, it is not surprising that Fafhrd at one point feels the temptation to "live on in the stony rock giants [. . .] and know with them the joy of crushing cities and trampling armies and stamping on all cultivated fields" (2.176); this typical response of the barbarian, however, seems to the Mouser mere madness. Women with their natural opposition to civilization are immune to these temptations, which they deprecate as "drunken male revelry" (1.177).

Death offers itself as an escape throughout the saga, as Freud suggested always seeking "*to repeat past experience*" (2.109). Death is a character in the work, at one point a cowled man with a bulging forehead (2.100). He has some affinity with Ingmar Bergman's figure in *The Seventh Seal*. He is, we learn in the last volume, a rather minor death insofar as he is only the death of Nehwon, subject to the lords of Necessity; but the language that describes his thought, "a vast coolness that yet had a tiny seething in it," hints that he is as close to absolute zero as anything mythic can be (6.2). The quantum laws of chance allow escapes from Death, as Death knows when he considers "that there *might* be powers in the universe unknown to him and subtler even than his" (6.13), though we feel certain that such powers do not include silly gods like Mog and Issek who live at the antipodes from Death. A wise woman's statement that both the heroes were in love with death (5.118) receives its perverse proof when the Mouser is masturbated by Pain, the sister of Death (7.230).

Much that we have said applies to Leiber's style in the saga, a style strikingly different from the realistic, detached style that he employs in his science fiction and horror fiction. This style is dramatic, often with a nod toward the stage; it often seems an intricate décor, a mask if you will. Its flamboyance is considerably more fecund than his other styles; it is rather hairy at times. But whatever we say of it, it is preeminently his style in a way that the other styles he employs are not. It is, Fafhrd would argue, an eminently civilized style because it pays such close attention to the proper word.

One of the most prominent elements of this style is its doubling. The fact that Leiber is dealing with two protagonists seems to generate a doubling upon every level of the stories. First, the two heroes are faced by antagonists that are doubled: two lovers, two companions, two wizardly mentors, two opponents, two deaths, two gods, two children. In "Adept's Gambit" they confront a sister and brother. The two lords of Quarmall are their demonic doubles:

> Hasjarl cultivating his passions as if in some fiery circle of Hell, making energy and movement and logic carried to the ultimate his greatest goods, constantly threatening with whips and tortures [...] Gwaay nourishing restraint as if in Hell's frigidest circle, trying to reduce all life to art and intuitive thought, seeking by meditation to compel lifeless rock to do his bidding and constrain Death by the power of his will. (4.116).

This doubling often leads to a doubling in structure as Fafhrd's and the Mouser's adventures are alternately dealt with. This parallelism of structure often produces parallelisms in imagery: "Only a great whale blowing after a deep sound" and "Only an iceberg hardly half that size" (6.80-81). This doubling can be casual, as when the Mouser's spying on Hisvet's sadistic play with her maids is echoed by Fafhrd's memory that he and Frix had once watched "two of her waiting ladies tall and mantis-slender as herself while they were mutually solacing each other" (7.235). More strikingly, this doubling sometimes manifests itself as imagery of doubles, the two heads of the dragon in *The Swords of Lankhmar* and in that same work the doubling of faces—for the Mouser the two faces of Hisvet and Frix are a "two-headed light-of-love" (5.99).

This doubling also shapes the rhetoric of the stories, doubling subjects, predicates, and objects: "glacier vast" and "ocean vast" balance each other at the end of two sentences (6.109). We find a frequent use of alliteration and an occasional use of rhyme, such as "Mingol jingle" (6.199). One of Leiber's most telling tropes is his penchant for compound words such as "palace-glimmer" (3.17), "leather-lunged" (3.51), "god-intoxicated" and "god-besotted" (3.56 and 3.59), "sow- and snail-changed" (3.117), "sparrow-watching and incense-sniffing and destiny-directing" (5.99), or "gray-smocked, gray stockinged" (7.64). On occasion these compounds become quite intricate: "clown-clad mad mahout" (5.69), "bone-tired, be-mired" (5.110), and "leather-skinned, death-skinny" (5.125). The compound haunts the sober style of Leiber's science fiction.

Leiber purposefully created a style highly influenced by Elizabethan English; this is not pseudo-biblical or pseudo-Malory, but a style inherited from London, 1600—a civilized tongue of the high Renaissance. It was an idiom natural to him from his early acquaintance with Shakespeare in his father's acting troupe; in the late 1950s he studied it conscientiously (Byfield, *Witches* 8). Elisions of the relative pronouns "which" and "that" occur, and sometimes elisions of prepositions also: for instance, "it was pure automatism made Fafhrd shift his guard" (6.11), or "tiptoeing next the wall" (7.275). Upon occasion a character will speak a monologue, as Skwee does as he meditates upon his ambition (5.187-88), as Glipkerio does in his melodramatic farewells to Lankhmar (5.201-17), or as Faroomfar does as he plots revenge (6.99); or in blank verse, as when Fafhrd orates, "I can't believe and yet cannot deny. I know when Mouser jests and when speaks true" (6.103). Both the narrator and the characters are fond of extended similes. Two assassins kill a man "as swiftly as ambitious men take last bite and wine-swig at a family dinner when unexpectedly summoned to the emperor's banquet board" (3.16). Above all, this rhetorical style favors the *mot juste*. Hrissa "haggles" her meat (4.31). Fafhrd's plight when captured by the rats is for the Mouser a "divertissement" (5.60). A bed is "frowsty" (6.44). Kreeshkra, whom Fafhrd calls Bonny Bones (5.115), has invisible flesh that encases her "distinguished bones" (6.39). A fishing boat with a full catch comes "creaming" back to harbor (6.133).

In contrast to this high style Leiber also employs several comic devices. Parentheses often break up artful sentences and qualify resounding epithets. Anticlimaxes abound: the eroticism of the Mouser's delicate play with plums, dropping them one after another into the sea, is undercut by the narrator who remarks that a shark "got a stomachache" (5.22). If euphemisms are frequent, so are puns, contemporary slang, anachronisms, and scientific phrases. To Fafhrd's charge that the Mouser would "turn a wizard's workroom into a brothel," his friend retorts, "Why not? [. . .] Both species of glamour at once!" (4.10-11). The Mouser thrusts through a man's chest "as if all were angelfood cake" (1.173). Slivikin and his ilk, who killed Vlana and Ivlis, are in the Mouser's flip words, "rodentine familiars" (2.12). The undersea landscape of "The Sunken Land" is both properly and hyperbolically an "abysmal scene" (2.144). With a nod to the political language of the 1960s, a momentary pause is called a "victory of the doves over the hawks" (3.39). With some anxiety in "When the Sea-King's Away" the Mouser thinks of himself as "an oiled needle floating in a bowl of water" that "sinks when one pinks it" (3.77). The mathematics of Cantor lie behind Keyaria's amorous insistence, "Think, we have half an eternity left us yet—which is also an eternity, as your geometer, whether white-bearded or dainty-breasted, should have taught you" (4.68).

Frequent enough to strike some readers as a stylistic tic are words ending in "-some"; "shuddersome" (4.25), "gaysome" (6.44), "boresome" (6.200), "ticklesome" (7.44), and "toilsome" (7.192) are a few examples. This choice style runs counter to the high-heroics that it purports to narrate.

Finally, we should note that Leiber discovers a number of solutions for the relentless allusiveness in his other works. Rather than naming an author, except for the footnote in the last volume that frankly identifies a poem of Webster's (7.283-84), he will freely quote the author. Fafhrd's phrase "the city and the stars" calls our attention for a moment to Arthur C. Clarke's novel (3.16). Sheelba's reference to the tightrope humanity walks recalls an image in *Also Sprach Zarathustra* (3.84). Some of the central allusions are to Shakespeare and H. P. Lovecraft. Hristomilo cackles, in a parody of Duncan, "I'll see it done [. . .], What Slevyas lost my magic has rewon!" (1.224-25). "No time now for slings and arrows," the narrator assures us, when the black priests are upon our heroes (2.171). Sheelba is a "king of shreds of lies and patches of hypocrisy" (3.114). Blithely Glipkerio reminds the Mouser that "all's well that ends well" (5.87); and the Mouser plays on Puck's line, *"Lord, what grotesques we mortals be!"* (6.174). Mog cites Hamlet's admonition, "Thrift, thrift!" (7.68); and Fafhrd seems to have the Prince in mind when he speculates, "Perchance we dream" (6.46). When under the curse of the small the Mouser renounces Lankhmar, he seems to half recall Prospero's farewell to his art: "Nor all the gorgeous palaces, piers, pyramids, and fanes, all that marble and cloud-capped biggery!" (7.82). "The second-best guest bed" on which Cif has a prophetic dream probably alludes to Shakespeare's will, deeding his second-best bed to his wife (7.149). These many allusions reinforce the theatricality of the stories.

The allusions to Lovecraft have a different effect. Fewer in number, they are much more direct. The clubhanded Slivikin, the familiar of the magician in "Illmet in Lankhmar," is reminiscent of Brown Jerkin (1.222-23). In the early "The Jewels in the Forest" a whippoorwill is "an augury of ill omen" (2.30) just as in "The Dunwich Horror." Simorgya, which shall rise from the sea in proper circumstances (2.144), is reminiscent of the Lovecraftian gestures of undersea threat in "Dagon," "The Temple," "The Shadow over Innsmouth," and "The Call of Cthulhu" (Joshi 68). The brother's usurpation of his sister's mind in "Adept's Gambit," perhaps the most Lovecraftian of the stories in the way that Ahura's story usurps the story of Fafhrd and the Mouser, reverses the misogyny operating in "The Thing on the Doorstep" (cf. Mason Harris's speculation quoted in Byfield, *Witches* 16). In a more comic vein, the treatment of the invisible skate that flies through the air is reminiscent of Lovecraft's material in "The Dunwich Horror" (4.53). In a direct allusion we have Ningauble's reference to the cockroach Scraa "who existed contemporaneously with those monstrous reptiles which once ruled the world, and whose racial memories go back into the mistiness of time before the Elder Ones retreated from the surface" (4.110). Lankhmar Below has a certain resemblance to Innsmouth, as we can see in Hisvet's explanation: "We have interbred with the rats, resulting in divinely beautiful monsters such as I am, but also in monsters most ugly, at least by human standards. These latter of my family stay below ground, but the rest of us enjoy the advantages and delights of living in two worlds" (5.179). When Leiber allows the Mouser to summarize his career, he realizes that he has always been an outsider (7.265).

Other allusions are not difficult to recognize. Fafhrd's expostulation on the wonders of the seabed, "IT'S AMAZING, IT'S FANTASTIC!" refers to pulp magazines of the '30s and '40s (3.76). Gwaay extends Clausewitz when he argues that "just as sword-war is but another means of carrying out diplomacy, so sorcery is but another means of carrying out sword-war" (4.166). Alyx the Picklock is a tribute to Joanna Russ (4.83). It is very fitting that in the middle of the satire of the rats the Mouser should remember "that proverb about little bugs having littler bugs, and so on," a reminiscence of a Swiftian epigram (5.145). Reetha recalls the several fairy tales in which "lizard- and frog-princes [were] restored to handsomeness and proper height" (5.160). When the narrator writes, "The brazen bells shrieked, clanged, clashed, roared, twanged, jangled, and screamingly wrangled," we realize that Leiber is attempting to best Poe's "The Bells" (5.205); and in another story the phrase "Rimic runes" (7.276) plays with a phrase from the same poem, "runic rhyme." Both Poe (6.163) and Coleridge (6.53–54, 56, 115) provide phrases and events that Leiber makes use of in the Rime Isle sequence. And with the irruption of Karl Treuherz into Nehwon, the German makes a direct allusion to Homer, whom the Mouser imagines "a minor scribe of Quarmall" (5.29). Hisvet's insistence that the Mouser enjoy the body of her maid Frix may recall the triangle in Yeats's sequence "The Three Bushes." Possibly the situation in "The Snow Women" recalls Wilhelm Meister's introduction to life by an actress in Goethe's *Bildungsroman*. Though the detail is doubtless realistic in the context of Rime Isle, one cannot help but hear an echo of Eddison, one of Leiber's models in heroic fantasy, in the "modest fish-dinner" that Afreyt prepares (6.238). When the Mouser's attempt to speak to Hisvet goes "most grievously agley," he owes the Scots phrase to Burns (7.212). Much more sinister are the map made of "well-tanned and buffed human skin" (5.161), Hisvet's proclamation, "Tonight, Lankhmar! Tomorrow, all Nehwon!" (5.182), and the Mouser's speech, with its shadows of *Götterdämmerung*, "of the glories of death, and of what a grand thing it was to go down joyfully to destruction carrying your enemies with you (and as many as possible of your friends also)" (6.230); the legalisms of the nihilist Mingols in "Rime Isle" are a part of the pattern. Newhon cannot escape the shadow of Nazi Germany. When Farnsworth Wright rejected "Adept's Gambit" because its style seemed to exceed the excesses of *Ulysses* (Byfield, "Fafrhd and the Scot" 109), he little knew how mannered the saga would become.

In *Our Lady of Darkness* Clark Ashton Smith's style is characterized as "very rich, doomful stuff. Arabian Nights chinoiserie. A mood like Beddoe's *Death's Jest-Book*" (14), not a bad description of the style of the saga except that Leiber inherits something from each of the major *Weird Tale* authors: the style and interest in decadence of Smith, except that Leiber's humor is more robust and more rooted in language; the lure of action we find in Howard, except that Leiber quite consciously looks askance at Howard's amoralism; and the dread and skepticism of Lovecraft, except that Leiber is quite aware of the neurotic roots of his monsters and extends the skepticism into Humean problems (Justin Leiber, "Fritz Leiber" 31-35). It is an equivocal style that lets the author stand to and not stand to. Though it is difficult to generalize the mode of the entire saga, my analysis makes clear that this is a highly literate fantasy in terms of rhetoric, vocabulary, and allusions, which consistently makes use of comic devices. But the comedy does not exist for its own sake.

If, as we claimed at the beginning of our analysis, the basic theme of the saga is the complicity and war between Eros and Thanatos and their threats to the human psyche, then we find that only comedy can dissolve this war. On the one hand comedy combats Thanatos. It is possible, the narrator suggests in "The Howling Tower," that laughter may be stronger than the howl that draws men to their death (2.115). On the other hand, only comedy can qualify the threats of erotic and romantic love. In the final works comedy ameliorates the pain of age and allows the two men to mature. Comedy dominates the saga because it is an eminently civilized mode; the Word manifests itself here in a way that tragedy prefers not to enter into. Despite these points, comedy is also the great escape from civilization. When erotic pleasure is not available, whether because of absence or age, when drink reveals that it is an accomplice of Thanatos, and when the sublimations of religion and philosophy have begun to lose their savor, the art of comedy remains. For though comedy depends upon civilization for its existence, its critical edge turns against civilization in a way that the other escapes cannot.

Comedy, however, implies a balance, but we cannot say that the saga is balanced, certainly not in central images and not in its treatment of the two men. Cats are much more important to Leiber's vision than dogs; spiders are mentioned much more often than snakes—it is not fortuitous in *The Big Time* that our desperate group of Demons is fighting for the Spiders; and much more emphasis is laid from story to story upon the Mouser's point of view than upon Fafhrd's (Justin Leiber, "Fritz Leiber and Eyes" 94). Despite Ilhililis's attempt in *The Big Time* to assert an ideal balance, this imbalance in the saga runs counter to his attempt. Necessarily, this imbalance affects our view of the two heroes. We know much more of the Gray Mouser's mental life than of Fafhrd's. Though Fafhrd thinks of his companion as civilized, coming from the south of Lankhmar the Mouser does not represent the typical life of that city; though he appreciates it, he is also critical of it and critical of himself. Once "a slum boy" (2.15), he is in Glipkerio's eyes "sleazily civilized" at best (5.88). Both men are in love with death, Fafhrd perhaps more so than the Mouser, but the Mouser is considerably more perverse in his erotic life than the barbarian. Fafhrd's face is much more open than the Mouser's, which is often tinged with "sneering contempt, self-conscious cleverness, and conceit" (1.170). He is competitive with his friend, even in their dreams; perhaps they share a collective unconscious, "a vast, black basement mind" (6.29). Though Fafhrd was trained as a skald and healer and the Mouser as a magician, neither remain committed to either trade; yet one still has a taste for that formal style and the other still dabbles in magic. Since, however, the Mouser is a rationalist who believes in no god (3.51), except upon whimsical or desperate occasions when he nods to the spider-god Mog (6.34), he finds that he must struggle "in the ocean of inexplicably strange intuitions engulfing him" (3.51), whereas Fafhrd is a natural polytheist (6.34).

The Mouser does appreciate puzzles, though he prefers to complicate them rather than solve them (5.84). Though Fafhrd is dubious of the Mouser's magic (3.109), he has close experiences with magic throughout the series, especially in "The Snow Women." It is Fafhrd who realizes that their lives have become stagnant, that they have not become leaders, that they have no homes, and that they lack commitment to women (6.76-77). Without realizing that he is also subject to a certain degree of courtliness, the Mouser considers himself free of Fafhrd's "romantic streak that sometimes was as thin as a thread yet sometimes grew into a silken ribbon leagues wide in which armies might stumble and be lost" (5.50); in "The Mouser Goes Below" it is a combination of sexual compulsion and romantic idealism that leads to the ribbons tied on Fafhrd's cock as onto a maypole. Despite his height and strength, Fafhrd seems the more vulnerable of the two; and the sign of his vulnerability is his loss of his left hand. Also, in part, his vulnerability flows from his expansive urge that often finds its expression in a drunken binge, whereas the Mouser attempts to hold things together: "if you tie things up carefully enough—your purse, your produce, or your enemies, and eke your lights of love—nothing can ever surprise you, or escape from you, or harm you" (7.50). Thus the one is tempted by the stars, the other by the pebbles. Only in the most roundabout way can the Mouser admit that he does "not like being in bondage to the idea of himself being a monstrous clever fellow" (6.201). Since Leiber is a monstrous clever fellow himself, as this survey of his style demonstrates, this admission is remarkable; it is as though near the end of his career he were attempting to dispossess himself of his treasures.

II

> Though his barque cannot be lost,
> Yet it shall be tempest-tossed. (*Macbeth* 1.3.23-24)

One of the most evident characteristics of *The Big Time* is its structure as a play (Staicar 53; Byfield, *Witches* 36). As the first-person narrator Greta pointedly says, the Place presents "a regular theater-in-the-round with the Void for an audience" (16). What kind of a play it is, however, turns out to be a complex question. It obeys the Aristotelian unities of time and place, but it does not quite obey the unity of action, for we have here a number of subplots in motion. As the title of chapter 9 suggests, the main plot develops into a locked-room mystery, rather like those that John Dickson Carr wrote, though it is more than such a mystery, since that development only occurs at chapter 9, at the precise halfway point when a pause of three hours occurs—let us all enjoy that intermission (72). A few love stories are at work here also, of various degrees of intensity. In addition, Greta is a confidential protagonist, given to asides to the reader that make her resemble one of those intellectual protagonists we find in such plays as *Hamlet* or *The Dutchess of Malfi*; and as so often with Leiber, the baroque similes are also in conflict with the purity of an Aristotelian play.

The Place, Greta believes, is "like a ballet set and the crazy costumes and characters that turn up don't ruin the illusion" (16). In terms of tone this is an excessive melodrama that turns out to be a comedy, but a denouement becomes a *threnos*. The love Bruce feels for Lili is not as unconditional as he had declared, for "a Demon is always an actor" (84); off he trots in the conclusion with the other male warriors. On the last pages Greta ruefully turns from the humans to the alien Ilhilihis. We might wonder whether the novel represents for Leiber Aristotle's lost discussion on comedy. On the other hand, turning inward, given the several suggestions that the place resembles a brain, we might think of the novel as an expressionist play, something like the psycho-dramas Strindberg composed in *The Road to Damascus* or *Dream Play*. Later we shall ask what kinds of roles, in terms of such a reading, the characters might play as internal urges. This is all to say that the structure of the novel, as a novel, is a metaphor of its very playful literary qualities. The Word appears here first as a structuring element that distances the reader from the melodramatic events.

There are other aspects of literature with which *The Big Time* plays. As Byfield points out, each of the characters has her or his own particular style, an aid to characterization when twelve characters are treading the boards (*Witches* 36). Kaby chants a trochaic tetrameter, Leiber's version of the meter Longfellow had adapted from *The Kalevala* to serve as the meter of *The Song of Hiawatha*, crossed at one point by a pastiche of Lady Macbeth's invocation of night to unsex her: "Triple Goddess, draw the milk now / from the womanhood I flaunt here / and inject the blackest hatred!" (50). We find allusions to Shakespeare, Tennyson, Stein, Carlyle, Dante, Aquinas, Keats, Homer, Wagner, Horace, and Ovid (not surprising, since one of the characters is a Roman soldier), as well as parodies of "Lili Marlene" and "The Whiffenpoof Song." In addition, the epigraphs refer to Hodgson, Aucassin, Eliot, Ibsen, Graves, Poe, Sassoon, Spenser, Webster, marquis, and Heinlein. Albeit not as erudite as *The Wanderer* or *Our Lady of Darkness*, in its small space this novel is learned, though it wears its learning lightly. The Place is an arena of literature and song.

In more general terms, the Place is the arena in which art finds itself at work. Not only is the Place an arena in which various theaters and mores collide, it is a major example of interiority in Leiber's work. When the Place nears its pick-up of the three hussars, "the gray velvet of the Void [. . .] was curdled with the uneasy lights you see when you close your eyes in the dark" (8). At the conclusion, Ilhilihis compares the Place explicitly to a brain: "its floor is the brainpan, the boundary of the Void is the cortex of gray matter—yes, even the Major and Minor Maintainers are analogues of the pineal and pituitary glands" (128). One of the more remarkable areas of the space is its art gallery, which plays a significant part in the action and which, Greta reveals, is the only history the Demons possess, "because the things in it and the feelings that went into them resist the Change winds better than anything else" (31). The arena where literature, song, and art find their homes, the Place exhibits itself as the major symbol of art in the book and indicates that the nature and function of art is one of the book's major themes.

The Place is not the arena of art, however, without the Change War for which it has been constructed—a fearful war, but we must admit that Bruce is accurate when he speaks of its allure:

> It's sweet to know there's no cranny of reality so narrow, no privacy so intimate or sacred, no wall of was or will be strong enough, that we can't shoul-

der in. Knowledge is a glamorous thing, sweeter than lust or gluttony or the passion of fighting. [. . .] It's sweet to jigger reality, to twist the whole course of a man's life or a culture's, to ink out its past and scribble in a new one. [. . .] It's sweet to feel the Change Winds blowing through you. (56-57)

Like magic, which is also glamorous, art takes apart its material, lives and cultures and philosophies, in order to reconstitute them in a new order. And in Bruce's view this activity is an act of knowledge; yet that view is not fully the view of the novel, for the winds of change, though they are quite random in their effects and we know not whence they come (John 3:8), are a part of this sweetness also.

Our account of the Place as the stage of art is not the only description of it, however. When Lili cuts the Place off from the cosmos the winds no longer exist, in a horrifying version of writer's block or the horrors of going cold turkey: "You're just you, and the facts you think from and feel from are exactly the same when you go back to them. [. . .] We were nothing but ourselves and what we meant to each other and what we could make of that" (81). Earlier one of the epigraphs compared the Place to Aucassin's hell, the world of energy into which the most stylish and wittiest people descend (28); but the Place also resembles, cut off from the world of change, the hell of Sartre's *Huit Clos*. At this point we realize how claustrophobic life within a brain playing to the void can be; that is what it is like to play to nothing and no one. On the other hand, once the Place is cut off from the world of change that the Demons had controlled for the purposes of art, time begins to tick and they once more enter the world of generation. Maud realizes that she has her period. But the vision that the world of generation offers them, one in which they can make the Place to serve their own needs, horrifies Erich: "The cave, the womb, the little gray home in the nest—is that what you want? It'll grow? Oh yes, like the city engulfing the wild wood, a proliferation of *Kinder, Kirche, Küche*" (99). Without the Change Winds, the Place becomes a sentimental art that symbolizes to Erich, who is Thanatos incarnate, everything that is smothering within the biological imperative.

In opposition to the Word as art there are the six warriors, the three black hussars, Erich, Mark, and Bruce, and later the more bizarre Kaby, Ilhilihis, and Sevensee; they introduce death into the Place, above all the small tactical atomic device. Thus it is not possible for the Place to become the tame parody of art Erich fears, for the bomb makes the Demons feel as uncomfortable "as atomic scientists would feel if a Bengal tiger were brought into their laboratory" (52), hence the title of chapter 13 after Erich arms the bomb, "The Tiger Is Loose" (103). Thus aggression disrupts their attempt to seal themselves off from the demands of reality and the Wind. In addition, through confronting the three women, Lili, Greta, and Maud, the triple goddess whom Erich characterizes as "the birther, bride, and burier of man" (99), the presence of the soldiers creates a sexual tension absent earlier. Thanatos and Eros are juxtaposed and interact. The three men are the warriors; the later group are warriors also, but they also represent that which is alien to the majority of the people in the Place: the implacable devotee of the Triple Goddess, the centaur who represents anger and lust, and Ilhilhis, a much more ambiguous figure who combines the imagery of the Spider and the Snake, the male/female polarity that so much concerns the sexual politics of the novel (Byfield *Witches* 36–38).

The most ambiguous image of opposition is the Change Wind, which the characters both fear and long for. We have noted that the art gallery best resists those winds, but we have not yet understood why. The Wind reaches into the characters' most intimate beings, affecting their slightest whims and desires, "down to the featheriest fancy" (31), without their being able to account for themselves; in this aspect the Wind represents the unconscious, that which lies beyond the world of reason represented by the cortex of gray matter. There is no way to predict that Wind. But in addition, the change that the Wind bears into the Place may snuff a character out of existence at any moment; the Wind is the breath of contingency with which rationality cannot cope. During the battle on Crete, Kaby suffers both aspects: "On the quiet sun-lit beach there, I could feel a Change Gale blowing, working changes deep inside me, aches and pains that were a stranger's. Half my memories were doubled, half my lifeline crooked and twisted" (48).

The Change Winds, however, are not peculiar to the Demons. When Greta challenges the reader in the first chapter, she raises issues central to the book:

> Have you ever worried about your memory, because it doesn't seem to be bringing you exactly the same picture of the past from day to day? Have you ever been afraid that your personality was changing because of forces beyond your knowledge or control? Have you ever felt sure that sudden death was about to jump you from nowhere? (6)

In part this vision certainly originates in the alienation, insignificance, and paranoia of modern life (Staicar 55–56), but it questions the personality so deeply that more is at stake than the existential fear of the assembly line, because the Winds are not only terrifying as emblems of our individual deaths; they are emblematic of Leiber's acceptance of that Humean skepticism which questions not only causality but the basis of human integrity (Justin Leiber, "Fritz Leiber" 32–35). When Greta reverses the inversion and connects the Place to the cosmos, the Winds hit her "like a stiff drink, [. . .] the uncertainties whistling past, and ice-stiff reality softening with all its duties and necessities, and the little memories shredding away and dancing off like autumn leaves, [. . .] and all the crazy moods like Mardi Gras pouring down an evening street" (115–16). The Change Winds are related to the primitive *ruach* invoked by the bull-roarer in Conjure Wife. The work of art depends upon danger, irrational inspiration, skepticism; no life is lived with thorough attention without accepting the contingencies of death, as Fafhrd and the Mouser know so well.

Like several Elizabethan plays, the novel has an epilogue in which Ilhilihis seems to step out of character, admitting that Greta may be surprised at his language (128), to comment upon the action. In this commentary Demons are the fourth order of life, possibility-binders who "make all of what might be part of what is," thereby leaping out of the world as it is into the immortality symbolized in the world's religions (127). Combining in themselves the principles of wisdom and patience that seem to be at war, like all artists who bind "the mental with the material," a principle of form embodied in words, or notes, or paint, they thereby "live inside and outside all minds, throughout the whole cosmos" (128). This is a claim as megalomanic as any made at the high point of German Romanticism, such as we might find in Schlegel or Novalis; but though Ilhilihis invites Greta to share in this "high existence" of a *poet maudit*, "a mixture of horror and delight" (128), she feels in a more muted fashion that "we've got to win and lose all the battles, every which way" (129). Philosophy is all very well, but she has the black eye.

Written not long after *The Big Time*, *The Wanderer* significantly shares some of the earlier novel's imagery, but the scene differs radically from the claustrophobia of the Place: characters from one side of earth to the other are involved, as well as the moon and the enormous planet that suddenly appears next to it, and much of the action occurs out of doors, the main exception being the boudoir of Tigerishka, though a reader never forgets that her boudoir is a flying saucer that at a major climax lifts very far above the earth; pejoratively, the trap in which General Spike and his extremely competent officer find themselves and the room in which Fritz Scher boasts, "Here we have the moon nailed down" (71), demonstrate that life is to be lived outside, without protection. It is as though Leiber set himself two very different narrative challenges in the two novels, the one that explores the inner world through a first-person narrator and the other that explores the outer world through an omniscient narrator, strategies that make the styles of the two novels very different.

In one regard, however, the two works are very alike. Each has an episode near the conclusion in which a moment of mythic self-reflection occurs. We have called that moment the epilogue of *The Big Time*, but in *The Wanderer* it is a moment of erotic foreplay between Tigerishka and Paul before the gigantic planet arrives that is in pursuit of her planet. In her mythic account she directly accuses the Word that has made a city of the universe; Leiber develops Erich's image in *The Big Time* of "the city engulfing the wild wood" (99). The solar system according to her "is one of the few primitive spots left, like a small, weed-grown lot overlooked by builders in the heart of a vast and ancient city that has overgrown all the countryside" (247). Suns and moons and gas-giants have been used as material for artificial planets, so extensively that, "throughout the universe, natural planets are as rare as young thoughts." So successful is this culture that "ten million trillion galaxies can become infected with the itch of thought—that great pandemic!" which spreads "faster than the plague"; the universe has become a slum (248), massively centralized and dedicated to "security and safety" and, with the conservative nostalgia of the old, to memory (249). To protect this vision they want "a police station winking blue by every sun, [. . .] fuzz everywhere, blurring the diamond-pristine, lucent stars" (251), to pursue its enemies, "hoping," as Tigerishka says, "we'll see the arc light of their reason that glares always above the cosmic prison yard" (252). The Stranger confirms this image when it appears, "all an unvarying, bright steely gray except for one glittering highlight midway between its round rim and its flatter rim" (287); the pursuer looks like a police car. Later Paul thinks of the Stranger in a more childish light: with a "cold, reptilian boredom [. . .] the grade school principal was listening to the painfully honest story without hearing it" (297). It is like the people in the novel "with proofreader minds" who joyously point out the slight mistakes of others (139). In this extended conceit the rationalized universe is a dystopian city sick from too much mind, an authoritarian, repressive, and punitive nightmare that benignly wishes to infect others with its own disease.

As this imagery suggests, civilization prefers to stay in one place, rooted in the past. Tigerishka's people, on the other hand, are on the move. In her flying saucer she travels swiftly across California, into far space, and to the Wanderer, ripping Paul away from his staid, paralyzed existence. Other characters are either natural wanderers, such as Barbara Katz stalking her millionaire, reduced from her perspective to the size of a mouse, or people who must wander to survive. Tigerishka's people are young races evolved "from solitary killers." Living with a taste for death, they value "style more than security, freedom more than safety; races with a passionate sadistic tinge; or coldly scientific, valuing knowledge almost more than life" (250). They do not do without knowledge, not at all; unlike the older races, which are now content with their ancestors' knowledge, these Marlon Brando bikers—Tigerishka calls them the Wild Ones (250)—wish to explore two fields. On the one hand they wish "to range through *mind* more thoroughly—that crumpled rainbow place inside our skulls. [. . .] We still don't know if there are other worlds upon the other side of the collective inward darkness" (250). But they also wish to explore hyperspace where they believe other cosmoses lie, worlds that would be radically different from this universe: "Worlds with no wall between mind and mind, [. . .] worlds where thoughts are real and every beast's a god" (251). Clearly these two goals are aspects of the same phenomenon, a cosmic celebration of interiority.

This mythic account, which concludes when Tigerishka and Paul make love, is paralleled earlier in the novel when Don is sent upon an astral voyage through the Wanderer to contemplate its several races. The one man is given a mythic history, the other man a mythic exobiology. The novel is filled with animal life, squirrels, pigeons, beetles, ants, dinosaurs, and bulls, but within the planet Don sees felinoids, horses, spiders, serpents, squids, basilisks, harpies, whales, intelligent plants, giant amoebas, "metal robots counterfeiting spiders, wheel-beings, and many other life forms" that Don supposes he can only intuit, "as if the Wanderer had more ghosts aboard than all her crew members" (231). In opposition to the Word, which is an abstract and fleshless bureaucracy, this catalogue concludes with a vision of a green-furred felinoid very like Tigerishka, leaping with the "almost incredible elevation of a ballet dancer executing a *grand jeté*" to capture a topaz bird and devour it: "There was a redness on her dull olive lips and on the one long white fang showing as she looked across the yellow feathers straight at Don with her large and flowerlike, jade-irised eyes. It may have been coincidence, but he felt that she saw him. And as she sucked the blood, with the blood-red sky behind her, she smiled" (234). This remarkable *sparagmos*, akin to the conclusion of Vlana's dance, summarizes the point made in the story that Paul hears; despite their scientific ability, the aliens in the planet have not left the body and its instincts behind. They are young, in contrast to the galactic society, which is "old, old, old," jealous of its order, and determined to hold on to its prerogatives (249). Like the Demons of *The Big Time*, the races aboard the Wanderer are *poètes maudits* who pursue their elusive goals through destructive actions not far from sadism.

These latter-day barbarians have two responses to their self-inflicted plight. One is a defensive braggadocio, very evident in Tigerishka, which challenges the older, stay-at-home personalities directly. More profound, the other response is a close translation of Schubert's "Der Wanderer": "Where are you, world that's all my own?— / Longed for and sought, but never known" (254). Though a more authentic response, it must deprecate itself because otherwise the personality would dissolve into a paralyzed depression; hence, in a similar moment, we have Fafhrd's melancholia and the pastiche of the Whiffenpoof song that concludes *The Big Time*.

The most direct way we learn of the nature of the Wanderer is through Tigerishka, whose name of course she projects from Paul's perception of her: she is a tiger, a ballet dancer, and a Russian—a savage animal, a symbol of civilized, artful eroticism, and within the context of the Cold War the ultimate enemy. The image of the tiger occurs early in the novel as the narrator describes the earth and moon aligning themselves for the lunar eclipse, "almost alone in a black forest twenty million miles across. A frighteningly lonely situation, especially if you imagined something wholly unknown stirring in the forest, creeping closer, shaking the starlight here and there as it bent the black twigs of space" (4). Something of the same imagery surrounds Barbara Katz, "hunting millionaires in their home lair in Florida" (13), one of whom she has already attracted through her "black-and-yellow striped bikini" (14). The colors of the Wanderer, purple and yellow, which its population has selected for the pure splendor of its decor, have something akin to Barbara's bikini and Tigerishka's green and violet pelt. On the Wanderer Don meets a creature that looked "like a high-foreheaded cheetah a little bigger than a mountain lion and standing as a man stands, or like a slim, black-furred, red-pied tiger wearing a black turban and a narrow red mask" (137).

So general is this imagery that it is unclear whether the references to Blake's tiger "burning bright / In the forests of the night" (i, 251) apply to the planet or to Tigerishka. In her the planet becomes a personal encounter. Besides being an animal of prey, however, she is also a creature that looks like a ballet dancer and thus speaks to Paul's eroticism. Undoubtedly a part of this attraction is fetishistic, especially in the aspect of costume; it was this very aspect that led Greta to appeal to the image of the ballet stage when trying to describe the appearance of her very differently accoutered friends in the Place.

Another way in which this novel resembles the earlier work is its gesture toward interiority, a gesture we have already noted in the program of the Wanderer. Midway through the novel Don finds himself on the surface of the planet looking up at an artificial sky that "resembled somewhat the marbling of a film of oil on water, and somewhat Van Gogh's wild painting, 'The Starry Night,' and even more the deep, glinting hues that flow churningly past the mind's eye in the dark," an image that "seemed to put him on the inside of some vast mind" (130). Later, during his astral circuit inside, he wonders whether "stars and galaxies and universes are truly such unreal things, no more than the dim points of light that swim before one's eyes before one sleeps" (233). When Margo and Hunter make love the landscape becomes "fixtures of the room that is the mind, or—truer—the mind reach[es] out to embrace them" (280). Before approaching Tigerishka in her flying boudoir Paul thinks of it as "the viewpoint of a dream," so that he "could hardly say whether he were living only in his fancy or in the whole great starry cosmos; for once, imagination and reality were seamlessly mated" (253). These two passages take seriously Hemingway's phrase in *For Whom the Bell Tolls*, "make the earth move," which is parodied when Sally, "in the blind egoistic world of sexual fulfillment that lies exactly on the boundary between the conscious and unconscious mind, [. . .] knew that the stars were a provincial district of herself." When the stars do move, as the Wanderer twists the gravitational field around the moon, she cries out in her climax, "I did it, Christ! I said I'd do it and I did it!" (32). For her the sudden appearance of the Wanderer is "a bonus" (33). The extreme of this attitude, however, is represented by the reefer brothers, by the alcoholic Dai Davies, by General Stevens and Colonel Wallingford, and by the narcissistic Guillermo Walker, an actor turned revolutionary, all of whom play out their fantasies indifferent to the world around them and die in a rush of waters. The porous division of the inner and outer world requires a careful respect.

This tendency toward interiority is one reason for the many different reactions to the Wanderer. At its first appearance some of the characters react with fear, some with ecstasy, a few dispassionately; the rationalists, the representatives of the Word on earth, try to reduce the monstrous phenomenon to a measurable and comfortable scale, as Hunter attempts to do on the beach until Rama Joan calls him to order (41). Fritz Scher is carried away with his machines by a tide that he still attempts to master, shouting as he drowns, "Multiply everything by eighty!" (188). Clarence Dodd is incorrigible, still making notes when the second planet appears and shatters every expectation they have of the universe. Leiber never scorns a rationality that attempts to pay attention to the world with care and respect, never dismissing it and never becoming reductionist.

Given the number of characters in the novel, it is difficult to pick out the significant categories. I shall focus on those characters who pair off into sexual couples and those who choose to be alone. The first example of this latter group has the significant name Wolf Loner; attempting a solo voyage in a small boat from England to America, he handles his situation self-contentedly and rationally and at the end of the novel has very little idea of the tremendous events that have occurred, though he has sailed to the top of the steeple of the Old North Church and rescued a child from Boston's North End. Another example is Asa Holcombe, an old man who has climbed a mesa to enjoy the night sky and who dies ecstatically when the Wanderer appears; the small tissue of his aorta tears away as the stars shake, and "a great golden and purple gateway" (32) seems to open in the sky, pushing away the darkness. In his last moments it seems to him that the great society of heaven is about to receive him into its bosom.

Two other significant loners are Dai Davies, a Welsh poet who is something of a parody of Dylan Thomas, and his friend Richard Hillary. Davies's language is ecstatic, given to such ejaculations as these, "Frore Mona in your meteor-skiff . . . Girlglowing, old as Fomalhaut . . . Trailing white fingers in my pools" (142); but we receive the strong impression that his praise of the moon and of girls is only so much blather and thereby we distrust his myth-making ability. He drowns because of his devotion to the myth of drink; fantasy uninstructed by knowledge is impotent, a megalomania of the imagination that cannot recognize the external world. Richard condemns him self-righteously, but as the disaster swells he finds companionship in Vera Carlyle, a woman rendered hopeless by the floods; in this development he rather resembles the brother of the narrator of Wells's *The War of the Worlds*, drawing the same moral that in times of disaster it is best that the human animal huddle with its kind. She is, she boasts, "strong, strong sleeping medicine" (269). Sex, for all its dangers, is a better defense against cognitive distress than drink. The extreme loners are the murderous Black Dahlia and Pops, the school bus driver whose attitude to the Wanderer is violently vituperative: "Fry 'em, oh, fry 'em!" he screams. "Keep it up! Kill yourselves!" He thereby associates himself with the Stranger (301). Toward any sexuality he maintains a judgmental frigidity.

The major loner is Don, the fiancé of Margo—an interesting example, since he is apparently alone by preference despite their engagement, fulfilling his work as an astronaut on the moon. Seldom in all the tremendous events does he consider her fate upon the earth. When the omniscient narrator introduces him he is upon the lunar surface remembering the snow of his childhood (29); he is inwardly chill. At the end of the novel Paul has a major insight into his former rival's condition: "You always liked loneliness better than you liked people" (305).

The example of Richard and the counter-example of Don lead us to the question of the couples. The loners stand out all the more in the fabric of the novel because so many diverse couples are brought together by the arrival of the magical planet. Richard and Vera, Sally and Jake, Katz and Kettering, Rama Joan and Doc, Margo and Hunter, and Paul and Tigerishka, all experience an unleashing of the biological imperative. One of the more bizarre couples is General Spike Stevens and Colonel Mabel Wallingford, whose coupling is thoroughly perverse, a mindless rut on his part determined to assert his military masculinity in the face of death and very conscious on her part, a preparation for strangling the man she despises; she uses her lesbianism as a weapon. Despite the hostility they have for each other, this is a couple that seems ordered from the beginning, since each is an expression of the military complex that the novel associates with the pursuers of the Wanderer; they represent the extreme manifestation of the Word as an aggressive instrument of individual pathology. And given their hostility, we should probably associate them with such loners as the violent Pops.

Turning from the loners and the couples, let us consider the flying saucer students, who receive the arrival of the Wanderer as a more impressive confirmation of their beliefs than most felt they had any right to expect. They are quite diverse; some are fervid believers, like the Ramrod, and some are skeptics; some are utterly down-to-earth, like Wojtowicz and Macheath, and some are exotics, like Rama Joan, who dresses as a man and whose adopted name, Rama, is that of a male Hindu god. Given these several polarities, the group is difficult to characterize. Three of the men are identified by two different names, Rudy Brecht a.k.a. Doc, Ross Hunter a.k.a. Beardy, and Clarence Dodd a.k.a. the Little Man. For the first third of the novel it is difficult to take a fix upon the three men who are at first loners: Doc is randy but unattached, a Priapus-figure; Hunter is married, but far from his wife and children; and Dodd is dedicated to a rather prissy albeit amiable taking of notes. The flying saucer students are people willing to believe, but they exhibit a spectrum of critical responses.

Despite the difficulties with which their diversity challenges our reading—on a basic level a diversity of biological life that opposes the categories the Word favors—a number of the students are very important for the novel. One of the most interesting is the Ramrod, a.k.a. Charlie Fulby, the most intense of the group because he claims to have been abducted by a saucer and taken to the planet Ispan; though benign, his madness seems patent. Gradually, however, Leiber reveals the complexity of the man. Married to Ida and Wanda, one for the sake of the flesh and the other for the sake of the spirit (182-83), he represents both a parody and an idealization of the conjunction of opposites, an important stage in the Jungian individuation of the spirit. His belief in the intrusive planet is more complex than it seems. He is something of a Platonic fabulist, mythologizing a planet in which he believes because he knows that no one will believe him (42-43); in the conclusion he confesses that the universe is much more complex than he himself can imagine (288). When Rama Joan employs the Platonic image of the cave, claiming that humanity knows less of the universe than a man "imprisoned from birth in a cell under the city would know of the millions in Calcutta or Hong Kong or

Moscow or New York" (30), she describes the fate of Fulby. Whether through his imagination or through a flying saucer, he has left the cave and returned, only to discover that in order to be understood he must tell myths. Thus he represents some of Leiber's attitudes toward his own fictions.

Finally, let us note that some of the characters are associated either with cats, whether domestic or tigers, and some are associated with dogs or are dogs. Miaow belongs to Margo, who shares some of the characteristics of cats; aloof but not aggressive unless their hunting instinct is roused, their cruelty is abstract, accidental, or passionate, the kind of slash that Tigerishka claws across Paul's face or the destruction that the Wanderer wrecks upon earth. At the conclusion Miaow recognizes that Margo has deserted her through her connection with Hunter and vanishes into Tigerishka's boudoir with "a synchronized spitting hiss" (284). MacHeath thinks that Wolf may not be a bad name for the Stranger who pursues the Wanderer (288). Bagung Bung, in his ship the *Tiger of the Mud,* determines to "try conclusions with the Wolf of Gold," a Spanish treasure ship called the *Lobo del Oro* (202), and at the end of the novel discovers a handful of rubies; the tiger guts the wolf. Dodd, the obsessive note-taker, has a German police dog called Ragnarok, but the poor beast never has a chance to achieve an apocalyptic moment because the guard at Vanderhill shoots it. Soldiers shall always kill soldiers, but if the enemy is not in their crosshairs they shall slay each other, as Mabel slays Spike. Dogs seldom fare very well in Leiber's fiction.

The handful of rubies that Bagung Bung digs out of the mud is one example of the pervasive imagery of jewels and crystals in the novel, imagery to be found throughout Leiber's work. Flying through the moon as it splits under the pressure of the Wanderer's tidal influence, Don imagines himself "a glass bee with a Prince Rupert's Drop tail buzzing through a ripple in a stack of metal sheets" (69). In *Conjure Wife* Norman also compares himself to a Prince Rupert Drop when he is beginning to "let go" (72), because as he had learned earlier if "the delicate filament in which the drop ended" were "flick[ed] with a fingernail" the drop would explode (39). In both cases the personality is compared to something beautiful, artificial, and fragile. Destroyed by the Wanderer the moon becomes "a filmy diamond-studded scarf" (272).

Like *The Big Time,* this novel is learned. In its three hundred pages it alludes to a number of science fiction authors, E. E. "Doc" Smith, Robert A. Heinlein, H. G. Wells, Arthur C. Clarke, Edgar Rice Burroughs, John W. Campbell Jr., and perhaps most importantly Olaf Stapledon; to poets, Homer, Daniel and St. John, Blake, Edward Thomas, Milton, Pound, Goethe, Heine, and Francis Thompson; to dramatists, Shakespeare, Webster, and

Shaw; to novelists, Hemingway, Stendhal, Blackmore, Caldwell, Chesterton, and Masoch, for Tigerishka seems very much a *Venus im Pelz* (255); and to musicians, Beethoven, Schubert, and Wagner. The allusions to science fiction reveal that *The Wanderer* is a very conscious reconstruction of several science fiction tropes; but, as John Langan has shown, Leiber also employs horror tropes here (127-28). The poets form a framework for the apocalyptic tenor of the work, though Heine's presence reminds us how much Leiber employs an ironic mode. The references to the novelists and dramatists are relatively minor. There is a more than a touch of Wagner's "Ride of the Valkyries" at the melodramatic moment of Sally's orgasm at the top of the roller coaster as the Wanderer flashes into being next to the moon and the stars move; and Schubert's Lied "Der Wanderer," set to words of Schmidt von Lübeck as Leiber meticulously notes, provides the transition between Tigerishka's mythic account of the Wanderer and the end of the chapter when she and Paul make love. There are two forms of the Word in the novel: the bureaucratic word, obsessed by "a great cosmic death-dread" (249), that attempts to rationalize the universe in the name of safety and close it down; and the artistic word that attempts to open wide the universe.

Finally we should note that the world of *The Wanderer* and the world of *The Big Time* are set within a churning chaos, a hyperspace within which improbable Winds may suddenly sweep away any orders we believe immutable. In the large novels these Winds are sometimes gravity forces, such as those that brush through the twigs of space (4) or those that tear apart the moon and raise the earth tides eightfold; or those Winds are the sudden churning waters within which so many of the characters drown. In each of these novels we are "tempest-tossed."

III

> And thence it is
> That I to your assistance do make love,
> Masking the business from the common eye
> For sundry weighty reasons. (*Macbeth* 3.1.124-27)

Leiber's early novel *Conjure Wife*, which takes place in a small private college, has the basic premise that all women are witches, secretly advancing the careers of their husbands. Here the occult, which seems to oppose the Word directly, erupts within the middle of a college and within the middle of domestic relations. For the witch-wives, the college is not a place of the Word, which they secretly envy and despise, but a place in which their husbands' status and thereby their status can be increased. They do not use their power for the sake of research but for the sake of aggression.

Their spite and aggression, however, is not unfounded. Rather than being an institution wholly devoted to knowledge, Hempnell is an extension of 1940s society, "an abnormal, story-book wholesomeness" (147): the society and the college are both repressive, competitive, and political (its platitudinous president has political aspirations); and both draw a façade across themselves. Women who had little position within mid-century American society, as Byfield noted in one of the Fafhrd and Mouser stories, have good reason to attack it (*Witches* 33). Hempnell's façade, however, the fake Gothicism of its architecture, possesses more energy than the college understands. In the heart of a space that ought to show forth the Word, a dragon co-opts the enlightenment challenge of Galileo, "Eppur si muove," and begins to move slowly upon the protagonist (56). As shall happen in *Our Lady of Darkness*, stone, the emblem of the word, assumes an aggressive life that mimics flesh.

The professors are direct products of the college; each man's "pursed lips, frightened eyes, and tyrannical jaw" (5) proclaim that he strives to arrange his life within the narrow limits the college prescribes. Yet within this "over-organized, tension-shot, [and] somewhat artificial" society (7), which at one point seems "to symbolize a whole world of barren intellectual competition and jealous traditionalism" (95), there is nevertheless a devotion to knowledge that is sometimes not tainted by the professor's ego. The protagonist, Norman, who lives in a house that "wear[s] bravely its middle-class trappings," has established himself as an effective ethnologist despite his own ambition that at some point "one of the big universities [would come] through with the right offer" (7). When his battle with the witches' attack reaches its crisis, he constructs an algorithm of magic through casting the traditional formulas of witchcraft as propositions found in the symbolic logic of Whitehead and Russell's *Principia Mathematica*, appealing to Professor Carr who decides that they are allowable equations and who then, swept up by the intellectual puzzle, reduces them to simpler and more powerful forms. His humility at his own achievement is touching: "I believe that behind those symbols, [Norman] is revolutionizing the science of sociology. [. . .] I'm just being a sort of electronic brain" (158). Though the novel does not emphasize the point, Carr's collegiality represents the finest tradition of the intellectual quest. Unfortunately, he is so abstracted in this intellectual world, living in an office that "seemed an attempt to reduce the lusty material world to the virginal purity of geometry" (154), that he does not understand the mania of his wife who is the most virulent of the witches. "In effect," Byfield concludes, "the women act as the unconscious mind of their rational husbands" (*Witches* 18).

Norman certainly is revolutionizing sociology, but his attitude toward the work that the events of the novel thrust upon him is ambivalent. Unlike the other husbands, who are uninterested in their wives, he sets the action in motion through his naughty decision, part trespass, part rape, and part titillation, "a gesture of illicit love" as he tacitly confesses (10), to investigate the drawers (such an old-fashioned, naughty word!) of Tansy's dressing table. In doing this he disturbs the balance that exists at the beginning of the novel, for without his awareness his knowledge coexists with his wife's magic and through its protection. The Word and the Flesh need not be opposed; but they can avoid such opposition only through tact. If the wives of Norman's colleges are evil, it is through their failure to observe such tact.

Opposing the Word and a healthy recognition of the Flesh, therefore, is the perverse aggression of the other wives, represented in a number of ways. For Norman this aggression is certainly represented by his phobia of trucks; connected with this phobia but perhaps more hidden from him and thereby all the more powerful is his characterization of the primitive societies he studies and thereby rationalizes, "an area plunged in darkness, acrouch in fear, blown by giant winds" (17). A recurrent image is a great wind, specifically the wind called up by the bull-roarer on Mrs. Sawtelle's tape recorder, which at crucial points Norman associates with the sound of a truck bearing down on him. This is, however, an ambiguous image, for the bull-roarer and the wind are numinous images, suggestive not only of primitive rites but of the Holy Spirit that moved as the breath of God upon the waters at the beginning of creation; this is the *ruach* and *spiritus* that give life to the word—the letter kills (2 Cor. 3:6). Not for nothing had Leiber spent some time at General Theological Seminary. Though his spiritual life is strongly tempered by skepticism, it is also allowed a certain freedom through his graduate work in philosophy and psychology, which leads here to the argument that "many seemingly impersonal forces, when broken down sufficiently, become something very much like personality" (140)—the other version of which would be that elements of the personality, achieving a sufficient synthesis, would seem very like impersonal forces. When the wives destroy Tansy, they leave her rationality, a purely mechanical matter, and obliterate her personality (Byfield, *Witches* 21). A further crucial image of the wives' magic aggression, therefore, is that of the material world, which is too prone to turn against the individual; this is "the cussedness of things" (47), the nick Norman gives himself shaving or his inadvertently biting his tongue. When Norman later interprets this tendency of matter as "the cussedness of the human nervous system" (69), however, he points at a further horror in the novel, the possibility that witches do not exist and that he is suffering a mental breakdown.

The symbol of this revolt of matter is the semi-animated stone dragon that is steadily and inexorably approaching his window but which is "solid and inert as only the inorganic can be" (87). As a dog-like creature, "a dog the color of concrete" (82), in one of the climaxes of the novel it attacks and destroys Tansy's cat Totem, which functions as her familiar. We have seen this persecution construed in galactic terms in *The Wanderer*, but in horror Leiber's symbol of the cat is much more under threat than in a science fiction novel. In terms of his later development of the opposition between the cat and the dog, this horrifying moment suggests that the wild and the mysterious, the truly feminine, is under serious threat in a world where inanimate buildings are liable to send forth maleficent male powers.

The threat is baldly realized when Tansy suffers a literal alienation from herself, announcing, "'I' is not here" (125). In a novel in which Leiber does not indulge in the dense literary allusions of his later works, overtly referring only to Barrie, Frazer, and Whitehead and Russell, Tansy's sentence may allude both to the dissociation of the ego in Descartes' skepticism (Justin Leiber, "Fritz Leiber" 32) and to its later development in Rimbaud's poetic program: "C'est faut de dire: Je pense. On devrait: On me pense [. . .]. JE est un autre" [It's a mistake to say: I think. One should say: Someone thinks me (. . .). I is another] (344). But what Rimbaud intends as a sign of his becoming a magical *voyant* becomes here a sign of loss of affect, or to speak theologically loss of soul. Our uncertainty as to which language we ought to use points at a chief horror in the novel.

Earlier Norman had good reason to fear he was losing control of himself. Twice he "lets himself go" in class, self-destructively cutting at the sexual repression that characterizes life at Hempnell. The first time his remarks are "a trifle raw," a bit against the grain of the restraint in which he had trained himself without, he hopes, "losing intellectual integrity" (37). The second time, when he tosses his notes aside, he cannot remember what he said except some words about "dirty-minded old women, in whom greed for social prestige has reached the magnitude of a perversion" (71). This is the same kind of fugue, taking over the human personality, that the Mouser suffered when he gave his *Götterdämmerung* oration. The ironies of the two passages in *Conjure Wife* are complex. First, we must wonder whether under the influence of Hempnell's proprieties he has indeed maintained his integrity; but his two speeches are not themselves examples of integrity but of a self-display and self-gratification that leave his students excited and puzzled, since he has given a speech very unlike him. He has "exploded" under the pressure of the academic life—the only excuse he can have for himself is that he has been bewitched, to opt for the theological language rather than the psychological, though the reader should remember that the other language may be more apt. One other detail of this passage is its emphasis on the age of the women; their husbands of course are old also, at least in relation to the young Norman, still attempting to find a firm place in the college hierarchy. As we saw in *The Wanderer*, age is one characteristic of the Word.

Something else is opposed to the Word in this novel, and to understand it we need to consider further the role of sexuality. Though the relationship between Norman and Tansy is certainly sexual, as any number of small physical details assures us, there is yet some question about its depth. As he considers her in the first pages, it is her professional skill as a professor's wife that he admires, not her allure, which he attempts to recapture when he opens her drawers; what we have earlier characterized as his search for knowledge is tinged with the quest for sexual knowledge, one that he had at one time possessed but which is now slipping from him. It is significant that Norman and Tansy have no children. But more importantly we should note that it is his colleagues' wives, the aggressive witches, who bear with them details of a perverse sexuality that the novel highlights.

This invasion of sexuality, which Norman invites, is symbolized first by the two young students he sees from the window, "sauntering in the trousers and flapping shirt tails forbidden in the classroom" (6), one of whom "laughed happily" as they turn a corner (9), immediately before he turns to Tansy's dressing table; these two girls shall reappear in *Our Lady of Darkness*, once more as forebodings of a psychic shift in the protagonist. On a much more sinister level the invasion is symbolized by the phone call from his student Van Nice: "I'll hurt you and you'll hurt me," she fantasizes, in a sado-masochistic fantasy that certainly has its attractions. "Nice, perhaps, if it were real," he had thought long before learning who person on the telephone actually was, though he recognized the unreality of the words (30). Her phone call has its parallel in the call from his student Jennings, who later attacks him with a pistol. Opposed to the Word in this novel are death and sexuality, the two irruptions that are the most difficult for any individual to control.

What kind of witchcraft does the novel present? The remarkable thing is that it is not supernatural. It is as natural and as capable of being rationalized as the sciences, as we have already noted when we saw that it could be brought under the rubrics of symbolic logic. White magic and black magic are characterized by their purposes, not by any inherent difference in their means; both come from the center of the wind.

A number of points stand out immediately as we turn to *Our Lady of Darkness*. First, much more than *Conjure Wife*, this is a thoroughly urban novel; San Francisco is the scene of the novel, and cities are the subject of de Castries's impossible book, *Megalopolisomancy*. Second, here much more directly than in his other works Leiber grapples with the nature of drink and other addictions, our questionable defenses against the pressures of civilization.

Several aspects of the city are once more touched upon: the maze with which it confronts the protagonist (91); the advertising slogans that form much of its surface, often in collusion with the breweries (26); and the "guards and idols" it offers, paper (which is either preserved or shredded) and money (75). Certain other aspects, however, are more important. The earthquakes of San Francisco, the great earthquake of 1906 and the great earthquake to come, emphasize that a city is always changing (114, 152). What you hoped to find is no longer there, and the building in which you live has changed its name. Next, the sheer mass of the city, what de Castries calls the "city-stuff" (64), is overwhelming; every individual must deal with the fact that a potent, inorganic, abstract work, haphazardly constructed by faceless corporations, transcends and always shall transcend the self.

Perhaps most important to the themes of the novel are the secret places of the city from which intrusions break through into our reasonable world. Meditating on the oddity of Corona Heights early in the novel, its protagonist Franz Westen thinks: "big cities certainly had some strange intrusions in them. This one was like a raw remnant of upthrust from the earthquake of 1906" (6-7). A few pages later he thinks of the black doors without knobs, "It was odd how old buildings had secret spaces in them that weren't really hidden but were never noticed" (9). From the roof of his apartment house, considering the San Francisco landscape, he looks at "the huge downtown buildings and whatever secret spaces they contained" (21). Fernando believes, and he is not far wrong, that witchcraft is hidden in the walls (44). The store where Franz bought de Castries's book and Clark Ashton Smith's diary, in which the curse is concealed, is hidden from Franz by his alcoholic fog, but he vaguely remembers the sexual attraction and threat the store contained (124). In something of the same state of mind, he had hidden in the back of his clothes cabinet a bottle of kirschwasser (155), which he discovers on the night that he encounters the Lady of Darkness.

Much of this material points at the discovery of de Castries's cipher at the climax of the novel, but Leiber is making a much more general point about the nature of the city, since these secret spaces and intrusions are not always threatening; the little girl in the store who had felt him up reappears to identify him (136), and "in a narrow lot the highrise moguls had somehow overlooked" grows Franz's favorite tree, an emblem of the wilderness that still exists within the interstices of the rationalized and commercialized city (80). In this light we should take seriously Byers's bon mot that every city should have ghosts, which are civilizing (97). But we must test the spirits.

One of the more bizarre aspects of urban life is de Castries's claim that every city of sufficient mass possesses an occult geometry that begets paramentals, its own host of spirits that intersect the lives of its human inhabitants; his curse is an attempt to arouse a spirit that the geometry of San Francisco manifests, an action upon a grander scale than the dragon that the magic of the faculty wives had activated. So the landscape here is tremendously important, one reason the novel begins with a description of the city that shall become personified in the action that follows. Long before he understands anything of his situation Franz is attracted by the TV tower, "broad-shouldered, slender-waisted, and long-legged, like a beautiful and stylish woman—or a demigoddess" (3), standing beyond Corona Heights where de Castries lies buried. The tower seemed to him at first "cheap and garish [. . .], an obscene embodiment of the blatant world of sales and advertising [. . .], an emblazonment of the American flag in its worst aspects" (5). Franz should not be too critical of this symbol, since he makes a living from the novelizations he writes, with a certain degree of realistic integrity, for a television series. At last, however, the tower represents reality; its lights lead him to the "sure and steady" stars beyond (63), of which he becomes an avid student, despite Saul's warning that it might not be a good idea to welcome "every new reality" into one's life (5). When Franz climbs Corona Heights for the first time he feels safe with the tower behind him "like a protective goddess" (26). Considerably later, on the night Franz is attacked by his scholar's mistress, he is willing to entertain the notion that the tower is the statue of our lady of darkness (166), a notion confirmed when the scholar's mistress rises in "very much the shape of the skeletal steel TV tower" (172).

Lying in front of the tower is Corona Heights, "as if it were a great predatory beast of night surveying its territory in patient search of prey" (1), we have seen that the hill is an intrusion, like a dog that appears tamed but is not or "some wilder and more secret animal that had never submitted to man's rule" (2). This language of the beast is persistently applied to the hill. When Franz approaches it for the first time it seems to hide itself "like a pale brown tiger" (24); later, when he flees the hill, like an earthquake it seems to shake buildings from its sides "preparatory to stalking down into the city" (88). The point of this imagery, of course, is that the tower and the hill mirror de Castries's veiled mistress and the black panther with which he arrived in San Francisco (99–100), imagery that pursues Franz at Byers's house when he hears a scratching at the door and imagines "a large black panther crouched close against the other side of the gold-traced white opacity, a green-eyed, gleamingly black panther that was beginning to metamorphose into something more terrible" (133). At the moment he is both right and wrong; the scratching comes from the two girls, masked as cats, beasts akin to Tigerishka, who enter to tease the two men, darker versions of the two girls Franz had earlier met on Corona Heights; the doubling we noticed in the saga is apparent here. Their comic and sinister intrusion does not, however, disinfect his imagination, for later he imagines something "midway between a black panther and a spider monkey" (154) in the elevator shaft, shortly before the attack comes. Franz, of course, is the target of this pair, the tower and the hill, the woman and the panther and the spirit of de Castries who is buried in the hill; but beyond Franz in his apartment lies the Transamerica Pyramid (153-54), emblematic in the book of the funerary imagery associated with large cities and of de Castries's hatred. For there is no reason to hate Franz, barely born when de Castries died; the weird story writer is simply in the wrong place when he activates the curse by buying the book in an alcoholic fugue and bringing it to the cipher hidden in the walls of his apartment, where he "unconsciously recreated de Castries' last years, brooding alone over the same concerns in the same room" (Byfield, *Witches* 66). The reign of Thanatos extends beyond our conscious guilts.

This description of the geometry, however, is liable to be misleading, since the discrimination between de Castries and his mistress is not as clean as the landscape suggests. De Castries fears her but he also needs her; and the panther is as much his as hers. He invents a very complex geometry and cipher—made up of random numbers. His first act of aggression is the mockery of taking Franz's place in his apartment; more significantly, his second act is reaching out to shatter Franz's binoculars, the symbol of his knowledge of the city. This act has the positive effect, however, of forcing Franz to surrender his distanced attitude.

Franz has every reason to feel paranoid about his situation, every reason to feel, irrationally, that the geometry of the city, which personifies forces coming into existence long before he is born, has him within the focus of an obscure curse; but his paranoia is heightened as a recovering alcoholic. Like Norman he comes close to losing control of himself, to the extent that late in the novel he discovers he was complicit with the secret places when he hid his bottle of kirschwasser in the cabinet. In Byers's apartment he remarks that Jack London's death was as much due to alcohol as to any supernatural attack by de Castries, a remark that puts the lie to Byers's response when he pours himself another measured tot of brandy (116). Byers's example and reiterated invitation, culminating in his offers of the girls and of cocaine, tempts Franz so much that his flight from the apartment is an act of salvation. Saul's story of the Invisible Nurse, "our mistress of oblivion, our queen of dreams," casts a strong light upon the anaesthetizing drugs that are extensions of Thanatos: "Here's your pass to dreamland [...], think of the dark salt waves [...].

Who'd ever think [. . .] they could put nine hours and maybe ten of good, good darkness into such a tiny time-capsule" (47). The great defense against the anxieties of civilization turns out to be in the service of death. And Franz confesses that he had used paraldehyde, the blissful drug of the Invisible Nurse, in his recent detoxification therapy (50). Even the fantasy that de Castries creates, a totalizing explanation for the ills of the urban world, is a drug, one that Clark Ashton Smith knows that he must escape (66).

Given these dangers, it is something of a surprise that only a few moments of interiority arise. Early in the novel, when Franz sees something disappearing down the stairwell, "just the suggestion of black hair and clothing and slim white wrists and ankles," he realizes "how the successive floors below were like the series of reflections you saw when you stood between two mirrors" (17). This moment almost leads to regret that he is determinedly sober, free from such guilty imaginings (18). The image of the mirrors is echoed by Montague's argument "that civilization is being asphyxiated, mummy-wrapped by its own records, bureaucratic and otherwise, and by its infinitely recessive self-observation" (69). Franz is so dedicated to reality that he is seldom a prey to the temptation of seeing things as mere projections of his own psyche. If, then, the hidden places are ambivalent and addiction is deadly, the only defense to anxiety is music, number, and order, brushed with a touch of Pythagorean mysticism. There is a rule of number and order in the universe, Franz believes, even though his experiences suggest that that rule can be affronted by human weakness and obsession and death (94). Music is a healing intrusion, if one pays close attention. As Cal says, "It's all release—and it has the power to release other things and make them fly and swirl" (11). Saul testifies to the effect of her music on the inmates of the psychiatric ward: she had "*melted* that tension, loosened and unbound it" (59). Once again, as in *Conjure Wife*, women are able to tap into this magic, whether it be the black magic hidden behind the veils and compacted intellectuality of our lady of darkness or the white magic Cal invokes to defend Franz and release him for a time from his obsessions. Both kinds of magic appeal to the imagery of the *ruach*; "magic is in all woodwinds," Cal remarks (10). But the image of the wind is much more associated with the influence pouring down from the hill. The stirring there in the early morning may be nothing more than the wind (2), but when Franz first sees the pale, brown thing "a sudden wind blew in," which he decides is nothing more than "a freakish gust" (7). There is "a lot of wind" on top on the hill (26), and when he sees the thing in his window he thinks again that it must be a result of "freakish winds among the high buildings" (30). At the end of the novel, on the roof of his apartment before the attack, he feels something sick in the air "as if the freshening wind had blown something malignant out of the west" (154).

If music is accepted as mere entertainment, however, if it becomes mere surface and not an intrusion, it offers a false escape from the threat represented by the geometry of the city, unless Franz pays attention to the command that also lies within its power to unloose (144); it is a command that he still obeys inside his room, remembering the music that Cal played within the concert hall (160). Despite Byers, who argues that there is "no distinction whatever between fantasy and reality," only a distinction between good and bad art, Franz believes that art, just as much as life, is bound up in integrity, truth, and moral imperatives. Cal can swear by order because order exists.

A typical gesture at the end of every one of these works is an uncertain hesitation, a refusal to assert fully that now, with these intrusions of the irrational in the middle of the Word, the protagonist knows at last everything there is to be known. Fafhrd and the Mouser have not fully settled into the democratic, uxorious semi-matriarchy of Rime Isle; though they admit that all desires cannot be fulfilled, they still respect the demands that desire makes upon them and leave their conclusions about the future open. Leiber never felt that he had finished with them (Byfield, "Fafhrd and Fritz" 55-56). Since Greta still does not know the ultimate aims of the Snakes and Spiders in the Change War, much less than anyone knows the ultimate teleology of the polarities we are faced with, she does not know her place within the universe; she only knows that the war shall continue and that whatever we know of good and evil is conditional (Justin Leiber, "Fritz Leiber" 34). Earth has lost the Wanderer and Paul has lost Tigerishka; whether she and her friends shall successfully sail "the whirlwind void of hyperspace" (251) and escape the galactic civilization, and whether Paul shall now construct a more balanced life for himself on earth, the narrative will not reassure us. Norman is uncertain whether the magic that women seem to possess exists, even though he has manipulated something very like it through symbolic logic; but he much more respects the independence of his wife. Calpurnia, with more assurance than her namesake, the wife of Caesar, reminds Franz that everything is "chancy" (183). Leiber is careful to leave his narratives open; one conclusion, however, he does assert, that the only arena in which a truly human life can take place, a life that is never yet achieved, is that where the Word and the Wilderness struggle to establish an uneasy coexistence.

Leiber Covers the Big Gambler Death

> Estimons ces deux cas: si vous gagnez, vous gagnez tous; si vous perdez, vous ne perdez rien. [Let us consider these two cases: if you win, you win all; if you lose, you lose nothing.] (Pascal 136)

One of the most extended gambles in fantasy is that which occupies the main scene in Fritz Leiber's Hugo- and Nebula-winning work "Gonna Roll the Bones." The identity of the antagonist in that work, however, is not clear. He may be Death, he may be the Devil; but if that character is Death, as I shall argue, Death also appears several times as a gamester and a gambler in Leiber's saga of Fafhrd and the Gray Mouser; and it is with those scenes that we shall begin. First, however, it will be useful to conduct a short meditation on gambling.

I

To gamble is to take part in a game—and it may imply by a play on words that when we gamble we gambol, behaving with reckless gaiety, whether we win or lose, because it is our addiction to the game that is the point, something beyond our humdrum lives. The game is constituted by rigid rules, by some rules that are more a matter of tradition, and by some rules that are simply understood but that have a certain amount of latitude, of play if you will. Every gamble, then, is a matter of discovery, uncovering the rules that are at work in the process of the game.

The complexity of this game appears in our recognition that we ourselves, mortals as we are, often place side bets in the game; if one of the players is Death, as he usually is in Leiber, we bet as much on the side of Death as on ourselves, recognizing the undeniable fact that in the long run the house always wins. Not only shall we die, we also yearn to die; Freud's Thanatos, the death urge that is rooted in the deepest parts of our cellular and psychic being, is often at work in our most casual acts. We cannot ignore that this is a dark recognition. For me it is symbolized by a woman I saw in the lounge of one of the more plastic hotels of Las Vegas, leaning over a cup of quarters filled with her vomit; she breathed, but she didn't move. Now many would argue that the woman dead drunk in the lounge is only one side of the archetype of the gambler; the other side of the archetype is the man or woman ecstatic at the throw of the dice, the turn of the card, the rush of the horse across the finish line. The archetype of the gambler is more complex than one side or the other, for on one side lies the rot of death, deep down death, and on the other side lies exuberant life, so much more life than we can imagine. As so often when we deal with a literary topos we are dealing with life and death; it is quite close to home.

The game, then, seems like a very apt symbol for our engagements with death. As Johan Huizinga points out in *Homo Ludens*, one aspect of the game is that it is limited in place and time; it has a beginning and an end (9)—just like life, I would add, although few of us can remember our birth, and Lucretius argues that we do not recognize our death (3.830-69). Moreover, unlike our lives a game is voluntary (7-8), unless you are playing the game with Death; unlike our lives, a game is not real (8), unless you are playing with Death; and unlike our lives, a game often seems beautiful, to be described in terms of rhythm, harmony, and tension (7, 10-11). Above all, Huizinga argues that a game is disinterested, though within the game as we play it we seem to be very interested indeed, just as we seem to be very interested in our lives (9, 13). A closer analysis of the German *Pflicht*, from which "play" is derived, suggests what happens when we are truly engaged in the game: play and danger, risk, chance, defeat—"it is all a single field of action where something is at stake" (40). That is the game as a high venture, a place where one's soul is risked. As soon as money becomes involved in the game, however, the game is clearly a matter of profit. And any game that is constructed by chance, whether it be cards or dice, loses in Huizinga's eyes its interest (198-99), perhaps because it then seems too real and too like life. "The virtue," he says, "has gone out of the game" (199). It has been transformed to a cupful of vomit and quarters!

In discussing these matters we should not ignore recent scientific work on gambling that strongly suggests that gambling is an addiction and thereby closely related to other addictions such as drugs, alcohol, and cigarettes (Volberg 3-10). The point of every one of these addictions is to numb a pain, and there is nothing that numbs pain so well as Death, even though the immediate result of gambling for the problem gambler may be depression, domestic violence, debt, and bankruptcy (12-13). One of the results of Leiber's alcoholism he feared was his wife's alcoholism, from which she was not able to escape, leading to their separation and her early death (Byfield 42, 51). The gaiety of his work, especially what we find in the series of Fafhrd and the Mouser, can be deceptive.

When in my title to this chapter I name Death the big gambler I do so to point out that Leiber has always had a healthy respect for Death, in part because of his power, in part because of his style. Death dresses well, and he thereby puts us to shame. This Big Gambler, however, according to Rachel A. Volberg's recent study, works on the margin and ignores dice; all the other games belong to the upper and middle class, but dice, whatever form they may take, belong by default to the back alleys and the back rooms (Volberg 30). This is the house that Joe Slattermill, the protagonist of "Gonna Roll the Bones," inhabits. He is poor, and only the loaves of bread that his mother-in-law bakes save his house from utter destitution.

One of the not so quiet arguments of this chapter, then, is that in Leiber's work gambling is often a symbol for alcoholism. Not that Leiber does not treat alcoholism itself, as he does in his last novel and as he does in Fafhrd's devotion to Issek of the bottle. It is simply that the games are games with Death, games that the protagonists shall one day lose. As the argument to the story "The Circle Curse" declares, "How Life is an Eternal Gamble with Death" (2.4).

II

The story "The Bleak Shore" opens with a language that alludes to a gamble, though it is only later that we learn that an actual dice game is happening. A "small, pale man, whose bulging forehead was shadowed by a black cowl," asks the Gray Mouser a pointed question: "So you think a man can cheat death and outwit doom?" The Mouser's answer, as he holds a dice box in his hand, ready for the next throw, is judicious: "I said that a cunning man can cheat death for a long time" (2.100). This admission of mortality does not, however, satisfy the small, pale man, who after an ironic list of their achievements repeats the words *the Bleak Shore* and thus places them under a curse to find their deaths in that distant region. The only thing that saves them much later is the Mouser's realization that *"he seeks always to repeat past experience, which has always been in his favor"* (2.109). This has been the great attempt of the two heroes, to avoid repetition in their lives.

How do we know that the small pale man is death? Well, he resembles strongly the death who plays chess with the knight in Bergman's 1957 film *The Seventh Seal,* sitting by the shore of the ocean; and Leiber knew that film well enough to comment perceptively on it (*The Second Book* 130-34). Here, however, the game is dice, and the Mouser wins by cheating and rakes in the coins by throwing the Lankhmar signs of the eel and the serpent, the sign of snake eyes, which on earth would signify a loss.

The great difference between the story and the film is that in one the game is chess, in the other dice. In chess the game is utterly open and rational, and we can trace its genesis; in dice the game is closed and a matter of chance; in addition, we might note that dice is probably one of the most ancient of games, although given its age we have no idea what the house rules were in the past. Leiber in the stories that follow will insert either chess or dice, depending on how far rationality or chance, openness or opacity, extends its power into the story.

The title of the early novella "Adept's Gambit" calls for the explanation that it receives in the argument to the work: "In his gambits a chess-player sacrifices pawn or piece to checkmate his adversary. But in his games, a black magician, in order to triumph, may sacrifice living pieces and even himself the player" (3.103). Like several authors who are fond of chess, Leiber cannot avoid the temptation of basing a work upon the game; but the game does not play a part in the story. Vis-à-vis Ningauble of the seven eyes, Fafhrd does once address him in this story as Snake Eyes, but dice plays no more part in the story proper than does chess (3.116).

Swords and Ice Magic opens with the solemn, intricate story "The Sadness of the Executioner," which recounts the woes of Death as he, or she (for Leiber in a number of stories prefers to leave the sex of Death unknown, perhaps because Death often proves to be a great emptiness; perhaps the sex of Death depends on the sex of the person who dies, but Leiber never asserts that), attempts to kill the requisite number of people in a given amount of time; in addition, Death must see to it that the Lords of Necessity, who outrank death, will be satisfied (6.2). It is as though Death were playing a four-dimensional game of chess as he, or she, casts the pawns in the box (6.6). Two of the pawns are Fafhrd and the Mouser, who do not know they are being played with in this fashion; they are not the opponents of Death, only the pieces of a player who can cheat a bit, as though this were a gamble, and who can improvise "as any good artist will" (6.6); and the story invites the reader to enjoy it as a connoisseur would. The work of Death is difficult, however, because "it may be that in the world of Nehwon there are gods of whom even Death does not know and who from time to time take pleasure in putting obstacles in his path. Or it may be that Chance is quite as great a power as Necessity" (6.9). Poor Death! expostulates the reader.

But despite this debonair Death, he has another aspect, another Death that Ourph claims the Mouser revealed when he spoke to his crew: "Why you spoke . . . of the glories of death and of what a grand thing it was to go down joyfully to destruction carrying your enemies with you (and as many as possible of your friends also), how this was the law of life and its crowning beauty and grandeur" (6.180). The horror of this speech is its elevation of death. If the person speaking these words were playing chess or dice, both games would end in the player's sweeping the pieces or the dice from the board. This person would not play the game; Death would collaborate with nothingness. This is a version of Hitler's last words to his troops at the end of the World War, but even a Mingol says no to this oration.

In the last book of the series *The Knight and Knave of Swords* Fafhrd and the Mouser are playing a game of backgammon, throwing the dice that dictate the moves of the pieces, as though "destinies in the larger world would jump with those worked out in the little world of the backgammon box" (7.100-101). But one of these games, one after another, is being played by the Death of Fafhrd and the Death of the Mouser, two quasi-supernatural doubles who are agents of the Assassins Order, remarkable men who slowly become their victims physically and mentally. When they come into the bar patronized by Fafhrd and the Mouser they immediately sit at the two men's table and begin backgammon, the game now favored by the two heroes. Though dice are used, this is not a game of pure chance insofar as it is played on a structured board with pieces, rather bony pieces at that; but several bets are being laid on the side. "Backgammon," Leiber later wrote, "is closer to real life [than chess] because the player has to follow a compromise path between, on the one hand, his desires and plans and, on the other, the blows and gifts of chance—or fate" (*The Ghost Light* 358).

The scene would be more eerie if the two Deaths were not so perplexed by the bizarre actions of the men they hope to kill. When Fafhrd leaves the bar on a madcap quest followed closely by his Death, the game is resumed by the Mouser and his Death, as though the Mouser were playing himself for his life; and game after game he plays with supernatural skill. After the two Deaths are dispatched, the Mouser speculates whether ghosts for revenge ever play backgammon; he has "heard of them contesting parties at chess with living mortals" (7.112). Their backgammon box is kept at the bar "as a curiosity of sorts, but it was noted that few used it or played with it, or got good games when they did" (7.115).

As the saga advances there are fewer references to Death playing chess or dice against mortals, and fewer references to games of chess and dice being played in the neighborhood of Death, a very polite and courteous Death always. We do not need, however, to accept this *politesse*, since death is often swift, violent, and baroque in Nehwon. Leiber is skating close to the cliché of that contest between death and humanity, often inventing new variations on the theme. Certainly this double contest of a game with one's own Death is such a superb variation on the game with Death that Bergman had staged.

III

Leiber had already written his classic story of supernatural skill in dice in a game with Death in the 1967 story "Gonna Roll the Bones," a story that he wrote "with the thought in [his] mind that [he]'d been playing dice with Death again in order to liven up [his] life" (*The Ghost Light* 357). There is little of the buffoonery, however, that Leiber invented in the later story; and one of the great virtues of this story, besides its serious aim, is the way Leiber exploits the language of craps. I want to analyze, however, the characterizations of the main people. Joe Slattermill, who is "just a dirty, working-still miner" (19), has an admiration for the big gamblers, no doubt because he can never be one; and this is his weakness, besides his taste for crap-shooting and his taste for gin. These are weaknesses that his wife despises, though we have a problem in analyzing his relations with her, who would seem to have a taste for gin also, given the row of gin bottles she keeps on the hearth; but he imagines her taunting him for these weaknesses: "You're going out and gamble and get drunk and lay a floozy and come home and beat me and go to jail for it" (2). The night might well have ended that way if something else did not stand in the way. In any case, he remembers her bringing him a pint when he was in jail in the past (2).

The only strength he would seem to have is a talent for "precision hurling" (19), which is a magic power that comes and goes for him, and nothing more; at least he plays as excellent a game of craps as the Mouser had played his games of backgammon. His ability transcends chance, the truth of dice upon which Huizinga looks so askance in its modern form (198); it is as though in this story Leiber returns the game to its early, numinous character (56–57). Early in the story we are reminded four times of his admiration for the big gamblers and the great gamblers, people for whom such strength does not come and go and who possess a great style (7, 9). His admiration reaches its apex when he imagines the Big Gambler in capital letters, as the man is known throughout the rest of the story. This man is not "a relatively minor death" such as the death that rules in Newhon (6.1); this is our death, that which we fear in the real world.

As Joe leaves the house for his night on the town he notices in passing the loaves of bread his wife is baking, loaves that he later realizes have the shape of the Big Gambler's head, which the reader now knows is the skull of Death. As he walks past the graveyard he feels "the equally unseen breezes and ghosts. [. . .] The breezes were gentle, but unusually restless and variable" (3), such as often accompany eldritch moments in Leiber's fiction; and soon, as though it comes into being from the breezes, he sees the Boneyard, the casino that everyone expected but everyone doubted would ever appear. Inside his confidence "sift[s] through him, like a breeze that heralds a gale" (5). Is Joe's wife a witch, with her traditional familiar Mr. Guts? And has she brought it all into being in order to debase him, because she knows that he will have nothing but admiration for a man he regards as the Big Gambler? In addition, as the events in the casino grow increasingly weird, is the Big Gambler in fact Death? We have no answers to these questions, but the more we consider the story the more we believe this is the truth.

What is so admirable then about the Big Gambler? He is a perfect gentleman, always generous to the poor, as is evident when he accepts Joe into the crap game (9). He has a whispery, gentle voice when he asks Mr. Bones to tell Joe the house rules; it is not blustery (11). "He exhibits courtesy in the smallest matters, [thinks Joe] another mark of the master devotee of games of chance" (12). Joe thinks that the Big Gambler is a paragon of courtesy, even after the poet, driven mad by jealousy as the man passes his hand across the rump of the poet's beloved, dies when he touches the man.

If Joe had been thinking clearly he might have remembered the worldweariness exhibited by Death in *The Seventh Seal,* or perhaps he would have remembered the savoir faire of Death in the American drama *Death Takes a Holiday.* He might even have considered the comforting, edgy voice of Death in Schubert's great lied, "Der Tod und das Mädchen," the death that "masquerad[es] as the merciful releaser" (Graham Johnson 10). As the left hand on the piano deftly manages the chords, it is as though "death the puppeteer manipulates human destinies with the tiniest of hand shifts" (10):

> Gib deine Hand, du schön und zart Gebild!
> Bin Freund und komme nicht zu strafen.
> Sei gutes Muts! Ich bin nicht wild,
> Sollst sanft in meinem Armen Schlafen.
> [Give me your hand, you fair and tender being!
> I am your friend, I do not come to punish.
> Be courageous! I am not cruel,
> You will sleep softly in my arms.] (Schubert 9)

True, Joe cannot bring to mind such works, because he is a "working-still miner," but this is the context we should consider for the Big Gambler's gentle voice. We trust him and his sweet voice, though as the narration proceeds we trust him less and less.

In the climax of the story Joe flees with, it seems, all the people in the Boneyard, clientele and employees, upon his heels, in a scene reminiscent of the climax of Burns's "Tam o'Shanter." Every terror in the magic space rushes after the man who has trespassed the rules, even if the trespass is such a compliment as "Weel done, Curry-sark!" (Burns 72). But the horse in Leiber's story does not lose its tail. Instead, Joe is thrown out of the establishment to land on his bottom in what feels like "a kick of encouragement" (23). He had gambled with Death and lost to Death, but he has come out alive. The doorway to the Boneyard is no longer an inviting swinging door but "a padlocked sheet-iron door" (23). He has to go home, if that home still exists and if we are to take seriously his vision of it burning, but he will go to it the long way, taking the long circle around the world. For a time he has won, as he really could not have imagined that he could. Even Death might ruefully smile on him—until next time. Every victory is more than chancy, though it does depend upon how you throw the dice; it is conditional.

There are so many details here that might have been tragic, above all the folklore story of the bet with the devil; but Joe is so courageous and so needy to escape. And finally there is no escape except for the place in which the protagonist is found. So he throws the dice.

Pascal would have bet on Joe.

Stage Violence, Stage Resurrection in Tiptree and Leiber

> Wit with his wantonness
> Tasteth death's bitterness:
> Hell's executioner
> Hath no ears for to hear. (*Elizabethan Lyrics* 167)

There is no doubt that Fritz Leiber's *The Big Time* is a novel that he carefully constructed according to the rules of a neo-Aristotelian drama. Many have said so (Staicar 53; Byfield 36), and I have argued so in this collection. It is more than that, but its basic structure, occurring within one location and within one narrow time and a relatively limited group of dramatis personae that is focused by its a single narrator, participant, and monoloquist, clearly follows that form. In the same way, James Tiptree, Jr.'s novel *Brightness Falls from the Air* is also modeled upon a rigorous ideal of drama. It takes place within one locale. True, some of the characters are received from a space ship and jitneyed to the station, and later that day they are taken to observe the aliens, the Dameii, of the planet; and true that a day upon Damiem is thirty hours long, not twenty-four, allowing Tiptree more time to develop the intricate relations of her characters. But most of the action takes place on the station, within its lounge and terrace, during some ten hours of the night. The two-day action thereafter is denouement, occupying only 65 pages in a 375-page work. The great difference is that Leiber's action takes place in an enclosed space compared to a brain (8, 12), with a claustrophobic effect, whereas the main action of Tiptree's novel takes place on a terrace as exotic colors tear apart the night sky; and this difference, as we shall see, leads to others.

I

If time and space are narrowly maintained in both novels, so are the characters. The characters of the *The Big Time* appear on stage in a very symmetrical fashion. The six entertainers who maintain the station welcome six soldiers. Associated in various ways with Eros, these entertainers are three men and three women. The six soldiers, associated with Thanatos, are three human men who are joined by two aliens and a warrior woman from Bronze Age Crete; the alien satyr and octopus accompany her as a part of the mythic décor of her time and place. These are the characters, no more and no less. In *Brightness Falls from the Air*, the greater number of characters is not at all as symmetrical, providing Tiptree the opportunity to develop interlocking subplots: Linnix's quest to find her father, Pardalianche's quest to resurrect her sister, and Vovoka's quest to enact justice on the person who destroyed his people. Three characters, two men and a woman, maintain the station and provide cultural entertainment. Among the visitors are two men and two women who are clearly associated with Eros, stars of a soft-porn drama who are under contract to their cameraman and who with him maintain a tradition of dramatic propriety. Two of the visitors are twin women, one of them in a coma; and two others are young, each in search of herself and himself. Finally there are the four murderers clearly associated with Thanatos, three of them connected with each other, and the fourth an alien loner. The alien Dameii are at first beautiful, passive victims, who only assume responsibility for their fate at the end of the novel when their beauty begins to fall away; the various spacers are not important to the main action except insofar as they suffer the accidental forces in the universe. It is not possible to fit these characters into neat categories as one can Leiber's characters; but with Leiber's characters in mind it is possible to see certain groups emerge that are roughly congruent. It is hard to deny that in both works Thanatos and Eros are thoroughly at war.

One of these groups is the triune mother, to whom Kaby openly refers in Leiber's novel; but the goddess, young girl, mother, and hag are fulfilled in the novel by the characters of Lili, Greta, and Maud, openly called the old girl. By the time Leiber wrote the novel he was very excited by Robert Graves (Byfield 26-29), whom he cites in the heading of a chapter: "Maiden, Nymph, and Mother are the eternal royal Trinity of [Crete], and the Goddess, who is worshipped there in each of these aspects, as New Moon, Full Moon, and Old Moon, is the sovereign Deity" (46). The goddess is more complex in Tiptree's novel. The young girl is Linnix, Bridey, and Paralomena, who has been frozen in time by her accident; the mother is Cory and Pardalianches, the Lady Marquise who is very experienced in sexual matters for the sake of her sister; and the hag is Cory at the end of the novel. But Cory is also the Kore, the Greek word for the young girl at the beginning of the novel, especially for Persephone, stolen from her mother by the god of the underworld—material we shall allude to in greater depth when we consider the theme of resurrection. But we cannot ignore Cory, also known as Cor, who in Kip's careless words is "the core" and "the heart" of their work (21), and thus intimately connected through his words to the star she killed, fulfilling Tiptree's assumption that "everybody wants to wipe the world out a couple of times a day" (cited in Phillips 26). As the young girl who in the past killed a race and who has since had that memory suppressed, as Cory in the present, and as the old woman she becomes, Cory fulfills each aspect of the goddess. Veiled in the second half of the novel to conceal her growing age, she recalls Isis, the goddess of Sais, veiled to conceal the power of her being. Cory possesses the power of witnessing; she speaks for Vovoka, as he has spoken for her. Together they mutually justify the other. But if Cory is the central character of the novel, similar in her function to Greta, she and Greta are quite different, above all in the way that Greta is active in her novel whereas Cory is remarkably passive after Vovoka shoots her. Each novel has its maintainers, its entertainers, and its destroyers; and various masochistic and sadistic relations arise from these groups.

This remark leads us to suspect that the two novels are not only similar in terms of place and time and characters. Though this chapter shall concentrate upon Tiptree's novel, I have found it fruitful to approach its themes through those of Leiber's earlier work. Both are concerned with theatricality and masks. Both are concerned with the human reaction to beauty, in Tiptree generating a highly symbolic use of colors, and both are concerned with violence. Both are concerned with resurrection; but the resurrections in *The Big Time*, although quite literal, are also highly metaphoric, given Leiber's interest in the nature of the imagination, whereas the resurrections in *Brightness Falls from the Air* are extremely ambiguous in nature. This theme of resurrection is associated with the theme of changing time, handled very differently in the two works but in each embodied by the imagery of wind—the change winds in one novel and the time-flurries in the other. There are, of course, major differences. Perhaps the greatest is that for Leiber the existence of the past, often a past that is other than the reader's past, is slight, despite his invention of the Conservation of Reality, whereas for Tiptree the past exists and returns with a vengeance, a rigorous, moral and mortal force.

This existence of the past in Tiptree's novel may not seem so evident at first, since the novel is written thoroughly in present tense. This stylistic decision may be understood in a number of ways. The present tense is often used to indicate habitual actions, such as, "Every Friday James visits the grocery." In *Brightnesss Falls from the Air*, especially in the early chapters, several actions are habitual, whether those are the actions of the station-maintainers or the actions of the entertainers. Even the violent characters, masked as they are by their assumed roles, assume the air of habituality. The other use of the present tense, however, is in the stage-directions of a script and the experience of the audience who see the action now. The effect in a novel is ambiguous. On the one hand it suggests a remarkable intimacy, perhaps owing to its suggestion of habitual action. On the other hand, owing to the fact that very few novels are written in present tense, the style seems arch, contrived, or artificial, a distancing device. I do not believe, however, that the reader receives any indication that dissolves the ambiguity; we are on our own, and this effect leads to a cumulative sense of unease as we read the work, an unease that is at work long before the grotesque violence erupts. Two other uses of the present tense in a normal novel are important here. On the one hand the present tense can indicate an intensification of the action and an increase in tempo. We may not notice this subtle effect in Tiptree, as the action moves from the habitual to the violent, but the effect suggests that violence is habitual. On the other hand, as an intensification, the present tense may also suggest a sense of awe at the sublime; and this use is clearly at work as the narrator describes the streamers of the murdered star or the beauty of the Dameii. But again a reader may feel ill at ease as the persistent present tense suggests that the sublime is at work in an habitual violence that is, as it were, mere theater. In the first chapters Cory and her husband Kip seem to be at home, but we are not at home.

In contrast to this present tense in Tiptree's novel, *The Big Time* is written in a jaunty, confidential first-person narrative that certainly conveys a sense of personal phobias, but these are not actuated for the reader until later in the narrative. The reader is asked in the first chapter to recall existential moments of unease, but such moments are not realized in the action, which despite the latent and actual violence of the work remains basically comic in style. The narrator, Greta, a tough party-girl from Chicago (where, coincidentally, the young Alice Sheldon a.k.a. James Tiptree, Jr. lived as a child when not traveling in Africa with her parents), cannot be overwhelmed by the action—Greta is too tough—and her attitude is conveyed by her style. Sid, the Elizabethan poet and playwright, exercising his authority broadly, is in charge of the Place, but she is in charge of the narrative.

Greta is, of course, very much masked by her style, for she is a more profound personality than the party-girl she announces herself to be on the first page. Every person in the novel is theatrical, wearing a mask. "A Demon is always an actor; no matter how much he believes in what he's saying," Greta remarks (84). Cut off from their natural times and places, transposed from their former contexts, each of the characters assumes something of the theatrical; the river-boat gambler, the Elizabethan writer, the poet from the Great War, the Roman soldier, and the devotee of the Great Mother are none of them natural when juxtaposed with one another. The aliens, cut off from their times, merely wear a costume. And even Erich the Nazi, responsible for the deaths of thousands in Chicago where Greta had lived when truly alive, is at least a Nazi with flare. He could very well be played by Conrad Veidt, the former German actor, whose greatest role was the somnambulist in *Das Kabinet des Doktor Caligaris*. Hollywood chose him to play the essential Nazi in *Casablanca*. The other women besides Greta are Maud, "the Old Girl, and Lili—the New Girl," (9) as Greta says in her introduction, in addition to Kaby from old Crete and the ghostgirls. To establish character, every person, except the ghostgirls who do not have a persona, has a monologue that flaunts his or her theatricality.

The theatricality of the characters in *Brightness Falls from the Air* is more complex, but in certain ways it is more thoroughgoing. Baram tries to play the role of a father to Linnix, who desires to play the role of a daughter; and each in their attempts knows that they are accepting a life that may be incestuous. At the least this life shall be a theater upon which they are mutually agreed. They shall achieve that Shakespearian couplet: "And so I lie with her, and she with me, / And in our faults by lies we flattered be" (Sonnet 138). The villains hide themselves behind various innocuous personas, the most striking of which is the jolly and intelligent Doctor Ari, limping and jesting his way through the early events of the novel, wearing a harness as painful as any that Lon Chaney created for his role as Quasimodo, a "mask of pathos" (372). More obscure and shattering is Ser Vovoka, who makes hardly any attempt to conceal his tragic nature, but no one can guess how tragic his fate is; and at the climax of the novel he first removes a literal mask from his face and then, more profoundly, removes his head by blowing it away to reveal the true nothingness of a creature that is the last of his race. This first act of violence in the novel also reveals the centrality of the mask in the work. These are the *sparagmoi* we cannot escape. And this is before we learn as readers how the Dameii have been tortured.

But no character is what he or she seems. Prince Pao, certainly a bit of a peacock (Portuguese *pao* means "peacock"), turns out to be a much more efficient and dazzling individual than his age or his position would seem to indicate. The troupe of *The Absolutely Perfect Commune* is much more complexly characterized than conventional clichés of a pornographic theater might suggest; and the different names they bear, their given names and their stage names, also remind the reader of how pervasive the theme of the mask is to this novel. Their contractor, Zannez, is a much more intuitive character than a zany, but in the climactic scene he acts the role of a zany when he jostles the mutilated body of Ari in front of him; though he "looks frighteningly like an ancient picture of the Lord of Evil carrying the damned to Hell," the text reminds us that he has "done the actor's magic of face and body change" (287). As the chapter puts it, he has simply acted in "The Gridworld Way" (280).

I repeat, no character is what he or she seems. Kip and Cory, presented as the peaks of normality and health at the beginning of the work, have profound problems they cannot admit. Kip likes to dramatize himself, suggesting that he has experienced events that were never his; and at the end of the novel he fails to accept the Cory who has become old in only a few hours. His moral failure condemns the young man who had seemed, at the beginning of the novel, so self-assured. More profoundly, Cory realizes that the life she lived upon the station masked her past in which, as a young spacer, she undertook to murder a race for the sake of an infatuation. She wears, however, another mask, one that the novel suggests every individual wears, the mask of health and youth, which is the mask of life; for at the end of the novel, as her youth and health are stripped from her, she can no longer hide the fact that she is an old woman about to die, about to ask for the phrase of release, "Green, go." The correlative to her situation is the situation of the alien Dameii, the incarnation of beauty throughout the novel; that beauty, however, is revealed to be false, something bestowed once upon the Vlyrocochans, the race that Cory slew, but only bestowed upon the Dameii now until the nova front passes and they are revealed to be the insectoids they always were, no longer "angels" (59) but merchants. *La beauté du diable* always fades away, but not to become an angel. In this novel neither humans nor aliens are allowed to wear the masks that have seemed to them and to the reader habitual.

Though Alice Sheldon always disapproved of any attention paid to the author rather than the work, it is useful in appreciating this novel to note that she had recently undergone the "shattering" experience of having the mask of Tiptree removed ("A Woman Writing Science Fiction" 390). Her first comments are nonchalant, but after a few years she began to miss the persona Tiptree had afforded her—"All my wonderful anonymity is gone," she lamented ("Contemporary Authors Interview" 350)—and to miss the kinds of themes that Tiptree seemed to make available, especially the theme of violence. With considerable ambivalence she wrote, around the time that she had begun *Brightness Falls from the Air*, "A woman writing of the joy and terror of furious combat, or of the lust of torture and killing, or of the violent forms of evil—isn't taken quite seriously. Because women aren't as capable of violent physical assault—not to speak of rape—as men are" ("Contemporary Authors Interview" 351).

She loses a very useful amoral credibility when she loses the phallic name of Tiptree, even though, in a passage she deleted, she later felt that the mask had established its own identity and will ("Contemporary Authors Interview" 370). Yet in this novel the most manic violence is committed by Bridey when, "her naked young body mounted on the bar, her white arms flashing like avenging lightning," she hurls one knife after another into Hiner and Ochter, "making their bodies quiver and convulse" (290) in an imitation of sexual climax. Considerable other violence is committed in the novel: the off-stage torture, Vovoka's grotesque suicide, the mutilation of Ari's legs and hands, Baram's ripping the poisonous scorpion from Linnix's neck, Zannez's tossing about Ari's body like a doll. Bridey's performance is the consequence, peak, and catharsis of the novel's violence; transformed into a many-armed Hindu goddess of death, she is more and less than human, and she needs Zannez's arms around her and his comforting voice to return her to her human state. The violence suffered by Patrolman-Tech First-Class Valkyr, who is not a woman, in the denouement of the novel is purely a part of the incidental violence that happens in the incidental world (354).

Violence is present in Leiber's novel, but it is more low-key than this scene. Kaby slaps Maud across the face "in a matter-of-fact way" that makes Greta sick to the stomach because it is a cold, casual violence that promises more to come, turning the woman inside-out in the Invertor (109). At the end of the novel Greta nurses a black eye from Erich, which he had given her after she had clawed him across the face—a violence that is much more emotional than the cold-blooded violence with which the group threatens Maud. Leiber's point would seem to be that mob violence is much more false than the violence that leaps from individual emotion. These acts of violence are overshadowed by the threat of the "tiny tactical atomic bomb" (50) that Erich arms. Nevertheless, except for this nod to the mass destruction threatened in the atomic age, violence is a less important theme for Leiber in this novel than it is for Tiptree.

Speaking more broadly of the theme of violence, we recognize that both novels concern war. In *The Big Time* the war is ongoing with no end in sight, a violence realized in Kaby's description of the sea-battle near Crete, made even more violent with the presence of the alien time-travelers; this violence is connected to the anxiety that the characters feel, fighting on the side of the Snakes but ruefully confessing that they have no idea whether they are on the right side. But be they right or be they wrong, they do handle the possibility of mass violence with the object Kaby announces in her chant: "It is nothing but a tiny tactical atomic bomb" (50), which Erich soon arms. This contemporary terror, however, is nothing to the planet-destroyer that Cory used in the past, which has destroyed a race and their magnificent art work, although it is clear that this science fiction trope points also at our contemporary terror. Sheldon shared her husband's anxiety that nuclear war had every chance of destroying humanity (Phillips 208).

At the end of Tiptree's novel, as Cory is dying, she reclaims her life through the intuition that "there are patterns, where I didn't know patterns were" (372). In a novel remarkable for its studied emotional intensity, unexpected violence, and concentrated action, it may be difficult at first to comprehend the patterns that bind it together, even beyond Cory's comprehension, but a study of them leads to a greater appreciation of the art, the suspect art—at least in the eyes of Alice Sheldon—and the themes of the novel.

II

This is a novel of brightness, not only of physical brightness but of moral brightness also; so let us consider the colors that we find in the novel. There are blues, most often as cerulean and azure. Gold and silver often form a pair in Stareem and Bridey. Emerald, vermilion, turquoise, amethyst, and violet are rich, deep colors. Purple is an important color connected with the arachnoid avray, "meaning doom or horror" (18), a color connected with Vovoka, whose actual skin is "a dusty-looking, pebbled, drab purple" (191), and connected with the treacherous bottle of a soporific that Ochter gives the company; the avray is in fact harmless, but doom does befall the company in the persons of Vovoka and Ochter. In a comic mode Kip swears by "the nine purple devils" (177). There is very little brown in the book, such a dull color, but black and silver form another pair in Paralomena's mount Comet and in Comet II and comets. There is opalescent and pearl. There is a planet called Rainbow's End, from which the two sisters come, and a remarkable variety of rainbows. The two colors most important in the novel, however, are red and green, with meanings reminiscent of contemporary signage. Red means stop or danger. Green means go or the permission to go, and the word allows Cory to die in the last sentence of the novel.

Another pattern that Cory may or may not see is pairing. Stareem and Bridey are dressed in the opposites of silver and gold. Star—whose real name, Sharon Roeback (344), may refer to erotic moments in the Song of Solomon— is asleep during the violence; but Bridey's violence concludes the crisis. Their partners Hanno and Snake are a gay couple, though in Zannex's film they perform heterosexual fantasies. Pardalianches, whose name suggests the pard/leopard and haunches (24), grips and rides her sister, not the thighs of the horse Comet; the lovely name of her sister Paralomena suggests the Greek verb "paraluein," to loosen from the side, or the adjective "paralutikos," paralytic. Two pairings suggestive of the Electra complex are those of Linnix and Bram, and Cory and Yaeger, in both cases a semi-incestuous relation that must be regarded dubiously. Cory's infatuation for Yaeger, "hunter," is truly disastrous; the mutual infatuation of Linnix and Bram may portend a threat for her in the future insofar as he will be the only person in her future who knows that she has died. Since he himself, and only he himself, recognizes that danger, is not the only moral act possible for him a renunciation? Or is he too fond? And is she truly as infatuated as he, or is it only the infatuation she brings with her in her search for her unknown father? And will she love him as much, the more she becomes drawn into that quest from which he withholds her?

As we have seen in these few cases, the naming of these characters is often significant. Cory's actual name is Corrison, which sounds like Corazon, heart or courage; as we have seen she is a kore, a young girl: but she is a married woman who has no children, perhaps because of her "muffled" state (374), and an old woman who dies in the place of Linnix (linnet, an old-world finch, or flax). A passage near the end of the novel suggests a connection between Cory the old woman and Linnix the bird, mediated by these lines in Yeats's "Sailing to Byzantium":

> An aged man is but a paltry thing,
> A tattered coat upon a stick, unless
> Soul clap its hands and sing, and louder sing
> For every tatter in its mortal dress [. . .] (193)

Cory thinks to herself, "All they can see is this rotting body; I'm perched in it like a bird in an old tree" (373); Sheldon was fond of Yeats (Phillips 156, 348). It is possible that Cory's death will loosen one more hold that Linnix's death has on reality. As for Kip, a kip is a rooming house or inn, a room to sleep, sleep itself—indeed, Kip asks himself shortly before the crisis erupts, "Have I been asleep?" (185). If so, it is a sleep that involves most of his life on Damiem, because after the war he had felt "that was over now. This stuff he didn't want to know" (185). That is to say, his sleep is culpable because it was willed, though that culpability is shared by his society, which refers to the war as The Last War; we recognize the irony because we are aware of what came of our War to End All Wars. The sleep also involves the first half of the novel, in which seven of the first twelve chapters are told from his point of view, a sleep the reader is therefore forced to share.

Ser Vovoka does move with a nobility that proceeds from his certainty that he has discovered his goal, having evoked the murdered star and the entity that inhabits it. Zannez recalls "zany" and "John"—his name on the one hand points at his profession, but on the other hand masks his true seriousness and ability; he is an actor, a professional actor, but he is no zany. Is he a John the Baptist, a forerunner who makes the way smooth for the Christ of the novel? That Christ is Paralomena, helpless in her crib and cared for by her sorrowing sister/mother in a scene that recalls the manger and the tomb, because she suffers a resurrection for a short time that initiates the others' salvation.

Mordecai, in the book of Esther, is the queen's pious relative who becomes the main target of Haman's planned genocide; and yule is the traditional English word for Christmas, the coldest time of the year—a word that Eric Partridge connects with the word "cold, gelid" (817). Mordecai Yule would seem to be a mask for that murderer. Nathaniel means gift of God and is one of the apostles, but Hiner suggests heinie or Heinrich. Aristrides means born of the best, but his nickname Ari may be suggestive in retrospect of Herod. But Ochter? Ocher, or octet perhaps? I think we are called upon to hear the resemblance of the name to the word Achtung, "Pay attention, danger!" But he is too good an actor and they do not pay attention to the man who looks like a gnome (32), a creature who would turn away from the glory in the sky.

The possibility that the three villains are in some fashion a blasphemous allusion to the three magi should alert a reader to a number of works to which Tiptree's novel responds. If, for instance, it is responding to the Christmas myth, which versions are at play here? Only the gospel of Matthew tells the story of the three magi, the three nameless wise men, and the story of the slaughter of the innocents. The names of Balthasar, Melchior, and Gaspar are traditional, dating from the eighth century. Modern versions of the myth involving them are *Ben-Hur* and *Amahl and the Night Visitors*. Wallace's novel is especially pertinent, with its famous chariot race that concludes with two men who should be brothers in a murderous competition, which leaves one of them in a semi-death and the other released to resurrect his sister. The novel opens with the meeting of the three wise men; but one of them stands out because he is later present at the crucifixion, Balthasar the Egyptian, who is described as "of admirable proportions, not so tall as powerful" (19), with thereby a rough resemblance to Tiptree's Ochter, the "small tufty gray-haired gnome" (24) who turns out to be quite strong in his upper body. With some irony the name "Balthasar" is given to Bram in Tiptree's novel. These three wise men do not bring gold, frankincense, and myrrh, but Ochter brings a very valuable gift, the Eglantine, a sweet briar with hooked spines, that masks his lust for the infinitely more valuable drug Stars Tears and that is an exudate like myrrh; the algotoxin he brings is also a horrendous gift, hooking into Linnix's neck with overwhelming pain. Wallace describes the angels at the birth in great particularity. What is merely "the glory of the Lord" (Luke 2:9) in *Ben-Hur* excites the cry of the shepherd, "The sky is on fire!" (61). The

Dameii fulfill this role in Tiptree's work pervasively, as Linnix asks in fumbling words, "What can you say when you see real live actual angels?" (59). In the story of the wise men the remarkable detail is the star that guides them. As he does with the angels, Wallace describes in detail the star's "roseate electrical splendor (58).

Wallace excludes the story of the slaughter of the innocents that Matthew tells so powerfully, transposing it to the destruction of the house of Hur:

> Then Herod, when he saw that he was mocked of the wise men, was exceeding wroth, and sent forth, and slew all the children that were in Bethlehem, and in all the coasts thereof, from two years old and under, according to the time which he had diligently enquired of the wise men. Then was fulfilled that which was spoken by Jeremy the prophet, saying, In Rama was there a voice heard, lamentation, and weeping, and great mourning, Rachel weeping for her children, and would not be comforted, because they were not. (Luke 2:16-18)

Tiptree makes the torture of a child and her death the great crime. But she climaxes the theme of the star, the great mystery in the Bible, in Vovoka's expostulation: "Enslaver! Radiant enchanter! Killer of worlds from none knows where—" (191), words reminiscent of Oppenheimer's quotation from the *Bhagavad-Gita* at the explosion of the first atomic bomb: "I am become Death, the shatterer of worlds" (Jungk 201). The star, perhaps the central icon of science fiction, is fused here with the Christmas star and nuclear destruction.

The possibility that the novel plays with the Christmas myth becomes even more certain when we examine another work to which the novel responds, Arthur C. Clarke's famous short story "The Star." Here also in the face of its racial death an alien race builds a monument to itself, a monument that emphasizes its aesthetic triumphs; at least those are the elements of the monument to which the Jesuit narrator of the story reacts. It is not simply that the race is wise and good, it is beautiful and creates beauty; but it dies in a supernova that has become the star of the Christmas story. In his close analysis William A. Quinn points out that in Clarke's story we are facing either a natural accident in an indifferent universe or a God who becomes a mass murderer in the slaughter of the innocents (46). In Tiptree's novel God's culpability is shifted to the ease with which humanity resorts to murderous violence, even so engaging a woman as Cory.

In addition, through a free-floating irony that Clarke leaves difficult to resolve, the star lies within the Phoenix nebula (518). The narrator alludes to the irony but does not bother to point out that the Phoenix, which every thousand years builds its nest, burns, and rises from the ashes, during the Middle Ages became a traditional symbol of Christ's resurrection. In this story, however, which takes place a thousand years after the founding of the order of Jesuits to which the narrator belongs, the Phoenix seems to symbolize the end of his order. They have not destroyed the race, but it is involved in "the glory of God's handiwork" (517). In Tiptree's novel, the race of Vlyracocha builds a monument to the beauty that has leached and destroyed them. The young Cory's attack that triggers a nova in the star and releases its beauty to the galaxy, taking part in God's handiwork, destroys the race but does no more than release the race from its obsession; it does not announce a new deity to the world, but it does announce a new, terrifying entity. "A terrible beauty is born" (Yeats 180). In Leiber's novel we do not find the intimate connection of the star and the destruction of an alien, overwhelmingly beautiful race; the novel is, however, occupied with an ambivalent situation in which the demons, very aware of the seduction of changing the world through their time travel, their complicity with the change winds, finds them also horrified at their casual wiping out of different lands and cultures.

A further work to which Tiptree's novel may respond quite crucially is H. P. Lovecraft's "The Colour out of Space," which in some aspects parodies the Christian story. At the fall of the stone from outer space, which the narrator attempts to identify as either a meteor or a comet, three wise men from Miskatonic University come to test its nature (57); but their attempt is hopeless. At first the farm is as beautiful as a garden—the name of its owner is Gardner—almost as beautiful as the Garden of Eden; but it soon grays and disintegrates. At the climax of the story the beautiful entity in the stone tears away from the earth and moves into the heavens to bring its message elsewhere. It remains impossible, however, to define that entity or its purposes. It plays out as though it mimicked the emptying of Christ in the incarnation and his glorification after the resurrection (Phil. 2:5-11). The only hope for the humans that remain, like Ammi, is that the reservoir that shall drown the valley shall drown whatever remains of the entity, but the surveyor who narrates the story leaves the nature of the threat inconclusive at the end of the work; the innocuous lake that lies north of Cory's station would have enabled the aquaman Hiner to overload the power-cell and destroy the station and every evidence of the great crime (342).

In Tiptree's novel the history of the Vlyracocha, whose planet Cory had destroyed when a cabin girl, receives a new interpretation. Their planet had been invaded by a beautiful entity, "a seed from space" (210), that sucked the people dry of hope, leaving them lost in desire and compelling them to build a monument that gathers up all their achievement, through which it would go forth into the galaxy, "feeding . . . reproducing" (210). The beautiful, indescribable colors that have flooded the skies of Damiem have made the planet gorgeous, like "an enchanted garden" (370), and the Dameii beautiful, like angels, leaving them like the semi-insects they had been before the skies blossomed; and there is some question whether the entity represented by the colors shall now "infect other planets" (370). Lovecraft would have appreciated the various ironies of the color that displays itself as the nova front gains its fullest expression, when "a feeling of something huge and alien and unnameable coming onto them grips the watchers on the deck" (177).

With the works of Wallace, Clarke, and Lovecraft in mind it becomes possible for the reader to understand that Tiptree is in the novel playing off the story of Christ in a variety of ways, most of them ironic, just as Lovecraft did so consciously. But she is not developing an allegory. It rather seems that with Clarke's story as one of the seeds of her plot she used the Christmas story as an opportunity for a series of witty variations, all of which we need to take seriously as a part of the moral judgment that her novel slowly develops.

It is impossible to detail all the materials of the Christian story that Tiptree uses. Here is Eden, Christmas and Crucifixion, heaven and hell (287), angels (58) and devils, many devils, and demons (287); the three kings who bring their gifts of gold, frankincense, and myrrh, mainly represented by the Eglantine which Doctor Ochter presents. In Keats's "Ode to a Nightingale" "eglantine" provides a rhyme for "wine" in a stanza quite loaded with a number of significant associations, followed by the stanza so important for Tiptree, "in love with easeful Death" (371). The drink is purple, the color of Stars Tears, and seems contained in a purple bottle, banned by the Federation, wrapped in gold paper; but the gifts of the magi are most truly represented by what the three men mean to take, the Stars Tears, an unguent or balm-like substance scraped from the backs of the Dameii just as frankincense and myrrh are resin-like gums that drip from trees. The Stars Tears represents real gold, cold cash, to Ochter, Hiner, and Yule. We have here the brilliant star, the slaughter of the innocents, the outcast nuclear family of Wyrra, Juiyn, and Nyil. Finally, we have here the "Nunc Dimittis" that Cory speaks for herself as "green, Go" (375) and the face that she sees on the cross. The fabled phrase "In hoc signo vinces" comes to mind, the vision of a cross in the sky that Constantine had, hearing those words as he rode to the final battle with his counterpart in the west; Cory wins through the sign of the crosslines on her gun as she fires at the monument: "*That face . . . it slowly formed as I aimed—it wasn't there at first. . . . Beauty. Transcendence—no words. And I aimed and fired . . . right between the eyes*" (198). For this Cory suffers the fate of the Wandering Jew who when he strikes Jesus carrying the cross and says, "Go faster Jesus, go faster, why dost thou linger?" is answered, "I indeed am going, but thou shalt linger until I return" (Percy 2.22). In a similar way

Cory strikes the face of the entity, the beauty that transcends all words, dismissing it, and is forced to wait for its return in glory on Damiem to be released from the burden of her unconscious guilt.

But the Christian story also demands a resurrection. Paralomena is resurrected by Baram's repetition of the word "comet," which had been the name of the horse that destroyed her; she is resurrected, that is to say, by her love for the horse, dead long ago, so that her resurrection can cause enough chaos for Baram to move into action against the murderers. But her resurrection causes her true death, ripping her from the bed to which she is attached by an intricate life-support system that most of the characters except her sister regard as a mockery of life. But there are other resurrections in the novel, almost all of them at the least ambiguous. The motto to the novel, taken from a poem by Kipling, warns that the "Abominations of old days" can be raised from the dead (13); to emphasize the point, the words are repeated as the title of a chapter (61). Another chapter is titled "Baramji Summons the Dead," as he resurrects Comet in Paralomena's mind in order to resurrect her. When Cory remembers her firing at the star it is "as though ghosts are breaking through deep burial in her mind" (196). This inescapable past that demands resurrection is liable to hurt horribly.

III

In dealing with these books by Tiptree and Leiber it is impossible not to address the way they seem most similar, their positing of the change winds and the time-flurries. Kip's explanation of the time-flurries is quite bland: "You see a running backward of things that have just happened [. . .], like replaying a scene [. . .], and we don't think it took up actual time" (114-15). It is an unexpected, theatrical, impossible experience outside of time. Ser Vovoka's account is at first pedantic, but it becomes more passionate:

> It is perhaps not too biomorphic to say that the formerly organized matter does not yet "believe" in its disorganization; that the shadowy persistence of its former state—its memory, if you like—is so strong it can distort the local time-flow. It generates turbulence in a backward direction, as though the debris strove to reassemble, to reexist in that last instant before the catastrophe, when perhaps it could have been averted. (116)

Is this too biomorphic a language? Bram's language is more urgent: "It's as if some personal enemy keeps trying to return and kill her, using now her very mind. [. . .] The force of that other reality is pressing on her, pressing her to know herself dead" (334-35). Matter in all its inertia desires to remain as it was, "as if" it were a living being torn to shreds, still possessed of the memory and the will and the power to undo its undoing, "as though" all creation lived and died within the existential state of choice. It wishes to remain, to be as it was. This language bestows life on Newton's first law of motion, which is the law of inertia. But this inertia, which seems to argue for life, is under the sign of Thanatos, the human urge to repeat and to repeat itself. Resurrection does not save the demons from the repeated pains that their other suffers, as Lili recounts (89). She uses a different language later: "I was more alive than I ever had been before, but it was the kind of life a corpse might get from unending electrical shocks" (91). Greta says it is like an alcoholic, getting a stiff shot from the change winds (80, 115). Linnix and the scorpion of algotoxin have an affinity to come together once more to perform the pain of her death; if it cannot find her, she will unknowingly find it.

The change winds and the time-flurries represent a complex group of psychic urges with which we are only too familiar. I have already dealt with them in an earlier work (*The Monster in the Mirror* 118-19, 260-61) and do not mean to deal with them at great length here. The simple point is that *Trägheit*, inertia, the power and apparent desire of matter to remain at rest, and *Nachträglichkeit*, the deferred reaction of a trauma, its desire to repeat itself in a new pain and a new understanding, seem to be rather similar. The Conservation of Reality that Leiber's characters suffer and the compulsion of matter to reconstitute and resurrect itself that Linnix suffers are two variations of the same will of the individual to be crucified in the matter of the world. The great difference in the winds is Leiber's assertion that art is the best means to resist the change winds, perhaps because the change winds create the matter by which art is made (31, 128)

Does Leiber in any way refer to the Christian myth? Words connected with that myth permeate the novel, such as Demons and Resurrection; but Leiber has already in his career used the vocabulary and hierarchy of the religion to cloak a very different intent. I suppose the three wise men are represented by the Luna octopus Ilhilihis, who utters the words of wisdom in the denouement of the novel; the satyr Sevensee, half goat or horse and half human; and the bardic Cretan Kabysia Labris, with "a face like a beautiful arrowhead" (38), who given her antiquity is almost as alien as the other two—and this antiquity is the measure in time, a billion years in the past and a billion years in the future, of how far in space these aliens have come in order to dispense some wisdom and also in order to set down the chest that contains a "tiny tactical atomic bomb." Incarnate in power, this is a Christ-child with a vengeance.

Did Alice Sheldon ever read Fritz Leiber? I don't know. "A fan for forty years" before she began to write science fiction (Phillips 158), she read deeply in the field, and anyone interested in the genre would have been aware of *The Big Time*, which received the Hugo in 1958. More compelling to me is the subliminal conversation that these two deeply wounded individuals seem to have conducted through these two novels. In his life Leiber suffered from several episodes of alcoholic anaesthesia; and Sheldon suffered from several episodes of depression, concluding late in life with her suicide. Despite their armors, each suffered more pain than is bearable, worse than algotoxin, though each bore the pain resolutely through long years. Theater, masks, violence, myth and inertia, despite great beauty these are symptoms of such pain.

Despite, however, the deaths we deal out so callously, to others and to ourselves, we still dream of our resurrections.

The Deeps of Eryx

H. P. Lovecraft may not have often written science fiction, though he was interested in its nature and what we should expect of it. One of the last stories he wrote, in conjunction with his young friend Kenneth Sterling, "In the Walls of Eryx," was forthrightly science fiction, and that is the last story I wish to deal with; it is one of the least addressed stories in the canon of Lovecraft's works. But I do not wish to deal with the story for that reason only; for though the story is no doubt meant to fulfill the genre of science fiction, it has problems that seem to pull it back into the world of the weird tale and into tragedy. In the first part of this essay I mean to deal with earlier stories that are much closer to the narratives I have looked at in this book. These are narratives in which the tragic tradition shows forth unmistakably, the tragic arc and the tragic resolution: The proverbial adage, "Through pain we learn," and the exhortation on the entrance to the temple of the Delphic oracle, "Know yourself," appear in several of the Greek tragedies. Often, however, the protagonists learn such things only at the last moment.

This chapter is, as the reader may well imagine, an epilogue to the collection, but I have already indulged in a few epilogues.

I

Important as the stories seem to me that reverberate in the tragic mode, Lovecraft wrote in fact only a few of them, "Dagon" in 1917 was an early study in tragedy. The first story that truly expresses this view is "The Call of Cthulhu" in 1926, followed in 1927 by the novella *The Case of Charles Dexter Ward* and by "The Colour out of Space," and in 1928 by "The Dunwich Horror." Four more tragedies follow after two years pass, "The Whisperer in Darkness" in 1930, *At the Mountains of Madness* in 1931, "The Shadow over Innsmouth" in the same year, and "The Shadow out of Time" in 1934-35. I will not necessarily deal with them in this order. He wrote many other stories of course, several of them quite good, but none of them have the relentless motion that these eight have in which the small size of humanity is played out against tremendous, alien forces in an immense universe. Moreover, this immense universe belongs to Lovecraft, at once horrifying him and exhilarating him; he imagines before Hubble's discoveries that it is expanding.

"Dagon" is the first story in which a man is destroyed by unknown forces, cast out onto a swelling ocean that is a symbol of the infinite universe, but it does not seem to contain such horrors at first. The narrator cleverly escapes captivity from a German destroyer early in the war when "the ocean forces of the Hun had not completely sunk to their later degradation" (*Dagon* 14), just as he had not yet sunk to the degradation of morphine. But in this story nothing sinks. Instead, the narrator sees no land or ship to rescue him from "the heaving vastness of unbroken blue" (15) until one night the ocean rises to present him "a slimy expanse of hellish black mire which extended about me in monotonous undulations" (15). This is the rhetoric of the rest of the story, and a rhetoric to which Lovecraft often returns. The blue "heaving vastness" is revealed to be no more than the "undulations" of "hellish black mire." Even worse, however, is the black canyon he discovers that reminds him of the first and second books of Milton's *Paradise Lost*, of "a fathomless chaos of eternal night" (16), of Satan's climb through the space of Chaos, of pandemonium, and of Satan himself, for the Dagon, or Polyphemus, that the narrator sees is as large as Satan who "Prone on the Flood, extended large and long, / Lay floating many a rood" (*PL* 1.195-96). Given this use of Milton, probably through the art of Doré (*Dagon* 18), whom Lovecraft greatly admired (*Selected Letters* 2.219-20; 5.335), it is not surprising that Dagon fills a place in the great catalogue of the devils that became idols:

> *Dagon* his name, Sea Monster, *upward* Man
> And downward Fish: yet had his Temple high
> Rear'd in *Azotus* dreaded through the Coast
> Of *Palestine*, in *Gath* and *Ascolon*,
> And *Accaron* and *Gaza*'s frontier bounds. (*PL* 1.462-66)

This is a conflation of monsters, not to be gainsaid.

Perhaps as important as these details is the mount that the protagonist decides he must climb, introducing mountain imagery that has already been important in these chapters; this mountain allows this narrator to look down into the canyon, slopping in water that lies on the other side. I will not describe his climb as he "started for the crest of the eminence," a language that is verging on the numinous; but here he discovers below the cliff and the monolith the worshipper of the monolith, the creature that casts him into the madness from which he will die, throwing himself "into the squalid street below" (*Dagon* 14).

As we have said, many of these works present a challenge in language and style, just as David Lindsay does; but Lovecraft presents this problem also. He is not the only writer of his generation, nor the only writer of weird tales, who exhibits this problem; consider writers like Clark Ashton Smith or Robert E. Howard, for whom the exotic name meant precisely that, the Exotic. But Lovecraft is little interested in the Exotic, so in time he has come to remain more problematic than they. One of our problems, for instance, as readers, has been how we shall pronounce the name of Cthulhu and, more importantly, what we are to make of the name within the framework of the English langauge that we share with Lovecraft.

The first problem is not so great because of Lovecraft's conscious thematization of the problem. Human throats, he argues, cannot pronounce a word that originates in an alien mind and throat. Cthulhu, then, is only an approximation of the word (*Selected Letters* 5.10-11). Hence the game that so many fans indulge in, questioning one another how we pronounce the name. Lovecraft teases us when he offers us such possibilities as Clooloo and Tulu in "Medusa's Coil" and "The Mound." Each person has a favorite pronunciation, though some may be more correct than others. In any case, each of us is accused by our various inabilities.

But stepping out of that game, how are we to interpret such words as Cthulhu, R'lyeh, or Yog-Sothoth within the framework of the English tradition, or, perhaps more correctly since the word is foreign to English, we should look at our foreign words. Zulu springs to mind immediately, as it looks back to Lovecraft's racism. Another possibility is the hungry owls in Coleridge's *Christabel*, which almost wake up the crows, calling out "*Tu–whit!– Tu–whoo!*" (215). The animal cry may be a version of the alien. In R'lyeh we may hear "rill" or "real," which suggests that R'lyeh is definitely a challenge to the world as we know it, though these are strikingly pleasant sounds in "r," "l," and "ia." It is thus in contrast to the difficult sound of Cthulhu. And Yog-Sothoth goes in a different direction, suggesting Arabic or Hebraic sounds.

It is not, however, simply a problem in how we shall pronounce the exotic tongue. It is a problem of how we shall pronounce the tongue that has become ancient or marginal. This is the tongue that the old man in "The Picture in the House" speaks. Joseph Curwen speaks it in his letters. Zadok Allen speaks it. Old Castro would speak it if the narrator did not render it in indirect discourse. This tongue that Lovecraft is so fond of seems to presage such books as *The Sotweed Factor* and *Mason & Dixon*, albeit with very different aims in mind.

"The Call of Cthulhu" calls out of dreams and out of the ocean. The only heroes in the story are those protagonists, sharing their heroisms, who are aware of the danger to the world and also aware of the danger to them individually; and indeed each of them dies. Thurston has died, for nothing is left of him but his papers; Professor Angell's death is announced on the second page of the story; and Johansen has died before Thurston can consult him. Each is a post mortem, as though he has never lived. But it is Thurston who scours the seas and the papers. Professor Angell is too old, Johansen too rough and foreign. Only Thurston, the lightning bolt of Thor, seems to be of an age like Lovecraft to gather and collate the material; and only Thurston is given the space and time to bear the long, complex quest, though he will not survive it.

These protagonists as well as other important figures cross the waters. Wilcox, one of the few artists in Lovecraft's canon, dreams and recounts his dreams to Professor Angell. Inspector Legrasse recounts to Angell his crossing the waters, "the swamp and lagoon country to the south" (*Dunwich Horror* 136), that is to say the complex delta at the mouth of the Mississippi. At the death of the captain and first mate, Gustaf Johansen becomes the captain of the *Emma* and of the *Alert*, an interesting transformation, crossing the Pacific to confront Cthulhu; and Thurston crosses the Atlantic to hear Johansen's story directly. But Johansen has died. Near the Gothenburg dock "a bundle of papers falling from an attic window had knocked him down" (149), while the help of "two Lascar sailors" had proved no help, rather like the fate of Professor Angell, who had died near the waterfront in Providence, "jostled by a nautical-looking negro" (126). The waters of darkness are dangerous, but they must be crossed if one is to discover any truth.

The Case of Charles Dexter Ward admonishes the reader that the titular character of the story is not necessarily the protagonist of the work and not its heroic figure. Ward tries to act as the Faust of the work, as a young man venturing down into the "maelstrom of tottering houses" (*Mountains of Madness* 115), "searching out the docks" and later ransacking Europe to find the formulae that would return his dubious ancestor Joseph Curwen to life. Yes, he seems to resemble the Doctor Faustus of Marlowe's play. But he loses the game very early; and in any case he does not gain the twenty-four years that Faustus had bargained for. He is more like the pitiable Wagner, a bit weak and dogmatic, of Goethe's play. It is Curwen who bets his life for an extended life.

Curwen is not, however, simply the Faust; he is the Mephistopheles also, ironic, daring, and larger than life—as Mephistopheles should be, since he is a supernatural being; and Curwen should be larger than life insofar as he has lived through more life than mortal beings have. Of course Curwen is less than life also, since he is nothing more than "a thin coating of fine bluish-grey dust" (234).

It is in the middle of one of Curwen's letters that another theme is broached: "And of ye Seede of Olde shal One be borne who shal looke Backe, tho' *know'g not what he seekes*" (151). Ward is in fact obsessed by looking back and reaching back to bring Curwen forward in time. Only in this aspect does Ward become a tragic hero in attempting to manipulate time; in this manner he represents Lovecraft's own obsessions as a young man. Let us remember that this theme of the manipulation of time is to be found in Stapledon also in each of his major books; Lovecraft and Stapledon run upon parallel tracks in this regard. But they treat this theme in very different ways. "The Shadow out of Time" shall orchestrate this theme more broadly than Curwen does.

Turning to "The Call of Cthulu," we see another way in which Lovecraft and Stapledon encountered each other. Since Lovecraft encountered Stapledon toward the end of his career, we speak of influence at our peril, except in the fate of the fifth race of humanity in *Last and First Men* when the fifth race encounters the Venusians; certainly Lovecraft does meet in Stapledon a man very much of his own mind. He has himself imagined the endless, magical space that lies beyond humanity. This endless space is the background to "The Call of Cthulhu," for the action is dependent upon the time "when the stars were right" (*Dunwich Horror* 140) and the time when they shall be right again. These are "strange aeons" (141), immeasurable times that cannot be measured, and the spaces within which they take place are immeasurable also. In "The Colour out of Space" the phrase "strange days," occurring seven times in the story, possesses a good deal of restraint in the strangeness to which it points, but its repetition is another means by which Lovecraft underlines these different spaces and times. This is a rhetoric that would be impossible for Lovecraft to use if he had not to some extent digested Einsteinian concepts. Those spaces and times are evoked in "The Colour out of Space," those spaces out of which the thing has plunged to destroy Mr. Gardner, "[Ammi's] ill-starred friend" (*Dunwich Horror* 79). What has happened to the narrator of that tale has happened to Lovecraft, and it is this that he wishes to communicate to his readers: "An odd timidity about the deep skyey voids above had crept into my soul" (81).

But to what extent does a sense of the tragic truly rule in the story? One of the most moving passages occurs here: "[Gardner] and the boys continued to use the tainted supply [of the well], drinking it and as listlessly and mechanically as they ate their meagre and ill-cooked meals and did their thankless and monotonous chores through the aimless days. There was something of stolid resignation about them all, as if they walked half in another world between lines of nameless guards to a certain and familiar doom" (66). They have become machines, in a monotonous world that has no surprise in it. They are sufficiently aware of the horror of this world that they have resigned themselves to it. Though these days are aimless, seeming to have no direction, they are nevertheless marching between nameless guards to a "familiar doom," a doom that is familiar to them, something that without any given reason does belong to them. They are indeed the "famuli," the slaves of their farm, not its masters.

But though this doom is familiar to them, have they comprehended it? This is a question we have raised in the past, the extent to which the tragic hero has comprehended not only his or her fate but both the rationality of that comprehension and its intensity. In this regard Oedipus remains our exemplary figure; he cannot escape the pins he has stabbed in his eyes. Against this example Gardner is a pallid man, who can only complain rather helplessly that "it must all be a judgment of some sort; though he could not fancy what for, since he had always walked uprightly in the Lord's ways so far as he knew" (68). This weak theology hardly recognizes the tragic universe that the meteorite announces, "that lone, weird message from other universes and other realms of matter, force, and entity" (60).

We recognize this extent to which the tragic demand that the tragic hero should be intensely aware of the way in which the world fails us, and we recognize why in his world Gardner cannot live up to this demand—he is not Mr. Thurston or Charles Dexter Ward the First, he is not Old Whateley—but we look for signs of this comprehension given the brilliance of the story's structure. If we are to find the center of this tragic comprehension it must lie in the mind of this nameless surveyor who has digested Ammi's story and given it a shape and significance, and who cannot let it loose.

Lovecraft's admiration for Stapledon was so powerful that we cannot let it go. He recommends *Last and First Men* to a number of friends, among them Fritz Leiber, and in his recommendation tries to sketch as Stapledon does the shape of "The next general dark age" (*Selected Letters* 5.357). He does not mention the ecstatic element in Stapledon's thinking because he himself is not interested in the shape of divinity. Later, after Leiber has read the book, Lovecraft expands his judgment of the work: "Its scope is dizzying—" and though some of the science is weak, "it remains a thing of unparalleled power. As you [Leiber] say, it has the truly basic quality of a myth, and some of the episodes are of matchless poignancy and dramatic intensity" (5.375). The scope to which he refers is doubtless Stapledon's acknowledgment of the immensity of the universe in which humanity counts for little; and its mythic and dramatic quality is surely tragic. I would argue that Lovecraft very much appreciated the tragic irony in this description of the Last Man: "He is young, the last born of the Last Men; for he was the latest to be conceived before we learned man's doom, and put an end to all conceiving" (245). A few months before his death Lovecraft still had Stapledon on his mind, before he was himself beyond all conceiving (5.415). To say so, however, is beyond anything that we can truly say.

Let us consider once more our climbing of mountains and our encounters at the peaks. Only in "The Dunwich Horror" and "The Whisperer in the Darkness" (of this more later) does Lovecraft climb that mountain, but he does climb it several times. Goatish Wilbur climbs the mountain with his mother Lavinia; and his brother, the true Dunwich Horror, with his nemesis Professor Armitage hot behind him, climbs it to meet his father, Yog-Sothoth. The tragedy of this story is that this meeting is not successful, in part because Wilbur does not understand the way modern libraries operate. The brother who has been hidden away in the care of his brother cannot be accepted by his father; in fact, his resemblance to his father is pitiable. This pitiable quality turns us away from thinking of Wilbur and his brother as tragic figures; no, they are second-raters. The actual tragic figure is Old Whateley, who has placed so much trust in Wilbur but who dies before he can see that trust come to fruition. But when he dies, according to Wilbur's witness, the whippoorwills don't get him (*Dunwich Horror* 167). He dies in full defiance; there is nothing pitiable in him. Still, his death is clearly sooner than he expected as he rushes to give Wilbur more instructions, and thus his death foretells the failure of the Whateleys at the end of the story.

There is another tragedy in this ascent, for clearly something has gone wrong when the climber does not meet Beatrice or liberty. He kills his mother Lavinia and, full of utopian dreams, is as it were nailed to the peak, torn apart daily by anxieties as the eagle tears at his liver.

I believe there is no doubt that Lovecraft allows his characters to encounter the midwives, the second-raters; the juncture with divinity. This is not to disallow the scholarship of such characters as Francis Wayland Thurston or Dr. Henry Armitage; these are central protagonists of the stories in which they appear, but they are not the heroes who cross the Night Sea Journey or who face an ecstatic death. They do not need to endure pain or to know who they are, for they have always known who they are. But Wilbur is the second-rate hero; he fails to have his all-important encounter with the *Necronomicon* and he is not at all as powerful as his invisible brother, who looks so much more like his father than he does; but he does help his brother as best he can.

Just as Peake was aware of the waste land through Eliot's poem, Lovecraft was aware of it too. He parodied it, but the parody revealed the extent of his interest in it. And just as Eliot was moved by his wasted London, Lovecraft loved Providence and identified with it intensely, though he was also intensely aware of its decadence. The arrival of the immigrants was not the simple reason for the decadence of the urban landscape, though it was the world he accused for its decadence. It was a diabolic world that he feared and found himself attracted by. We should take very seriously then his declaration in May 16, 1926, "I am Providence, and Providence is myself" (*Selected Letters* 2.51). Not long before that declaration, on April 23 he had written, "I took a sunset-and-evening walk Thursday [. . .] and found many things of striking and even of terrible novelty. It is astonishing what a wealth of hidden and tangled lanes and obscure, surprising quarters Providence possesses. A good three-quarters of my recent trip took place over territory my feet had never before trodden, and I found one monstrous and blasphemous neighborhood whose existence I had never suspected" (2.43). Much space in the letter is then spent on the people of this area, the Jews and the blacks, "half Jew and half Negro, apparently" (2.44), the Papists and Italians; and all this he must accept for in them he is as much Providence as he is on College Hill. "A tangle of horrible and infinitely alluring alleys of blackness" still awaits his eager exploration (2.43). The rest of the letter behaves as though he were placing himself next to Robert Olmstead, the nameless protagonist of "The Shadow over Innsmouth" who undergoes an ecstatic acceptance of himself as someone who bears the Innsmouth look.

"I am Providence." We have come to take him at his word, so much that we have decided that his words should be engraved upon his headstone at Swan Point Cemetery, as though thereby we had immortalized his words. He was Providence, even its dark side; but was he really?

Though there was some truth to his claim, especially an emotional truth upon his return from New York, there are several ways in which there is no truth to the claim, and we are left floundering, as he would have been left floundering, to say what he was. The answer to this problem is, I believe, simply to say that he was an American, as deracinated as anyone in his generation and the generations that followed, but this was a deracination he could not admit unless in his fiction, and that in the most roundabout of fashions; for first the fiction had to insist upon the fiction of his life in Providence. "God Save His Majesty, George the Third [. . .]!" (*Selected Letters* 1.206). But how is this agnostic to explain himself?

To what extent is this man of Providence one truly? Yes, he grew up in Providence, through both happy and unhappy years that we need not describe. But if we are to be legalistic about the matter he was not born in Providence proper but in East Providence, and for some time the Lovecrafts did not live in Providence but in the suburbs around Boston (Joshi, *I Am Providence* 17–18). His mother had a solid New England genealogy, but his father was English; Lovecraft was proud of his father's background, but it is hardly a background steeped in the lore or blood of Providence. To achieve that he had to read a good deal. I have already developed the theme of the divided city that is first a Providence divided in class and country (*An Epicure in the Terrible* 230-36), so I do not need to say more about it here. Lovecraft was quite aware of that division in his city and made use of it in his fiction. It is for us to agree with him and not to idealize his city. Understood properly, the Whateleys live there.

Written two years after "The Dunwich Horror," "The Whisperer in Darkness" would seem to have little in common with that earlier story; I certainly believed in the great differences between the two for years. But as I reread that later story certain similarities began to press themselves upon me. For instance, the misspelling of Henry Akeley's name at one point as "A-K-E-L-Y" (*Dunwich Horror* 232) causes me to pay attention to the pronunciation of the name; and his full name, Henry Wentworth Akeley or H. W. Akeley, tempts me to hear that name as W. Akeley, so near as it is to Wakeley, or if misheard, Whateley. Which is to say that these two names, Whateley and Wakeley, are phonological cousins. We almost ask whether Wilbur and his whole family, whether decayed or undecayed, wait, and whether Henry Wentworth wakes; his guest Wilmarth did not sleep very well. But rather than being so presumptuous with waiting or waking, I will simply point out how often the two stories dwell on similar details.

Wittgenstein wrote, "The Fall is the Case," and that is all very well and not a bad way to introduce the horrors of Case in *Neuromancer*, as we have done; but it is difficult to imagine what Lovecraft would have made of the computer and its internal delights and terrors in this intensely fallen world. On the one hand he is a man of the Word; his belief in culture is unshakable, but in so many of his works the Word is attacked by external and internal forces—if we can disentangle them. In "The Whisperer in Darkness" the great horror lies in decapitation in the name of purity, ridding the mind of the body. The head of Henry W. Akeley is on its way to Yuggoth.

The narrations of both stories are overwhelmed by the mountains of Massachusetts and Vermont, and beyond the mountains overwhelmed by outer space beyond the newly discovered Pluto. In the story of Akeley, this theme is summed up in this sentence: "Dark Mountain and Round Hill were both notoriously haunted spots" (264), but these two mountains are not in fact haunted in the accepted sense of the word. They are the outposts of the outer aliens, especially Round Hill, which is full of a great variety of machinery, lenses, tubes, sockets, and dial switches, the kind of "mechanical mummery" that we associate with the "crazed inventors" (259) so dear to the writers of science fiction in the 1920s and '30s. It is as though Lovecraft wanted to make this story indeed something that belonged to science fiction at the same time as he laughed at it. Stylistically he has returned to the hyphenated words of his deeply horrendous period, a protection against the sobriety of science fiction. We do not find this kind of language in "The Dunwich Horror," in which we have no doubt that at the top of the mountain we shall meet Yog-Sothoth. The narrator of that story asks, "What walked on the mountains that May-Night?" (172). We know perfectly well, and we have faith in Dr. Armitage to take care of it.

I have used the language of decayed and undecayed earlier, which Lovecraft uses with his tongue in his cheek pervasively throughout "The Dunwich Horror" to draw a line between the people in Dunwich who have devolved toward the animal and those who have not. Once, however, in "The Whisperer in Darkness" he uses the same language when referring to "some hidden, night-haunting human being decayed to a state not much above that of lower animals" (220). Despite the arch phrase "night-haunting," rather like several phrases in the story, this sentence is upon the whole more serious than many we find in the earlier story.

In "The Dunwich Horror" a hired boy, Luther Brown, has the singular honor of being the first to confront the Horror and to live to tell the tale in the thick tongue of the back country. In "The Whisperer in Darkness" a furtive farmer called Walter Brown spies for the aliens and pays the price of dying for it. Again I believe we realize that it is the later story that is the more serious. In both stories a black stone is connected to the center of the alien cult. In both stories fierce dogs are used as guards, but those guarding Akeley's house die. And in both stories the characters track down invisible or hidden aliens by tracking down their footprints, but those prints in the later stories indicate the direction the alien is going ambiguously; the characters in the later story have to question the prints cautiously. But there is little question where the Horror is going, once it has taken its bearings.

I should at this point admit that I do not believe that Lovecraft was aware of these parallels and contrasts, though we should keep in mind in any question of this sort how carefully Lovecraft plotted and wrote his stories. But in doubting that he was aware of all this, I nonetheless believe that these are significant moments. It is as though Wilbur or his grandfather were the dark side of Akeley, both of them living in isolation, both of them learnèd in esoteric material.

But Akeley, or the dark side of him, wears a mask, as we learn in the last sentence of the story. Wilbur wears a mask also, for the same reason. The community must not learn that he is truly an alien. We learn that he wears a mask, however, some time before the last sentence of that story is uttered. His more profound mask is his invisible brother, so much more like his father than he is.

It is not strange that in Leiber and Tiptree the stage and the masks that play upon it manifest themselves; the tragic mode began on a stage and in the masks that were already present, which is simply to say that the stage demands the mask and the mask the stage. They appear together and yearn for each other. It is not surprising, then, that we search for their presence in Lovecraft. The stage and mask, however, are not as evident in these stories because they are stories in which everything that is of importance is interiorized; nevertheless, the traces of the mask and the stage do appear in them.

This mask appears for instance in "The Shadow over Innsmouth" in the mask of normality that the narrator unconsciously wears, only to have it removed as he looks upon his true appearance, a person who wears the Innsmouth look. In time his true appearance, rather like his mother's, will come forth. Once he has rescued his cousin from the madhouse he plans to "swim out to that brooding reef in the sea and dive down through black abysses to Cyclopean and many-columned Y'ha-nthlei" (*Dunwich Horror* 367). Once more as in "Dagon," the ocean serves as a symbol of the infinite universe; the narrator has accepted its checkered, multiform beauties, which would otherwise appear deadly, as so often they do.

The other aspect of the universe lies in "a frightful dream" (366) the narrator has had of the universe in his grandmother: "She lived in a phosphorescent palace of many terraces, with gardens of strange leprous corals and grotesque brachiate efflorescences, and welcomed me with a warmth that may have been sardonic" (366). This immortal beauty is qualified by such words as "leprous," "grotesque," "brachiate," and "sardonic." The immense universe allures us in every way imaginable, and it does not.

Something of this ambivalence appears in "The Shadow out of Time." Professor Peaslee discovers in his several breakdowns a more complex world than he had ever taught in his smooth and happy life as a professor of political economy (*Dunwich Horror* 370). He has talked with philosophers from up and down the universe as well as with magicians from various times of earth's own scattered history (395-96). We could detail other encounters, insofar as a part of the rhetoric of this section of the story is to insist upon the complexity of the universe as Peaslee reads the "horrible annals of other worlds and other universes" (394). It is possible that Lovecraft learned this static rhetoric from Stapledon, but he does lack Stapledon's philosophic background.

More to our point is the conclusion of the work. Peaslee receives the letter entreating him to join an expedition to the other side of the earth; and one of the men is "Professor William Dyer [. . .], leader of the Miskatonic Antarctic Expedition of 1930-31" (406). He has survived that expedition to the extent that he can once more go to the other side of the earth. Is it any wonder that we think of this story as an epilogue!

In this light the conclusion is all the more strange, when Peaslee confesses that in the central archive of the Great Race he discovered a book written in "our familiar alphabet, spelling out the words of the English language in my own handwriting" (433). We have met this situation in several of Lovecraft's stories, for instance in the conclusions of "Dagon" or "The Thing on the Doorstep," taking these moments as evidence of Lovecraft's profound faith in the act of writing, and no doubt we are right in to think so. This moment, however, in the conclusion of "The Shadow out of Time," means something else. Peaslee has been betrayed by his hand. He can no longer think that his experience is one that is mythic in its source. He can no longer be a novice of Joseph Campbell. His own hand is "a frightful confirmation of all [he] had sought to dismiss as myth and dream" (369). He owes this moment to reality, not to his pen or to a putative fiction.

Some of the argument that lies under the surface of these themes can return to us if we ask which of Lovecraft's stories, At the Mountains of Madness or "In the Walls of Eryx," fulfills better the genre of science fiction as he understood it. In his late essay "Some Notes on Interplanetary Fiction" Lovecraft runs through a catalogue of "stock devises" (Miscellaneous Writings 120) that must be avoided, all of which Edgar Rice Burroughs fails to create in Lovecraft's conclusion: "What must be present in a superlative degree is a deep, pervasive sense of *strangeness*—the utter, incomprehensible *strangeness* of a world holding nothing in common with ours" (120). He writes further that "the real nucleus of the story ought to be something far removed from the specific aspect and customs of any hypothetical outside race—ought, indeed, to be nothing less than the *simple sensation of wonder at being off the earth*" (121). In At the Mountains of Madness Lovecraft is determined to keep us on the earth, paradoxically through the details of the airplanes the exhibition is determined to use. "In the Walls of Eryx" clearly does not fulfill this demand of wonder until in one paragraph near the end of the story; the character never expresses such a sensation of being on Venus and thus off earth. We might, however, argue that this commercial undertaking leaves no room for wonder; and the description of the aliens is very good, though we might object to their arms and legs. At the Mountains of Madness does not take place anywhere else than earth, but surely Dyer does express a scholarly excitement if not wonder in the first half of the story; and in the second half his wonder is muted by his meticulous care upon which his and Danforth's escape from the city of the Old Ones depends. "In the Walls of Eryx," from this perspective, is much the more a science fiction story as Lovecraft demanded the genre should be; and it is in this way that we shall consider it.

II

First we should examine the extent to which we can expect Lovecraft really to have had a hand in this late story. According to Kenneth Sterling, the central idea of the story, the invisible labyrinth, was his. Joshi, however, points out that a story by Edmond Hamilton that Lovecraft liked may have influenced the story also (*I Am Providence* 963), though in 1929 he claimed that when he would "get around to the interplanetary field" he would not take Hamilton for his model (*Selected Letters* 3.88). Sterling gave him a draft of some 6000 to 8000 words, which Lovecraft expanded to 12,000 words that contain a number of apparently gratuitous puns aimed at various science fiction editors (*I Am Providence* 963). It is my experience and certainly the drift of modern criticism that this kind of extreme rewriting transforms the original material; though the invisible labyrinth was Sterling's idea, we can be assured that Lovecraft made it his, and it is that idea, transformed by Lovecraft's style, that we have confidently taken upon ourselves to read closely.

I want to examine "In the Walls of Eryx" in two ways. First, I want to look carefully at the details that clearly identify the work as one of science fiction; without them we might well think that we were reading something akin to "The Outsider"; the presence of these details assure us that we are not reading a weird tale. Then I want to look at those details that place the work within a different genre, one that may be more difficult to identify but which is certainly more tragic than the story that is merely to be found in the group of the first details.

First, it is easy to accept the physical details, preeminently of the planet Venus where the story takes place. Lovecraft wrote stories that also took place in other places in the solar system, above all Yuggoth, but it is striking that that planet is almost always named by its own name rather than that by which Earth has identified it, Pluto. In Lovecraft's hands Pluto is Yuggoth, not the indistinct planet discovered in our telescopes and now visited by our spacecraft. Venus is treated as it would have been when Lovecraft and Sterling wrote the story; Lovecraft could be trusted to possess the necessary astronomical details from the time that he was writing astronomical columns in various Providence newspapers. Venus, then, is hardly a mystery, and it does not seem a mystery until the narrator begins to deal with the man-lizards.

The story is palpably a science fiction story. Venus is Venus, and its cyanogen atmosphere must be counteracted with such gear as the mask and the narrator's chatter about the superiority of the Dubois mask with its sponge-reservoir to the Carter mask, the oxygen pipes, the water capsules and the food capsules. This is not the ritual mask that we find in the saga of the Mouser and Fafhrd. This section is probably Sterling's, but clearly Lovecraft has accepted it; it is very like the gear that he had swatted up for *At the Mountains of Madness*. Given these details in fact, this is much more obviously a science fiction story than is C. S. Lewis's *Perelandra*, which also takes place on Venus. Nothing surprises us yet.

One detail, however, that does surprise us is the name of the plateau on which the narrator finds the crystal—Eryx, a classical word that names a mountain in Sicily (*Aeneid* 12.701). Lovecraft's phrase, "Erycinian Highland" (*Dagon* 296, 319), which the narrator attributes to his map, alludes to three Virgilian lines, "tum uicina astris Erycino in uertice sedes / fundatur Veneri Idaliae, tumuloque sacerdos / ac lucus late sacer additus Anchiseo" [Then near to the stars in the summit of Eryx the temple / is founded of Idalian Venus, and the sacred clearing devoted to Anchises] (5.759-61). Not only sacred to the man who is a son of Venus (Ovid, *Metamorphoses* 14.82-85), the clearing at the summit of Eryx is sacred to a temple of Venus and to Anchises, the father of Aeneas (5.757-61). So the mountain of Eryx alludes to a broad range of sacred events. We are surprised, then, for we did not expect to find in this commercial undertaking upon which Lovecraft's story opens a man sufficiently learned to name the high plateau in this fashion. In any case, the word "eryx" in the title and the action suggests that the goddess Venus is much more significant to the story than we expected. The temple devoted to Venus was famous in the classical world, so we must be tempted to consider the labyrinth something of a stand-in for that temple. S. T. Joshi may be correct in thinking that the setting of Venus may be a conventional setting that Sterling had proposed ("Lovecraft's Revisions" 43), but Lovecraft was surely aware that the planet and the plateau reinforced each other in significance. What this significance is, however, we must wait upon. At least we can see that it is undoubtedly erotic.

One other detail we need to pay attention to is the presence and nature of the man-lizards. It is difficult, however, for us to say what they are truly like because of the fierce animosity the narrator has for them. They are "damnable," "damned things" (*Dagon* 293). The narrator would like to see "a single regiment of flame throwers [that] could raise hell with them" (294). Three times near the end of the story the narrator calls them "devils" (313-14). So fierce is this reasonless hatred that the narrator plans to "urge the wiping out of these scaly beggars by a good stiff army from home" (293), a notion that his superior after his death approves of, "to wipe out the natives altogether" (321). This man, however, has a reason for the genocide: "With a clear field, there can scarcely be any limit to the amount of crystal we can secure" (321). In the conclusion of this story financial considerations justify genocide.

Lovecraft had two models for this moment. On the one hand there is the governmental decision in "The Shadow over Innsmouth" that the people under the sea should be exterminated; and on the other he had a model for the genocide very near at hand, his admiration for the recent publication of Olaf Stapledon's description of the fate of the future human races in *Last and First Men*, especially in his complex description of the fifth race as it attempts to migrate to Venus. It becomes a question whether the highly advanced fifth race should survive or the native race that the humans discover upon the planet. They decide on the slaughter of the natives through an electrolysis of the ocean, a process they cannot halt. "It was therefore determined to put [the natives] out of their misery as quickly as possible" (190). But the fifth race cannot avoid the moral implications of their act; the guilt is too overwhelming, and they cannot escape the biological influence of the native race.

The narrator of Lovecraft's story, however, has no way to face the implications of any of these genocides, for he is dead before it can be enacted on Venus; but the people in the company exhibit no moral qualms. In any case it is possible that these aliens will defend themselves in a striking fashion. In the classical world Venus is not a goddess to be approached without appropriate care. She was born through the castration of her grandfather, the titan Cronus. The worship of another goddess on another island, Cybele on the island of Mount Ida, leads to self-castration in her worshippers, an event that Catullus treats in a poem that Lovecraft alludes to in his story "The Rats in the Walls" (*Dunwich Horror* 37). The name of this labyrinth may in fact warn the humans that this is a Venus fly-trap. "It was a trap—a trap set to catch human beings" (*Dagon* 312), the narrator writes, and later as he is dying he repeats himself (318). It is a Venus fly-trap.

I do not suggest this frivolously. In an off-handed manner the narrator mentions the "carnivorous plants" (*D* 294) on Venus and the mirage-plants with their "dangerous blossoms" (295). The narrator's supervisor had warned him of "the shaggy stalk, the spiky leaves, and the mottled blossoms whose gaseous, dream-breeding exhalations penetrate every existing make of mask" (295). More specifically the narrator wishes that "some really carnivorous organisms like the skorahs would appear" (310) that could lead him out of the labyrinth. No warning, however, will protect the narrator from the invisible labyrinth because of the crystal that lay in its center. It is an overpowering clitoris that no warning will save him from.

A part of the impact of this story lies in the meticulous style of the narrator as he attempts to describe the inward structure of the labyrinth in order to escape it. This style is very like the style and purpose of Professor Dyer in *At the Mountains of Madness*. The differences, however, are striking. The labyrinth at the summit of Eryx bears no historical obsession; nothing is written or

The Deeps of Eryx

drawn upon its invisible walls, so like the narrator we remain puzzled by this labyrinth's purpose. Also, the two structures vary greatly in construction and material. The city that Dyer and Danford explore is composed of a variety of formal motifs: round, straight, cylindrical, small, large. No shape is employed in any obsessional fashion, whereas the labyrinth of Eryx is composed of curves, curve upon curve, within a large circle. The great difference of course is the materials, the one of stone, the other of an unknown transparent material that unlike glass cannot be shattered, at least not in the experience of the narrator.

I said earlier that this story has an erotic theme, but we might understand that in some doubt when we consider how often a carnivore theme is raised. It is certainly suggested that the natives of the planet mean to eat the people trapped in the labyrinth, though they are very careful about it; in this care and covert aggression they behave like Lovecraft's usual ghouls. It is not surprising, however, to see oral aggression combined with phallic aggression. As the great example of this moment consider Penthesilea's action at the climax of Kleist's drama, joining her dogs in attacking her beloved Achilles and tearing him apart (22nd and 23rd scenes). That is the difficult action suggested by this story, melding the Venus at the top of Mount Eryx to the aroma of the dangerous carnivorous flowers.

In the conclusion of the story the narrator is at last granted a name, though no independence, "Our Operative A-49, Kenton J. Stanfield" (*Dagon* 319). If we were to play with numbers we might pay attention to 49, the square of the lucky number 7. But he does not need the nobility of the numbers. He has learned something about those crystals that is very important: "They belong to Venus alone [. . .] and I believe we have violated some obscure and mysterious law—some law buried deep in the arcana of the cosmos—in our attempts to take them" (318). The Greek tragedians said as much by referring to Δίκη.

Works Cited

Abrash, Merritt. "Utopia Subverted: Unstated Messages in *Childhood's End.*" *Extrapolation* 30 (1989): 372-79.

Adams, Henry. *The Education of Henry Adams: An Autobiography.* Boston: Houghton Mifflin, 1961.

Adorno, Theodor. *Minima Moralia: Reflections from Damaged Life.* Trans. E. F. N. Jephcott. London: Verso, 1978.

Aeschylus. *Aeschyli septem quae supersunt tragoediae.* 2nd ed. Ed. Gilbert Murray. Oxford: Clarendon Press, 1953.

Alighieri, Dante. *La Divina Commedia.* Ed. C. H. Grandgent; rev. Charles S. Singleton. Cambridge, MA: Harvard University Press, 1972.

———. *Tutte le opera.* 3rd ed. Ed. E. Moore, rev. Paget Toynbee. Oxford: Oxford University Press, 1894.

Aquinas, Thomas. *Summa Theologiae.* 5 vols. Madrid: La Editorial Catolica, 1955.

Arnold, Matthew. *The Poetical Works.* New York: Thomas Y. Crowell, 1897.

Ault, Norman, ed. *Elizabethan Lyrics.* Ed. Norman Ault. New York: Capricorn, 1960.

Bachelard, Gaston. *La Poétique de l'espace.* 4th ed. Paris: Presses Universitaires de France, 1964.

Baudelaire, Charles. *Les Fleurs du mal.* Paris: Garnier, 1961.

Beatie, Bruce A. "Arthur C. Clarke and the Alien Encounter: The Background of *Childhood's End.*" *Extrapolation* 30 (1989): 53-69.

"Bernoulli." In *The Encyclopaedia Britannica.* Vol. 3. 803-5.

Betteridge, Harold T., ed. *The New Cassell's German Dictionary.* New York: Funk & Wagnalls, 1958.

Blake, William. *Complete Writings.* Ed. Geoffrey Keynes. London: Oxford University Press, 1972.

Burns, Robert. *The Complete Works of Robert Burns.* Philadelphia: Lippincott, 1875.

Byfield, Bruce. "Fafhrd and Fritz." In Searles 44-56.

———. "Fafhrd and the Scot." In Searles. 102-17.

———. *Witchcraft of the Mind: A Critical Study of Fritz Leiber*. West Warwick, RI: Necronomicon Press, 1991.

Candelaria, Matthew. "The Overlord's Burden: The Sources of Sorrow in *Childhood's End*." *Ariel* 33 (Winter 2002): 37-58.

Carmen. Music by George Bizet. Words by H. Meilhac and L Halévy. Chester, NY: Schirmer, 1959.

Chaucer, Geoffrey. *The Tale of the Wyf of Bathe*. In *The Student's Chaucer*. Ed. Walter W. Skeat. Oxford: Clarendon Press, 1904.

Clareson, Thomas D. "The Cosmic Loneliness of Arthur C. Clarke." In *Arthur C. Clarke*, ed. Joseph D. Olanger and Marin Harry Greenberg. New York: Taplinger, 1977. 52-71.

Clarke, Arthur C. *Against the Fall of Night*. In *The Lion of Comarre and Against the Fall of Night*. New York: Harcourt, Brace & World, 1968.

———. *Ascent to Orbit: A Scientific Autobiography*. New York: John Wiley & Sons, 1984.

———. *Astounding Days: A Science Fictional Autobiography*. New York: Bantam, 1990.

———. *Childhood's End*. San Diego: Harcourt Brace Jovanovich. 1953.

———. *The City and the Stars and The Sands of Mars*. New York: Warner, 2001.

———. "Guardian Angel." In *The Sentinel*. New York: Berkley, 1986. 39-81.

———. "The Star." In *The Collected Stories of Arthur C. Clarke*. New York: Tor, 2000. 517-21.

Clute, John. "Introduction." In Lindsay, *A Voyage to Arcturus*. vii-xv.

Crossley, Robert. "Olaf Stapledon and the Idea of Science Fiction." *Modern Fiction Studies* 32 (Spring 1986): 21-42.

Coleridge, Samuel Taylor. *The Poems*. Ed. Ernest Hartley Coleridge. London: Oxford University Press, 1960.

Collodi. *Le avventure di Pinocchio, storia di un burattino*. Milan: Rizzoli, "Biblioteca Universale," 1949.

Curtius, Ernst. *European Literature and the Latin Middle Ages*. Trans. Willard R. Trask. New York: Harper & Row, 1963.

Davis, Philip J. *Spirals: From Theodorus to Chaos*. Wellesley, MA: Peters, 1993.

Delany, Samuel R., Jr. *The Einstein Intersection*. Middletown, CT: Wesleyan University Press, 1998.

Dick, Philip K. *Ubik*. New York: Vintage, 1991.

Eddington, Sir Arthur. *The Nature of the Physical World*. Ann Arbor: University of Michigan Press, 1958.

Einstein, Albert. *Über die spezielle und die allgemeine Relativitätstheorie*. 3rd ed. Sammlung Vieweg: Tagesfragen aus den Gebieten der Naturwissenschaften und der Technik. Braunschweig: Friedrich Vieweg, 1918.

Eiseley, Loren. "Afterword." In Lindsay, *A Voyage to Arcturus*. 269-72.

Eliot, T. S. *The Complete Poems and Plays: 1909-1950*. New York: Harcourt, Brace, 1952.

———. "A Note on Poetry and Belief." *Enemy* (Winter 1927): 15-17.

Engel, Claire Eliane. *A History of Mountaineering in the Alps*. 2nd ed. Westport, CT: Greenwood Press, 1977.

Epictetus. *The Discourses as Reported by Arrian, The Manual, and Fragments*. 2 vols. Trans. W. A. Oldfather. Cambridge, MA: Harvard University Press/Loeb Classical Library, 1979-85.

Eriksen, Inge. "The Aesthetics of Cyberpunk." *Foundation* 53 (1991): 36-46.

Ewing, Murray. "The Life and Works of David Lindsay." http://www.violetapple.org.uk/life/influences.php. [accessed 19 February 2014].

The English Bible. King James Version. Vol. 1. The Old Testament. Ed. Herbert Marks. New York: W. W. Norton, 2012.

The English Bible. King James Version. Vol. II. The New Testament and The Apocrypha. Ed. Gerald Hammond and Austin Busch. New York: W. W. Norton, 2012.

Fiedler, Leslie. *Love and Death in the American Novel*. New York: Criterion, 1960.

———. *Olaf Stapledon: A Man Divided*. Oxford: Oxford University Press, 1983.

Fischer, Roland. "A Story of the Utopian Vision of the World." *Diogenes* No. 163 (Fall 1993): 5-25.

Frazer, James. *The New Golden Bough*. Ed. Theodor H. Gaster. New York: Mentor, 1964.

Freud, Sigmund. *Civilization and Its Discontents*. Trans. and ed. James Strachey. New York: W. W. Norton, 1962.

Fussell, Paul. *The Great War and Modern Memory*. London: Oxford University Press, 1975.

Gibson, William. *Burning Chrome*. New York: Ace, 1987.

———. *Count Zero*. New York: Ace, 1987.

———. *Mona Lisa Overdrive*. New York: Bantam, 1989.

———. *Neuromancer*. New York: Ace, 1984.

Goethe, Johann Wolfgang. *Faust I und II*. Ed. and com. Erich Trunz. In *Goethes Werke: Hamberger Ausgabe*. Vol. 3. Hamburg: Christian Wegner, 1959.

———. *Zur Farbenlehre*. In *Goethes Werke: Hamberger Ausgabe*. Vol 13. Hamburg: Christian Wegner, 1962.

Goldman, Stephen H. "Immortal Man and Mortal Overlord: The Case for Intertextuality." In *Death and the Serpent: Immortality in Science Fiction and Fantasy*, ed. Carl B. Yoke and Donald M. Hassler. Westport, CT: Greenwood Press, 1985. 193–208.

Gond, J. *Kurze Elementar-Grammatik der Sanskrit-Sprache*. 4th ed. Leiden: E. J. Brill, 1963.

Goodheart, Eugene. "Stapledon's *Last and First Men*." In *No Place Else: Explorations in Utopian and Dystopian Fiction*, ed. Eric S. Rabkin, Martin H. Greenberg, and Joseph D. Olander. Carbondale: Southern Illinois University Press, 1983. 78–93.

Gordon, Lyndall. *T. S. Eliot: An Imperfect Life*. New York: W. W. Norton, 2000.

Grant, Glenn. "Transcendence through Detournement in William Gibson's *Neuromancer*." *Science-Fiction Studies* 50 (1990): 41–49.

Greene, Robert. *The Honourable History of Friar Bacon and Friar Bungay*. In *The Chief Elizabethan Dramatists*, ed. William Allan Neilson. Cambridge, MA: Riverside Press, 1939.

Hegel, Georg Wilhelm Friedrich. *Phänomenologie des Geistes*. Ed. Gerhard Göhler. Frankfurt am Main: Ullstein, 1973.

Herr, Cheryl. "Convention and Spirit in Olaf Stapledon's Fiction." In McCarthy, Elkins, and Greenberg. 23–37.

Hesiod. *Theogonia, Opera et Dies, Scutum*. Ed. Friedrich Solmsen. Oxford: Clarendon Press, 1970.

Hesse Hermann. *Magister Ludi*. Trans. Mervyn Savill. New York: Frederick Ungar, 1949.

———. *Narziß und Goldmund*. Frankfurt am Main: Fischer Bücherei, 1957.

Hollow, John. *Against the Night, the Stars: The Science Fiction of Arthur C. Clarke*. New York: Harcourt, 1983.

Holzel, Tom, and Audrey Salkeld. *First on Everest: The Mystery of Mallory and Irvine*. New York: Holt, 1986.

Howard, Robert E. *Conan the Warrior*. Ed. L. Sprague de Camp. New York: Ace, 1967.

Huizinga, Johan. *Homo Ludens; A Study of the Play-Element in Culture.* Boston: Beacon Press, 1964.

Hull, Elizabeth Anne. "Fire and Ice: The Ironic Imagery of Arthur C. Clarke's *Childhood's End.*" *Extrapolation* 24 (1983): 13-32.

Huntingdon, John. Huntington, John. "From Man to Overmind: Arthur C. Clarke's Myth of Progress." In Olander and Greenberg. 211-22.

———. "Olaf Stapledon and the Novel about the Future." *Contemporary Literature* 22 (Summer 1981): 349-65.

———. "Remembrance of Things to Come: Narrative Technique in *Last and First Men.*" *Science-Fiction Studies* 9 (November 1982): 238-64.

James, Edward. *Science Fiction in the Twentieth Century.* Oxford: Oxford University Press, 1994.

Johnson, Graham. Schubert's "Der Tod und das Mädchen." In *The Hyperion Schubert Edition.* Brigitta Fassbaender and Graham Johnson. London: Hyperion Records, 1991. 10.

Joshi, S. T. "Lovecraft's Revisions." In *Lovecraft and a World in Transition: Collected Essays on H. P. Lovecraft.* New York: Hippocampus Press. 2014. 31-45.

———. *I Am Providence: The Life and Times of H. P. Lovecraft.* 2 vols. Hippocampus Press. 2010.

———. "Passing the Torch." In Searles. 65-74.

Joyce, James. *Finnegans Wake.* New York: Viking Press, 1958.

Jung, C. G. *Psychological Types.* Trans. H. G. Baynes and R. F. C. Hull. Princeton: Princeton University Press, 1976.

———. *The Symbolic Life: Miscellaneous Writings.* Trans. R. F. C. Hull. Princeton: Princeton University Press, 1976.

———. *Symbols of Transformation: An Analysis of the Prelude to a Case of Psychophrenia.* 2nd ed. Trans. R. F. C. Hull. Princeton: Princeton University Press, 1967.

Jungk, Robert. *Brighter Than a Thousand Suns: A Personal History of the Atomic Scientists.* Trans. James Cleugh. New York: Harcourt Bruce Jovanovich, 1958.

Kaplan, Abraham. "Sociology Learns the Language of Mathematics: Some Recent Studies Analyzed." *Commentary* 14 (September 1952): 274-54.

Keats, John. *The Poems.* Ed. Jack Stillinger. Cambridge, MA: Harvard University Press, 1978.

Kinnaird, John. *Olaf Stapledon.* Mercer Island, WA: Starmont House, 1986.

Kleist, Heinrich von. *Werke*. 2 vols. Ed. Heinrich Kurz. Leipzig: Bibliogphischen Institut, n.d.

Kuttner, Henry. See Padgett, Lewis.

Langan, John. "Sailing the True Void: H. P. Lovecraft in Fritz Leiber's *The Wanderer*." In Searles. 124-36.

Lawrence, D. H. *The Plumed Serpent*. New York: Vintage, 1954.

———. *St. Mawr and The Man Who Died*. New York: Vintage, 1953.

Leiber, Fritz. *The Big Time*. New York: Collier, 1982.

———. *Conjure Wife*. New York: Award, 1970.

———. *The Ghost Light*. New York: Berkley, 1984.

———. "Gonna Roll the Bones." In *The Best of Fritz Leiber*. New York: Ballantine, 1974.

———. *The Knight and Knave of Swords: Fafhrd and the Gray Mouser VII*. New York: William Morrow, 1988.

———. *Our Lady of Darkness*. New York: Berkley, 1978.

———. *The Second Book of Fritz Leiber*. New York: DAW, 1975.

———. *Swords Against Death: Fafhrd and the Gray Mouser II*. Boston: Gregg Press, 1977.

———. *Swords Against Wizardry: Fafhrd and the Gray Mouser IV*. Boston: Gregg Press, 1977.

———. *Swords and Deviltry: Fafhrd and the Gray Mouser I*. Boston: Gregg Press, 1977.

———. *Swords and Ice-Magic: Fafhrd and the Gray Mouser VI*. Boston: Gregg Press, 1977.

———. *The Swords of Lankhmar: Fafhrd and the Gray Mouser V*. Boston: Gregg Press, 1977.

———. *Swords in the Mist: Fafhrd and the Gray Mouser III*. Boston: Gregg Press, 1977.

———. *The Wanderer*. New York: Tor, 1964.

Leiber, Justin. "Fritz Leiber and Eyes." In Searles. 81-97.

———. "Fritz Leiber: Swordsman and Philosopher." In Searles. 26-35.

Leopardii, Giacomo. *Canti*. Milan: Rizzoli, 1983.

Lindsay, David. *A Voyage to Arcturus*. Lincoln: University of Nebraska Press, 2002.

———. *The Violet Apple and The Witch*. Ed. J. B. Pick. Chicago: Chicago Review Press, 1976.

Lovecraft, H. P. *At the Mountains of Madness and Other Novels.* Sel. August Derleth. Ed. S. T. Joshi. Sauk City, WI: Arkham House, 1985.

———. *Dagon and Other Macabre Tales.* Sel. August Derleth. Ed. S. T. Joshi. Sauk City, WI: Arkham House, 1986.

———. *The Dunwich Horror and Others.* Sel. August Derleth. Ed. S. T. Joshi. Intr. Robert Bloch. Sauk City, WI: Arkham House, 1984.

———. *Miscellaneous Writings.* Ed. S. T. Joshi. Sauk City, WI: Arkham House, 1995.

———. *Selected Letters.* 5 vols. Ed. August Derleth, Donald Wandrei, and James Turner. Sauk City: Arkham House, 1965-76.

Lucretius. *De Rerum Natura.* 2nd ed. Ed. Cyril Bailey. Oxford: Clarendon Press, 1959.

MacClure, J. C. "Language and Logic in *A Voyage to Arcturus*." *Scottish Literary Journal* 1 (Winter 1974). 29-38.

Mallory, George Leigh. *Climbing Everest: The Complete Writings of George Mallory.* London: Gibson Square, 2012.

McAleer, Neil. *Arthur C. Clarke: The Authorized Biography.* Chicago: Contemporary, 1992.

McCarthy, Patrick A. "Stapledon and Literary Modernism." In McCarthy, Elkins, and Greenberg. 39-51.

McCarthy, Patrick A.; Charles Elkins; and Martin Henry Greenberg, ed. *The Legacy of Olaf Stapledon: Critical Essays and an Unpublished Manuscript.* Westport, CT: Greenwood Press, 1989.

McCaffery, Larry. "An Interview with William Gibson." *Mississippi Review* 16 (1988): 217-36.

Manilius. *Astronomica, Astrologie.* Trans. Wolfgang Fels. Stuttgart: Reclam, 1990.

Mann, Thomas. *The Magic Mountain.* Trans. H. T. Lowe-Porter. New York: Vintage, 1969.

Mead, David G. "Technological Transfiguration in William Gibson's Sprawl Novels: *Neuromancer, Count Zero,* and *Mona Lisa Overdrive.*" *Extrapolation* 32 (1991): 350-60.

Melville, Herman. *Moby-Dick; or, The Whale.* Ed. Harrison Hayford and Hershel Parker. New York: W. W. Norton, 1976.

Menger, Lucy "The Appeal of *Childhood's End.*" In *Critical Encounters: Writers and Themes in Science Fiction,* ed. Dick Riley. New York: Frederick Ungar, 1978. 87-108.

Merivale, Patricia. "Gothic Pedagogy in the Modern Romantic Quest." *Comparative Literature* 36 (Spring 1984): 146-61.

Milton, John. *Complete Poems and Major Prose*. Ed. Merritt Y. Hughes. New York: Odyssey Press, 1957.

Moore, C. L. See Padgett, Lewis.

Murray, Gilbert. "Excursus on the Ritual Forms Preserved in Greek Tragedy." In *Themis: A Study of the Social Origins of Greek Religion*. By Jane Ellen Harrison, with Gilbert Murray and F. M. Cornfield. 2nd ed. Cleveland: Meridian, 1962.

Neumann, Erich. *The Great Mother: An Analysis of the Archetype*. Trans. Ralph Manheim. Princeton: Princeton University Press, 1974.

Nicolson, Marjorie Hope. *Mountain Gloom and Mountain Glory: The Development of the Aesthetics of the Infinite*. New York: W. W. Norton, 1963.

Nietzsche, Friedrich. *Werke in drei Bänden*. Ed. Karl Schlechta. Munich: Carl Hanser, n.d.

Nixon, Nicola. "Cyberpunk: Preparing the Ground for Revolution or Keeping the Boys Satisfied?" *Science-Fiction Studies* 57 (1992): 219-35.

Oehler, Richard, ed. *Friedrich Nietzsche's Briefe*. Frankfurt am Main: Insel Verlag, 1993.

Olander, Joseph D., and Martin Harry Greenberg, ed. *Arthur C. Clarke*. New York: Taplinger, 1977.

Olsen, Lance. "The Shadow of Spirit in William Gibson's Matrix Trilogy." *Extrapolation* 32 (1991): 278-89.

Padgett, Lewis [Henry Kuttner and C. L. Moore]. "Mimsy Were the Borogoves." In *Science Fiction Hall of Fame*, ed. Robert Silverberg. New York: Avon, 1971. 226-60.

Pagels, Elaine. *The Gnostic Gospels*. New York: Vintage, 1981.

Partridge, Eric. *Origins: A Short Etymological Dictionary of Modern English*. 2nd ed. New York: Macmillan, 1959.

Pascal, Blaise. *Pensées*. Paris: Garnier, 1961.

Pagels, Elaine. *The Gnostic Gospels*. New York: Vintage, 1981.

Peckham, Morse. *Man's Rage for Chaos: Biology, Behavior, and the Arts*. New York: Schocken, 1967.

Peake, Mervyn. *Boy in Darkness*. In *Sometime, Never: Three Tales of Imagination by William Golding, John Windham, and Mervyn Peake*. New York: Ballantine, 1957. 127-85.

———. *Titus Alone*. Woodstock, NY: Overlook Press, 1982.

Percy, Thomas. *Reliques of Ancient English Poetry*. Ed. J. V. Prichard. London: George Bell, 1900.

Petrarca, Francesco. *Die Besteigung des Mont Ventoux*. Trans. and ed. Kurt Steinmann. Stuttgart: Reclam, 1995.

Phillips, Julie. *James Tiptree Jr.: The Double Life of Alice Sheldon*. New York: St. Martin's Press, 2006.

Plato. *Opera*. 3 vols. Ed. John Burnet. Oxford: Clarendon Press, 1958.

Poe, Edgar Allan. "A Descent into the Maelström." In *Collected Works of Edgar Allan Poe*. Vol. 2. Ed. Thomas Ollive Mabbott. Cambridge, MA: Harvard University Press, 1978. 574-94.

The Poetic Edda. 2nd ed. Trans. Lee M. Hollander. Austin: University of Texas Press, 1986.

Pohl, Joy. "Dualities in David Lindsay's *A Voyage to Arcturus*." *Extrapolation* 22 (1981): 164-70.

Quinn, William A. "Science Fiction's Harrowing of the Heavens." In *The Transcendent Adventure: Studies of Religion in Science Fiction/Fantasy*, ed. Robert Reilly. Westport, CT: Greenwood Press, 1985. 37-54.

Rimbaud, Arthur. *Œuvres*. Ed. Suzanne Bernard. Paris: Garnier, 1960.

Rose, Mark. *Alien Encounters: Anatomy of Science Fiction*. Cambridge, MA: Harvard University Press, 1981.

Samuelson, David. "*Childhood's End*: A Median Stage in Adolescence?" In Olander and Greenberg. 196-210.

———. *Visions of Tomorrow: Six Journeys from Outer to Inner Space*. New York: Arno Press, 1974.

Sayers, Dorothy L. *The Mind of the Maker*. 1941. New York: Living Age, 1956.

Schillebeckx, Edward. *Christ: The Experience of Jesus as Lord*. Trans. John Bowden. New York: Crossroads, 1983.

Schlegel, Friedrich. *Kritische und theoretische Schriften*. Ed. Andreas Huyssen. Stuttgart: Reclam, 1978.

Schopenhauer, Arthur. *Sämmtliche Werke*. 6 vol. Ed. Eduard Grisebach. Leipzig: Reclam, 1890.

Schumaker, Curtis Scott. "Exorcism from Heaven." In Searles. 57-69.

Searles, A. Langley, ed. *Fantasy Commentator* 11, Nos. 1 and 2 (Summer 2004). Fritz Leiber issue.

Shakespeare, William. *The Norton Shakespeare*. Ed. Stephen Greenblatt et al. New York: W. W. Norton, 1997.

Shelley, Percy Bysshe. "Mont Blanc: Lines Written in the Vale of Chamouni." In *The Complete Poetical Works*. Ed. Thomas Hutchinson. London: Oxford University Press, 1923. 528-31.

Slusser, George Edgar. *The Space Odysseys of Arthur C. Clarke*. San Bernardino, CA: Borgo Press. 1978.

Sigurðsson, Arngrímur. *Íslenzk-Ensk Orðabók: Icelandic-English Dictionary*. Reykjavík: Leiftur, 1975.

Slotkin, Joel Elliot. "Haunted Infocosms and Prosthetic Gods: Gibsonian Cyberspace and Renaissance Arts of Memory." *Journal of Popular Culture* 45 (2012): 862-82.

Spinoza, Benedict. *Die Ethik: Lateinisch und Deutsch*. Trans. Jakob Stern. Stuttgart: Reclam, 1977.

Squire, Charles. *Celtic Myth and Legend*. Hollywood, CA: Newcastle, 1975.

Staicar, Tom. *Fritz Leiber*. New York: Frederick Ungar, 1983.

Stapledon, Olaf. *The Flames: A Fantasy*. London: Secker & Warburg, 1947.

———. *Last and First Men and Star Maker*. New York: Dover, 1968.

———. *A Modern Theory of Ethics: A Study of the Relations of Ethics and Psychology*. London: Methuen, 1930.

———. *Nebula Maker*. New York: Dodd, Mead, 1983.

———. *Odd John and Sirius*. New York: Dover, 1974.

———. *Olaf Stapledon: Speaking for the Future*. Syracuse, NY: Syracuse University Press, 1994.

———. *Talking Across the World: The Love Letters of Olaf Stapledon and Agnes Miller, 1913-1919*. Ed. Robert Crossley. Hanover, NH: University Press of New England, 1987.

Sterling, Bruce, ed. *Mirrorshades: The Cyberpunk Anthology*. New York: Ace, 1988.

Sturluson, Snorri. *Snorra Edda*. Reykjavik: Iðunn, 1975.

Tasso, Torquato. *Gerusalemme liberata*. Vol. 3. In *Opere*. Ed. Bruno Maier. Milan: Rizzoli, 1963.

Tennyson, Alfred, Lord. *The Poetic and Dramatic Works*. Boston: Houghton Mifflin, 1927.

Tiptree, James, Jr. [Alice Sheldon]. *Brightness Falls from the Air*. New York: Tor, 1985.

———. *Meet Me at Infinity*. New York: Tor, 2001.

Tremaine, Louis. "Olaf Stapledon's Note on Magnitude." *Extrapolation* 23 (1982): 243-53.

Valéry, Paul. *Aesthetics*. Trans. Ralph Manheim. *The Collected Works*, Vol. 13. New York: Pantheon, 1964.

Verne, Jules. *Vingt mille lieues sous les mers*. Paris: Le Livre de Poche, n.d.

Volberg, Rachel A. *When the Chips Are Down: Problem Gambling in America*. New York: Century Foundation, 2001.

Wallace, Lew. *Ben-Hur: A Tale of the Christ*. New York: Harper, 1908.

Wasserzieher, Ernst. *Woher? Ableitendes Wörterbuch der deutschen Sprache*. 18th ed. Ed. Werner Betz. Bonn: Dümmler, 1974.

Whalen, Terence. "The Future of a Commodity: Notes toward a Critique of Cyberpunk and the Information Age." *Science-Fiction Studies* 56 (1992): 75-88.

Wheat, Andrew R. "Neither This, Nor That: The Apophatic Allegory of David Lindsay's *A Voyage to Arcturus*." *Scottish Studies Review* 9 (Spring 2008): 101-21.

Wilson, Colin; E. H. Visiak; and J. B. Pick. *The Strange Genius of David Lindsay*. London: John Baker, 1970.

Wittgenstein, Ludwig. *Tractatus Logico-Philosophicus; Tagebücher_1914–1916; Philosophische Untersuchungen*. Werkausgabe, vol. 1. Ed. Joachim Schulte. Frankfurt am Main: Suhrkamp, 1984.

Wolfe, Gary K. *The Known and the Unknown: The Iconography of Science Fiction*. Kent, OH: Kent State University Press, 1979.

Wordsworth, William. *The Complete Poetical Works*. Ed. A. J. George. Cambridge, MA: Houghton Mifflin, 1904.

Ybarra, T. R. *Bolivar: The Passionate Warrior*. New York: Ives Washburn, 1929.

Yeats, William B. *The Poems*. Ed. Richard J. Finneran. New York: Macmillan, 1983.

www.ingramcontent.com/pod-product-compliance
Lightning Source LLC
Chambersburg PA
CBHW051048160426
43193CB00010B/1102